THOUGHTS FOR
EACH DAY OF THE YEAR

St. Theophan the Recluse
1815–1894

Thoughts for Each Day of the Year

ACCORDING TO THE DAILY CHURCH READINGS
FROM THE WORD OF GOD

By St. Theophan the Recluse

Translated by Lisa Marie Baranov

Edited by Nun Cornelia and
the St. Herman of Alaska Brotherhood

SRETENSKY MONASTERY
MOSCOW

ST. HERMAN OF ALASKA
BROTHERHOOD
PLATINA, CALIFORNIA

2018

Printed with the blessing of His Holiness Patriarch KIRILL
of Moscow and All Russia

Copyright © 2010, 2018 by the St. Herman of Alaska Brotherhood
P. O. Box 70 Platina, CA 96076

website: www.sainthermanmonastery.com
email: stherman@stherman.com

First edition: December 2010. Second printing: March 2012. Third
printing: January 2018.
Printed in the United States of America.

Front cover: Portrait of St. Theophan the Recluse. Courtesy of Sretensky
Monastery, Moscow.

Originally published as *Mysli na kazhdyy den' goda po tserkovnym"
chteniyam" iz" slova Bozhiya* [Thoughts for each day of the year
according to the church readings from the word of God] (Moscow:
Athonite Russian St. Panteleimon Monastery, 1881).

The publishers express their thanks to Mr. Oleg Safonov for his help in
the publication of this book.

Publishers Cataloging in Publication

Thoughts for each day of the year : according to the daily church readings
from the word of God / by St. Theophan the Recluse ; translated by Lisa
Marie Baranov ; edited by Nun Cornelia and the St. Herman of Alaska
Brotherhood.—1st ed.—Moscow : Sretensky Monastery ; Platina, Calif. :
St. Herman of Alaska Brotherhood, 2010.—3rd printing, 2018.
    p. ; cm.
    ISBN: 978-1-887904-22-3
    Translation of a Russian book first printed in Moscow in 1881.
    Includes bibliographical references and index.

    1. Feofan, Saint, Bishop of Tambov and Shatsk, 1815–1894—Sermons.
2. Orthodox Eastern Church—Doctrines. 3. Spiritual life—Orthodox
Eastern Church. 4. Bible—Devotional use. 5. Russia—Civilization—
European influences. I. Baranov, Lisa Marie. II. Cornelia, Nun. III. St.
Herman of Alaska Brotherhood. IV. Title.

BX578 .F4613 2010 2010939921   2010939921
248.4/819—dc22   1012

CONTENTS

CONTENTS

Russian icon of St. Theophan.

INTRODUCTION

I

A Brief Biography of St. Theophan the Recluse

This biography of St. Theophan, a Holy Father of nineteenth-century Russia, was written by E. Sumarokov in the 1940s[1] and translated by Hieromonk Seraphim (then Eugene Rose) in 1966,[2] before St. Theophan's glorification as a saint of the Orthodox Church (in 1988). Following this biography, information is given on St. Theophan's posthumous miracles and glorification, and on the content of the present book.—Ed.

To Bishop Theophan belongs an immense significance in the history of the moral development of Russian society. That thirst for complete union with God which led him into reclusion did not deprive the world and his own people of his help. Even from his remote reclusion he was a great public figure, supporting and directing thousands of people and their spiritual life.

Acquiring great spiritual experience by means of complete self-renunciation and strict daily asceticism, Bishop Theophan generously shared with all who had need of it the treasures of his spiritual experience. No one who appealed to him in writing was denied advice. But he exerted a much wider influence by means of his books. How to live a Christian life; how, amidst the slough of temptations, misfortunes, weaknesses, and the weight of our sinful habits, not to fall into despair; how to desire salvation for oneself and begin the work of moral perfection; how to do battle

---

[1] E. Sumarokov, *Lectures on the History of the Russian Church,* vol. 2 (in Russian) (Harbin, 1945).

[2] English translation published in *The Orthodox Word,* vol. 2 (1966), no. 9, pp. 91–96.

on this path step by step, and to enter ever more deeply into the saving enclosure of the Church: it is of this that the books of Bishop Theophan speak.

In this connection he resembles the great laborer on the field of the spiritual rebirth of the Russian people, St. Tikhon of Zadonsk, who wrote so much, so well, and so penetratingly on the salvation of the human soul amid the dangers of this sinful world.

Behind all the spiritual wisdom that is expressed in his books stands the pure image of a great ascetic. Every word of Bishop Theophan produces all the stronger an impression for having been imprinted by his life. When he repeats: "Do not gravitate to the earth; all is corruptible; only the happiness beyond the grave is eternal, unchanging, true, and this happiness depends upon how we spend this life of ours!"—then we see, as a living example of this correct view of the world and the destiny of the soul, there stand his own self denial, his reclusion, and his desire to take nothing from life but a striving toward God.

✠ ✠ ✠

Bishop Theophan was named in the world George Vasilievich Govorov and he was born on January 10, 1815, in a village near Orel, where his father was a priest. Thus from the first impressions of his youth he lived with the Church. He studied first in the theological preparatory school in the city of Liven, then in the Orel Seminary. However difficult the severe, sometimes cruel conditions of the theological school were at that time, it gave its sons a strong mental temper.

From 1837 to 1841 he continued his education at the Kiev Theological Academy. One may confidently say that the young student often went to the caves of the Kiev Caves Lavra, and amid these recollections there could have been formed in him the resolution to leave the world. Even before finishing the course he was tonsured a monk.

After his tonsure Theophan, together with other newly

tonsured monks, went off to the Lavra, to the well-known Fr. Parthenius.[3] The Elder told them: "You, learned monks who have taken various rules upon yourselves, remember that one thing is most necessary of all: to pray and to pray unceasingly in your mind and heart to God."

Having finished the course with a master's degree, Hieromonk Theophan was assigned as temporary rector of the Kiev-Sofia Theological School; later he was rector of the Novgorod Seminary and a professor and aid to the supervisor in the Petersburg Theological Academy.

This purely scholarly work did not satisfy him, and he petitioned to be discharged from academic service. He was assigned as a member of the Russian Mission in Jerusalem; then, raised to the rank of archimandrite, he was assigned as rector of the Olonets Seminary. He was soon transferred to Constantinople as chief priest of the embassy church, then called to Petersburg to be rector of the Theological Academy and supervisor of religious instruction in the secular schools of the capital.

On May 9, 1859, he was consecrated Bishop of Tambov. Here he established a diocesan school for girls. During his stay in the Tambov Diocese, Bishop Theophan came to love the isolated Vysha Hermitage. In the summer of 1863 he was transferred to Vladimir, where he served for three years. Here too he opened a diocesan school for girls. He served in church often, traveled much throughout the diocese, preached constantly, restored churches, and wholeheartedly lived with his flock, sharing with them both joy and sorrow.

✠ ✠ ✠

In 1861 Bishop Theophan was present at the opening of the relics of St. Tikhon of Zadonsk. This event must have produced a very strong impression on him, since he had so much in common

---

[3] St. Parthenius of the Kiev Caves (†1855), commemorated March 25.—ED.

with St. Tikhon. He had so loved St. Tikhon from his very childhood and had always thought of him with such enthusiasm, that
when the time came for the glorification of this great teacher and
protector of the people, Bishop Theophan's joy was inexpressible.

In 1866 Bishop Theophan petitioned to be relieved as Bishop
of Vladimir and was appointed head of the Vysha Hermitage, and
soon, at a new petition of his, he was freed even of this duty.

What reasons induced Bishop Theophan, full of strength,
to leave his diocese and retire into solitude? Various are the
characters and gifts of men. It was difficult for him in the midst
of the world and those demands to which one must yield as a
consequence of human corruption. His unlimited goodness of
heart, a meekness like that of a dove, his trust of people and
indulgence of them—all this indicated that it was not for him
to live amidst the irreconcilable quarrels of vain worldly life. It
was very difficult for him to be a leader, especially in such an
important position as that of bishop. His trust could be abused;
he could never give necessary reprimands. Besides this, he felt the
call to devote all his energies to spiritual writing. As for himself
personally, he wished to give up all his thoughts to God alone,
Whom he loved so absolutely. He desired that nothing might
disturb the complete communion with God that was so dear to
him. And he left the world to be alone with God.

There was an example that Bishop Theophan kept constantly
before his eyes: St. Tikhon, to whom he had been so drawn from
his youth, and who also, leaving one diocese, became a spiritual
benefactor of the whole Russian people.

To be sure, in retiring from his diocese, Bishop Theophan
more than anything else thought about the salvation of his own
soul by means of the complete dedication of every thought and
breath to God. But the word of Christ was realized in him.
In reclusion, invisible to people, he became a public figure of
enormous magnitude. He sought only the Kingdom of God, and
his great significance for the world was added to him.

On Sunday, July 2, 1866, the Bishop bade farewell to his flock. After serving the Liturgy, the Bishop gave his last sermon amidst a death-like silence, in which could be heard only an occasional quiet weeping. And there began twenty-eight years of a solitary, full life of uninterrupted labors.

The first six years the Bishop went to all services and to the early Liturgy. In church he stood without moving, without leaning, with eyes closed so as not to be distracted. On feast days he usually officiated.

Beginning in 1872, however, he discontinued all intercourse with people except for the chief priest and his confessor. He went no longer to the monastery church, but built with his own hands in his chambers a small church dedicated to the Baptism of the Lord. For the first ten years he served the Liturgy in this church every Sunday and feast day, and for the next eleven years every day. He served completely alone, sometimes in silence, but sometimes singing.

He seemed to be no longer a man, but an angel with a childlike meekness and gentleness. When people came to him on business, he said what was necessary and plunged back into prayer. He ate only enough so as not to ruin his health. Everything that he received he sent by mail to the poor, leaving himself only enough to buy necessary books. From his publications, which were quickly distributed, he received nothing, hoping only that they might be sold as cheaply as possible. In the rare moments when he was free from prayer, reading, or writing, he occupied himself with manual labor. He painted excellent icons and was skilled in woodcarving and the locksmith's trade.

Every day Bishop Theophan received from twenty to forty letters, and he answered them all. With extraordinary sensitivity he penetrated to the spiritual situation of the writer and warmly, clearly, and in detail replied to this confession of a distressed soul.

His letters, which appeared in print after his death, strike one by their freshness, sensitivity, depth and boldness of feeling, simplicity, warm concern, and cordiality.

And thus he lived, directing from his reclusion believers who came to him from afar, thirsting for salvation.

A few words should be said on the books of Bishop Theophan. He spoke on everything from experience and systematically, as a man who had himself passed through the stages of spiritual development on which he wanted to lead others. His works include:

On moral theology: *Letters on the Spiritual Life; Letters on the Christian Life; Miscellaneous Letters on Faith and Life; The Spiritual Life and How to Attune Oneself to It; The Path to Salvation; On Repentance, Communion, and Amendment of Life; On Prayer and Sobriety.*

Commentaries on Holy Scripture: *Commentaries on the Epistles of St. Paul* (all, with the exception of Hebrews); *Commentaries on Psalms 33 and 118.*

Translations: *The Philokalia,* in five volumes; *The Ancient Monastic Statutes; Unseen Warfare; The Sermons of St. Symeon the New Theologian.*

✠ ✠ ✠

The life of Bishop Theophan passed unseen by the world, and death too came to him in solitude. In his last years his vision began to fail, but he did not abandon his constant work, continuing to portion his time in the same strict fashion as always. In the evenings his cell-attendant prepared everything for the celebration of the Liturgy. After the Liturgy the Bishop asked for tea by a knock on the wall. At one o'clock he ate—on non-fast days an egg and a glass of milk. At four o'clock he had tea, and after that no more food for the day.

Beginning January 1, 1894, there were several irregularities in his schedule. On January 6, at 4:30 in the afternoon, his cell-attendant, noting the Bishop's weakness during these days (although he nonetheless continued to write after noon), looked into his room. The Bishop lay on the bed lifeless. His left arm rested on his breast and his right arm was folded as if for a bishop's blessing.

For three days the body remained in the small church in his cell, and for three days it was in the cathedral—and there was no corruption. When he was vested in his bishop's vestments, the face of the dead man was brightened by a joyful smile. Bishop Theophan died at the age of seventy-nine. He was buried in the unheated Kazan Cathedral.

In Bishop Theophan's cell everything was extremely simple, even meager. The walls were bare, the furniture old: a cupboard worth a ruble, a two-ruble chest, an old table, an old reading stand, an iron folding bed, and sofas of birch wood with hard seats. There was a trunk with instruments for lathe-work, carpentry, and bookbinding; photographic equipment, a bench for sawing, and a joiner's bench. There was a gray cotton robe, a wooden panagia, a wooden pectoral cross, a telescope, a microscope, and anatomical and geographical atlases.

And then the books—books without number, without end, in Russian, Slavonic, Greek, French, German, and English. Among them were a complete collection of the Holy Fathers; a theological encyclopedia in French in 150 volumes; Soloviev's *History of Russia*; Schlosser's *Universal History*; the works of the philosophers Hegel, Fichte, Jacobi, and others; works on natural history by Humboldt, Darwin, and others. One calls to mind his words: "It is good to understand the structure of plants, of animals, especially of man, and the laws of life; in them is revealed the wisdom of God, which is great in everything."

In addition there were an immense number of icons, a picture of St. Seraphim of Sarov,[4] and many icons painted by the Bishop himself.

---

[4] Before his glorification, which occurred in 1903.—TRANS.

The great hierarch is hidden from us in body, but his spirit lives in the divinely wise printed works which he left. In the person of Bishop Theophan, as Archbishop Nicander of Vilnius has said, we have a universal Christian teacher, even though he did not speak; a public figure, though in reclusion; a preacher of the Church who was heard everywhere, even though in his last years he appeared in no Church see; a missionary convictor of sectarian errors, even though he did not step out onto the field that was open to missionary activity; a bright lamp of Christ's teaching for Orthodox people, even though he concealed himself from the people's gaze; possessing scarcely a sufficiency of earthly goods, yet enriching all with the spiritual wealth of his teaching; seeking no temporal, earthly glory, yet glorified now both by people and by theological science, as well as by various institutions.

II
THE GLORIFICATION OF ST. THEOPHAN

AFTER the Bolshevik Revolution, the Vysha Monastery of the Dormition of the Theotokos suffered a fate similar to that of most of the monasteries and churches of Russia. During the 1920s the monastery was closed, and the monks were scattered. One church, the Church of Christ's Nativity, was left in use as a parish church. During that time, the monastery territory was logged and also used as a pig farm. However, at the time of the purges of the late 1930s, the last church was closed, and a psychiatric hospital was housed in the monastery buildings.

Finally, in 1973, Archpriest George Glazunov of the Church of St. Sergius of Radonezh in the nearby town of Emmanuilovka, along with Archimandrite Eleutherius (Didenko), carefully removed the relics of St. Theophan and brought them to the former's home. A short while later they were taken to the Holy Trinity–St. Sergius Lavra, where they rested until 1988.

At the Russian Church Council of that year, held in connection

The St. Sergius of Radonezh Church in the village of Emmanuilovka,
where the relics of St. Theophan reposed for fourteen years.

with the thousand-year anniversary of the Baptism of Russia, the
holy Hierarch Theophan was glorified in the ranks of the saints,
and his relics were translated to the St. Sergius of Radonezh
Church at Emmanuilovka. At the Liturgy that was celebrated at
translation of the relics, which took place during Soviet times,
there were over two thousand communicants.

During the period that St. Theophan's relics were at the St.
Sergius Church, numerous miracles took place through the prayers
of the Saint. Among them are the following:

> 1. A young child who was unable to walk was brought to the
> church from afar three times. He would be bathed in the
> nearby holy spring of St. Theophan (located by the St. Sergius
> Church) and then Fr. George would place him on the Saint's
> reliquary. The third time, the child asked to be put down on
> the floor, and began to run around the church.

The reliquary of St. Theophan in the St. Sergius Church
in Emmanuilovka.

2. A military pilot from Volgograd was suffering from
chronic lower back pain. He had spent a great deal of money
on treatment, but to no effect. He was completely healed at
the spring of St. Theophan.

3. A woman who had a herniated disc in her spine arrived on
pilgrimage. Doctors had listed her as an invalid. After bathing
in the holy spring her pain ceased, and after her return home
the doctors informed her that her problem had disappeared.

The holy spring of St. Theophan, near the
St. Sergius Church in Emmanuilovka.

In 1990 part of the Vysha Monastery was given back to the
Church, and by 1993 a women's monastery was opened there.
The only functioning church in the monastery at that time was
the Dormition Church. The nuns had to live outside the walls of
the monastery, since the psychiatric hospital still occupied most
of the buildings.

On June 16/29, 2002, the relics of St. Theophan were brought
home to his beloved monastery. They were placed in the Dormition
Church until March 2/15, 2009, when they were finally placed
in the newly restored Kazan Church, where they had originally
been laid to rest. At this time the nuns were finally able to settle
within the walls of the monastery. To this day, the psychiatric
hospital occupies a portion of the newly restored monastery while
the authorities prepare a new place for the patients. The nuns live
a quiet, cenobitic monastic life, receiving blessings from God
through the prayers of their heavenly benefactor, St. Theophan.

The log house inside the Vysha Dormition Monastery, in which
St. Theophan lived the last twenty-two years of his life in reclusion.
Photograph taken in the late 1990s.

III

About this Book

THE PRESENT BOOK, *Thoughts for Each Day of the Year,* was
first published in Moscow in 1881, under the auspices of
the St. Panteleimon Russian Orthodox Monastery on Mount
Athos, Greece. The book was compiled by St. Theophan primarily
from passages of his previously published works. Many of these
excerpts are from the Saint's articles printed in the magazine
Domestic Conversation in 1869, such as "I Sit and Think," "Reply
to a Question" (from a letter to the editor about Spiritism),
"Resolution of a Perplexity" (about mental prayer), "Alpha and
Omega," "The Renewal of the World," "The Fate of the World,"
and others.

Thoughts for Each Day of the Year was reprinted in Moscow in
1890, 1897, and 1904, and in St. Petersburg in 1903 and 1915. Each

year it was published, the text was arranged to fit the structure of the Church calendar for that particular year. The present English translation was made from the original 1881 Russian publication (which would have been used for 1882), republished by Sretensky Monastery, Moscow, in 1995.

Since each year is structured differently, we ask the reader to refer to the Scripture readings primarily according to the Paschal cycle of each year. Thus, one may orient oneself by looking in one's Orthodox calendar, finding out which week after Pentecost (or Pascha) it is, and turning to the corresponding entry in this book for a commentary on the reading(s) for that day.

While most of the daily entries in this book refer to the Scripture readings assigned to those particular days, St. Theophan occasionally comments on other Scripture passages, or even on cultural and philosophical trends of his time. His aim is always to provide nourishing food for the soul. Contemplating his words on a daily basis, the reader is given continuous encouragement to strive more diligently in cutting off unbelief and sin, growing in faith and virtue, and drawing closer to our Lord and Savior. An Orthodox Christian cannot read this book without feeling convicted in his conscience by the holy Recluse's powerful exhortations. If one takes up the challenge raised by the Saint, one can find true and lasting benefit for one's soul.

St. Theophan's comments on the intellectual trends of his time can also be of benefit to us who live of the twenty-first century, for, in delineating earlier stages of the modern apostasy from the Christian Faith, he helps us to understand what is happening in the world today. The truth of his words is corroborated by their prophetic import. With the clarity of a mind enlightened by Divine grace, he identified the spiritual sickness of the modern West, with its symptoms of materialism, naturalism, deism, atheism, neopaganism, hedonism, and other antichristian belief systems. With sorrow he saw that this sickness had infiltrated his native Russia, and he prophetically warned his fellow countrymen that

The newly restored Kazan Church in the Vysha Monastery,
where the relics of St. Theophan now repose.

this would result in a revolution with cataclysmic consequences, including an open and widespread persecution of the Church.[5]

Within four decades after the publication of this book, all his words came to pass. This thought can only be sobering to us who live nearly a century after the Communist Revolution in Russia, which brought untold misery not only to St. Theophan's homeland but to the many countries which subsequently fell to Communist domination. In this we see that, just as there are dire personal consequences to a loss of Christian faith, so are there terrible national and worldwide consequences. Conversely, just as St. Theophan's warnings to Russia about its loss of Christian faith were borne out by subsequent historical events, so also his personal warnings to us about laxness in Christian life and faith will be borne out by consequences which will be far worse for the fact that they will be eternal—unless, as he continually exhorts us, we truly make an offering of our lives to the Lord. May St. Theophan's grace-filled words sink deep into our hearts, that we may find in them both a support and a push on the path that leads to Christ, Who is *the Author of eternal salvation unto all who obey Him* (Heb. 5:9).

Editor's note: Throughout the text, the King James Version is used for New Testament citations. The English translation of the Psalms is from *The Psalter According to the Seventy* (Boston: Holy Transfiguration Monastery, 2007). The translation of all other Old Testament books is from *The Septuagint Version, Greek and English* (London: Samuel Bagster & Sons, Ltd., 1851).

---

[5] See especially pp. 134–35, 156–57, 271–73, and 292 below.

Iconographic portrait of St. Theophan from
the Holy Dormition Convent at Vysha.

THOUGHTS FOR EACH DAY
OF THE YEAR

According to the Daily Church Readings
from the Word of God

New Year's Day
The Circumcision of the Lord
St. Basil the Great
Col. 2:8–12; Luke 2:20–21, 40–52

Since New Year's Day is the beginning of the days of the year,
we ought to gather in our soul those thoughts, feelings, and
dispositions that would direct our affairs throughout the year in
a Christian way. We will find these the moment we bring to mind
the meaning of New Year's Day in the spiritual life. In the spiritual
life, New Year's Day is when one who has been living carelessly
becomes zealous about salvation and pleasing God. When one
makes this resolution, then all is rebuilt afresh both internally
and externally, upon new beginnings—the old passes away and
all is new. If you have this, renew it; if not, acquire it—and for
you this will be New Year's Day.

A worthy celebration of the Feast of the Circumcision of
the Lord and of the commemoration of St. Basil the Great is
also connected with this. The essence of the change we have
mentioned is that a person begins from this moment to live solely
for his salvation, for God; whereas previously he lived exclusively
for himself, preparing destruction for himself. Now he abandons
former habits, all comforts, and all in which he found pleasure.
He cuts off passions and lustful dispositions and takes on works

of strict self-denial. Such a change precisely represents that which, according to the Apostle, the circumcision of the heart should be. The celebration of the Circumcision of the Lord reminds us of this and obligates us to do it, while St. Basil the Great provides us with an example to follow. So all the themes which crowd our consciousness on New Year's Day come together into one—our inner renewal through the circumcision of the heart. If it pleases the Lord to give someone this mind-set on New Year's Day—that is, not only to think in such a way, but also to bring all of this into his life—he will celebrate New Year's Day in a most perfect Christian manner, and will prepare for a Christian passage of the whole year. On the subsequent New Year's Day he will only have to renew and enliven what he has now taken on.

SATURDAY BEFORE THEOPHANY[1]
I Tim. 3:14–4:5; Matt. 3:1–11

The house of God, which is the Church of the living God, the pillar and ground of the truth (I Tim. 3:15). Consequently there is no need for us to look here and there to search out where the truth is. It is near. Be in the Church, maintain all that it maintains, and you will be in the truth. You will possess the truth and live by it and in it, and you will overflow with true life. The truth does not exist outside of the Orthodox Church. It is the only faithful guardian of all that was commanded by the Lord through the Holy Apostles, and therefore it is the true Apostolic Church. Some lost the Apostolic Church; but since their Christian conscience tells them that only an Apostolic Church can truly preserve and manifest the truth, they decided to make such a church, and they made it, and called it by that name. They could call it the Apostolic Church, but they could not impart the essence to it. For

---

[1] Theophany (in Russian, *Bogoyavleniye*), otherwise known as Epiphany, means "the appearance of God."—TRANS.

the Apostolic Church was created according to the good will of the Father by the Lord and Savior, and by the grace of the Holy Spirit through the Apostles. Such a church cannot be created by people. Those who think they can create such a church are like children playing with dolls. If there is no true Apostolic Church on the earth, there is no need to waste the effort on the creation of it. But thanks be to the Lord, He has not allowed the gates of hell to prevail against the holy Apostolic Church. It exists and will remain, according to His promise, unto the end of the world. This is our Orthodox Church. Glory be to God!

SUNDAY BEFORE THEOPHANY
THIRTY-FIRST SUNDAY AFTER PENTECOST
II Tim. 4:5–8; Mark 1:1–8

Before the Lord's appearance to the people, before He began the work of Divine economy[2] of our salvation, St. John the Forerunner was sent to prepare people to receive Him. This preparation consisted in a call to repentance. Since then, repentance has become the path to the Lord and Savior and the threshold to faith in Him. The Savior Himself began His preaching with the words: *Repent ye, and believe the Gospel* (Mark 1:15). Repentance and faith lead a person who seeks salvation back and forth between each other. Repentance weighs him down with the burden of his sins and frightens him with the impartial judgment of God's righteousness. But faith comes along and shows him the Deliverer Who has taken away the sins of the world. He who repents cleaves to the Deliverer and, having laid down the burden of his sins through Confession, joyfully runs after Him along the path of His commandments. In this manner faith is born of repentance and is

---

[2] Throughout this book, the Russian word *domostroitel'stvo* will be translated as "Divine economy," which refers to God's ordering of and plan for His creation. The epitome of God's economy is Christ's Incarnation, and our salvation through Him.—TRANS.

founded on it. He who repents holds firmly onto faith according to his feeling of deliverance. Faith is alive through repentance. Without repentance faith would be like a sapling which is without a life-giving flow of sap—withered and incapable of giving life.

MONDAY
James 2:14–26; Mark 10:46–52

What doth it profit, my brethren, though a man say he hath faith, and have not works? Can faith save him? (James 2:14). The path to faith is repentance. In repenting what does one say? "I have sinned; I will not do it again. I will not sin; therefore I will live by the commandments." Repentance does not depart with the acquisition of faith; but uniting with faith, it remains through to the end. So too this resolution to live by the commandments remains in force in the presence of faith. Consequently, if the believer has come to faith by the direct path—that is, the path of repentance—he is a zealous fulfiller of the commandments, a doer of good works. Faith gives him a most powerful motivation for this; faith also gives him grace-filled strength to accomplish this through the Holy Mysteries. Thus, faith furthers works. Works in turn make faith perfect, for until that which someone believes is done in deed, faith is not really faith. It becomes apparent only in works—not only apparent, but strong. Works influence faith in return and strengthen it.

TUESDAY
James 3:1–10; Mark 11:11–23

The Lord took away His blessing from the fig tree which was rich with leaves but had no fruit, and it dried up. This is a lesson in action. The fig tree represents people who in appearance are in a good state, but in essence are not worthy of approval. Who are these people? They are those who eloquently discourse about faith, but do not have that faith; they hold the objects of faith in the intellect only. They are those whose outward behavior is proper but their feelings and dispositions are very improper, and they manifest proper works only to hide their impropriety from people. Whenever possible, they do not do these works. For example, such a person gives alms when someone asks him in front of people, but ask him in private and he will berate you. He goes to church to pray to God, prays in sight of everyone, and prays at home as well, so as to not bring shame upon himself before his household. But as soon as he is alone, he does not even make the sign of the Cross on his brow. He does not have any idea about turning to God with the mind and heart. Let us pray that God will not allow us to be like that, for then we will not escape the judgment pronounced over the fig tree.

THEOPHANY
WEDNESDAY
Titus 2:11–14; 3:4–7; Matt. 3:13–17

The Baptism of the Lord is called Theophany because therein the one true God, worshiped in Trinity, revealed Himself palpably: God the Father through the voice from heaven, God the Incarnate Son through His Baptism, and God the Holy Spirit through His descent upon the One baptized. Here the mystery of the relationship between the Persons of the Most Holy Trinity is also revealed. God the Holy Spirit proceeds from the Father and rests in the Son, but does not proceed from the Son. Here also is revealed the fact that the incarnate Divine economy of our salvation is accomplished by God the Son Incarnate, consubstantial with the Holy Spirit and God the Father. And it is revealed that the salvation of each person can be accomplished in no way other than in the Lord Jesus Christ, through the grace of the Holy Spirit, according to the good will of the Father. All the Christian Mysteries shine here with their Divine light and enlighten the minds and hearts of those who with faith celebrate this great festival. Come, let us mentally hasten on high and immerse ourselves in the contemplation of these mysteries of our salvation, singing, "When Thou, O Lord, wast baptized in the Jordan, the worship of the Trinity was made manifest"[3]—a salvation which establishes us in the Trinity, and saves us in the Trinity.

SYNAXIS OF ST. JOHN THE FORERUNNER
THURSDAY
Acts 19:1–8; John 1:29–34

St. John bore witness to Christ Jesus, that He is in truth *the Lamb of God, Who taketh away the sin of the world* (John 1:29), that He is the promised Deliverer, awaited by all. Those who were near him heard this and believed. From them this witness passed on to the people, and everyone began to think that He to Whom John bore witness was not an ordinary man. The Savior pointed this out when, during His last days, he posed a question to the chiefs of the temple: *The baptism of John, was it from heaven, or of men?* (Mark 11:30). They refrained from answering, because it was impossible for them not to see that John, baptizing with water, had not come of himself. But if they were to say this, they would immediately have to acknowledge John's testimony that the Promised One was before them, and would therefore be compelled to submit to His teaching. But they did not want to submit—not for any well-founded reasons, but solely because of their prejudice. However, their obstinacy does not in the least lessen the power of the witness of St. John. To this day, it is as certain as it was when it came forth from his mouth. We hearken unto John, who shows us the true Deliverer; and through this we enliven our faith, as a faith that has tangible proof behind it.

---

[3] From the troparion to the Feast.—ED.

Friday
I Peter 1:1–2, 10–12; 2:6–10; Mark 12:1–12

On the day of Theophany it is shown in action that the Divine economy of our salvation is accomplished by the Lord Jesus Christ, according to the goodwill of the Father, together with the Holy Spirit. But now, through the word of the Apostle, it is suggested to us that the salvation of each person, according to that Divine economy of God, happens in no other way than through the operation of the Most Holy Trinity: the Father, the Son, and the Holy Spirit, *according to the foreknowledge of God the Father, through sanctification of the Spirit, unto obedience and sprinkling of the blood of Jesus Christ* (I Peter 1:2). God the Father, foreknowing that a man is capable of faith, meets him in His goodwill and calls him to salvation through the grace of the Holy Spirit. The Holy Spirit, having called him to faith and strengthened him therein, sprinkles the believer with the blood of the Lord and Savior in the Sacrament of Baptism. Through this the Holy Spirit, receiving entrance into him, Himself abides in him and cooperates with him in every way possible to provide for his salvation. Let us praise, hymn, and magnify the Most Holy Trinity, the good Helper of our salvation. *Giving all diligence*, let us hurry to adorn ourselves with every virtue, in the image of Him Who created and re-created us; that we not be shown to be *barren nor unfruitful in the knowledge of our Lord,* and bar ourselves from entrance *into the everlasting Kingdom of our Lord* (II Peter 1:5, 8, 11), to which we are called.

Saturday after Theophany
Eph. 6:10–17; Matt. 4:1–11

The Apostle clothes Christians in the whole armor of God. It is appropriate that this follows the previous lesson. For if someone, heeding the call of God, has taken on the beginning of a new life through God's grace, providing for his own part *all diligence* (II Peter 1:5), then he must not expect to rest on his laurels, but rather to struggle. He has left the world, and for this the world will begin to press him. He was saved from the power of the devil, and the devil will chase after him and set snares before him, to throw him off the path of good and drag him back to his domain. He has denied himself and denied selfishness, along with a whole horde of passions. But this sin which lives in us will not suddenly relinquish its free and self-pleasing existence, and every minute it will attempt, under various pretexts, to establish once more the same routine of life that so richly filled and fed it earlier. Three enemies,[4] each with innumerable hordes; but the commander-in-chief is the devil, and his closest helpers are the demons. They are in charge of everything in a sinful life; they are the opponents of spiritual life. That is why the Apostle arms the Christian against them as if there were no other enemies at all. He says: *We wrestle not against flesh and blood, but against principalities, against powers, against the rulers of the darkness of this world, against spiritual wickedness in high places* (Eph. 6:12). If they did not exist, perhaps battles would not exist either. Likewise, as soon as they are repelled and struck down, it takes nothing to repel and defeat the others. So, each of you—look to see where you need to direct your arrows, or at least look to see from which side you particularly need to defend yourself. Then, defend yourself! The Apostle prescribed several weapons, but all of them have power only through the Lord. That is why experienced spiritual fighters have passed on to us this instruction: "Flog your enemies with the name of the Lord Jesus!"[5]

---

[4] I.e., the world, the devil, and the flesh.—ED.

[5] St. John Climacus, *Ladder of Divine Ascent,* Step 21.—ED.

SUNDAY AFTER THEOPHANY
THIRTY-SECOND SUNDAY AFTER PENTECOST
Eph. 4:7–13; Matt. 4:12–17

Yesterday the Apostle armed with the whole spiritual armor the Christian who sets out upon the path of salvation. Now, for our inspiration in times of hardship, he shows who the leaders are in this battle procession, and what is the final bright goal of everything. The leaders are pastors and teachers, whom the Lord has given to the Church, and through whose mouths He Himself utters the guiding direction needful for all, as soon as one turns to such leaders with faith and prayerful appeal to the Lord. Those who selflessly walk the Lord's path know this truth, as do those who conduct a struggle against the enemies of salvation without pity for themselves. In their pastors they always find help and are brought to understanding, while, looking from the outside, such help could not be expected. For they are not coming to men, but to the Lord, Who is always ready to direct and give understanding through such men, to anyone who sincerely and with faith seeks help from Him. The final bright goal is *the measure of the stature of the fullness of Christ*—the stature of *a perfect man* (Eph. 4:13). We all know what a perfect man is in the usual order of things, and we could hardly find a person who would not wish to attain such perfection. But the meaning of *a perfect man* in the Lord is something not known to anyone other than those who have entered into that stature. This, however, should not cool one's fervor for the attainment of such a stature, but on the contrary should kindle it even more; for this lack of knowledge is due to the height of that spiritual perfection which is called a manly stature in a life according to God. The Apostle defined this as taking on the fullness of perfections revealed in the Lord and Savior. Anyone can see that there is reason for us to apply *all diligence* (II Peter 1:5) toward our calling.

MONDAY
I Peter 2:21–3:9; Mark 12:13–17

The Apostle now points out to us the *hidden man of the heart* (I Peter 3:4) as the object of our most painstaking concern and care. We are to adorn ourselves through the formation of this man within ourselves. What is the meaning of the *hidden man of the heart*? It is that man which forms in the heart when only good dispositions and feelings come to dwell therein. Examine these dispositions and feelings, and you will see the face of the man hidden in the heart. Here are these dispositions: *His Divine power hath given unto us all things that pertain unto life and godliness* (II Peter 1:3), and on your part, *giving all diligence,* writes St. Peter, *add to your faith virtue; and to virtue knowledge; and to knowledge temperance; and to temperance patience; and to patience godliness; and to godliness brotherly kindness; and to brotherly kindness love* (II Peter 1:5–7). In a similar fashion St. Paul lists the inner good dispositions of the Christian heart: *The fruit of the Spirit is love, joy, peace, long-suffering, gentleness, goodness, faith, meekness, temperance* (Gal. 5:22–23). Also: *Put on therefore, as the elect of God, holy and beloved, bowels of mercies, kindness, humbleness of mind, meekness, long-suffering … and above all these things put on love, which is the bond of perfectness. And let the peace of God rule in your hearts* (Col. 3:12–15). Bring together all of these good things into one spiritual body with its various members, and you will see the divinely beautiful face of the hidden man of the heart. You must fervently establish the same in your own heart.

TUESDAY
I Peter 3:10–22; Mark 12:18–27

But sanctify the Lord God in your hearts (I Peter 3:15). Sanctifying the Lord in one's heart is the soul and spirit of the hidden man of the heart depicted above. As in the beginning God created the body of man out of particles of dust, breathed into him the breath of life (cf. Gen. 2:7), and man became as he ought to be, so the hidden man of the heart, created on the inside from the indicated virtues, is only a real spiritual man when his heart sanctifies the Lord God. Thus, we read in the Lord's Prayer, "Hallowed[6] be Thy name." If this does not occur, then a man modeled from the aforementioned virtues will end up a stillborn child, without the spirit of life. Let this be known to those who think they can get away with a few virtues without having anything to do with God! What does it mean to sanctify God in the heart? It means showing great reverence before Him unceasingly, always bearing in mind the thought of His omnipresence; being eager at every instant to zealously please Him, and with all fear to beware of everything unpleasing to Him. Especially, it means committing all of your temporal and eternal life unto His fatherly care; to accept all that happens humbly, submissively, and thankfully, as coming straight from His hand.

WEDNESDAY
I Peter 4:1–11; Mark 12:28–37

One lawyer asked the Lord: *Which is the first commandment of all?* The Lord answered: *Thou shalt love the Lord thy God with all thy heart, and with all thy soul, and with all thy mind, and with all thy strength: this is the first commandment. And the second is like, namely this, Thou shalt love thy neighbor as thyself. There is none other commandment greater than these* (Mark 12:28, 30–31). This also serves as a supplement to the portrayal of the hidden man of the heart. Sanctifying the Lord is his spirit, and love is his soul; all the other virtues are his various members—arms, legs, eyes, ears,

---

[6] In the Slavonic, the word "sanctify" from the Epistle and the word "hallowed" in the Lord's Prayer are the same.—TRANS.

tongue. Remembrance of this is very needful, because it sometimes happens that, considering the doing of good to be the final virtue, people think they can get by with only this, not thinking about the Lord and forgetting about love. Doing good without faith and a desire to please God is not holy; it is like a house that has not been blessed, or a room without icons. Without love, the doing of good is like a building filled with lifeless sculptures, which succumb, moreover, to mustiness and mold. Pay attention to this, each of you; and setting out to create a new person in yourself, try to place him before the Lord, Who is without any flaw.

THURSDAY
I Peter 4:12–5:5; Mark 12:38–44

The widow placed in the treasury (the church collection box) two mites (a half-kopeck piece,[7] approximately); but the Lord said that she had cast in more than anyone, although the others were casting in rubles and dozens of rubles. What gave extra weight to her mite? It is the disposition with which the offering was made. Do you see the difference between the doing of good without soul, by habit, and the doing of good with soul and heart? It is not the external aspects of a deed which give it value, but the inner disposition. It may happen that a deed which is outstanding in every other regard has no value whatsoever before God, yet a deed which is insignificant in appearance is valued greatly by Him. What follows from this is evident in and of itself. But do not take it into your head to be careless about external things, intending to limit yourself only to inner things. That widow would not have received approval if she had said to herself, "I too have the desire to put in money—but what should I do? I only have two mites. If I give them away, I myself will be left with nothing." She had the desire and acted upon it as well, committing her life into God's hands.

---

[7] This would equal the buying power of a few U.S. cents.—ED.

No one would have condemned her if she had put in nothing—neither people, nor God. But then she would not have revealed the disposition which singled her out from the ranks of others and made her renowned throughout the entire Christian world.

FRIDAY
II Peter 1:1–10; Mark 13:1–8

Having enumerated the virtues which we must seek with all diligence, and having received grace-filled power, the Apostle says by way of encouragement: *If these things be in you, and abound, they make you that ye shall neither be barren nor unfruitful in the knowledge of our Lord Jesus Christ* (II Peter 1:8). The virtues to which he refers here were mentioned in I Peter 2:21–3:9. Now we shall add only that we are required to manifest these virtues not just once, but rather to make them always abide in us, to be part of our essence, to take root in us. Thus, they must not remain on one level, but must ever multiply and grow in strength and fruitfulness. Only then, he says, will we not be barren and unfruitful *in the knowledge of our Lord Jesus Christ.* He who believes in Him and confesses Him enters into the knowledge of the Lord. "You believe?" says the Apostle. "See then that your faith be not barren and unfruitful." What should I do, so that my faith will not be like that? Prosper in every virtue. Where are those who repeat over and over that believing is enough: that nothing more is needed? Whoever thinks this way is blind.

SATURDAY
II Tim. 2:11–19; Luke 18:2–8

To more strongly impress the truth *that men ought always to pray, and not to faint* (Luke 18:1) and that they should continue to pray if their prayer is not soon heard, the Lord told the parable about the judge who neither feared God nor regarded man. The judge complied at last with the widow's petition, not because he feared God and regarded man, but only because that widow gave him no peace. So, if such a callous man could not withstand the persistence of this woman's petition, will not God, Who loves mankind and is filled with mercy, fulfill a petition raised up to Him persistently with tears and contrition? Here is the answer to why our prayers are often not heard: Because we do not send up our petitions to God zealously, but as though in passing; furthermore, we pray once today, then expect our prayer to be answered by tomorrow, not thinking to sweat and trouble ourselves any more in prayer. That is why our prayer is neither heard nor answered. We ourselves do not fulfill as we ought the law laid down for prayer—the law of hopeful and zealous persistence.

Sunday of the Publican and the Pharisee
II Tim. 3:10–15; Luke 18:10–14

Yesterday the Gospel reading taught us persistence in prayer, and now it teaches humility, or the feeling that we have no right to be heard. Do not assume that you have the right to be heard, but approach prayer as one unworthy of any attention, allowing yourself only the boldness needed to open your mouth and raise up your prayer to God, knowing the Lord's boundless condescension toward us poor ones. Do not even allow the thought to come to your mind, "I did such and such—so give me such and such." Consider whatever you might have done as your obligation. If you had not done it you would have been subject to punishment, and what you did deserves no reward; you did not do anything special. That Pharisee enumerated his rights to be heard and left the temple with nothing. The bad thing is not that he actually did as he said, for indeed he should have done it. The bad thing is that he presented it as something special; whereas, having done it he should have thought no more of it. Deliver us, O Lord, from this sin of the Pharisee! People rarely speak like the Pharisee in words, but in the feelings of their heart they are rarely unlike him. For why is it that people pray poorly? It is because they feel as though they are just fine in the sight of God, even without praying.

MONDAY
II Peter 1:20–2:9; Mark 13:9–13

The fear of God leads to the beginning of a holy and God-pleasing life and is its most faithful guardian when one follows the inspiration of the fear of God and makes such a beginning. The present Epistle reading teaches us this, bringing to mind the threatening judgments of God and the punishments which are manifest even here upon those who do not submit to His will. He, it says, *spared not the angels that sinned* (II Peter 2:4). They were pure and dwelt in a most radiant habitation. But as soon as they sinned, they were cast down into the nethermost darkness. Will He spare you and me if we go against His will? Impiety overflowed in the days of Noah. God brought a flood upon them and destroyed them all, except for the eight souls of Noah's family. He did not take into account that there were many people. Will He deliberate over you alone, whether to destroy you or not, when you do not to listen to His voice? For a long time the Lord spared Sodom and Gomorrah. But instead of coming to their senses, they rushed to the height of impiety. Therefore, they were struck by fire when they did not expect it. This fire is an image of the eternal fire, which awaits the impious. Neither will you escape this fire if you walk the same path as they did. Bring all of this to mind when sitting by yourself, especially in the silence and darkness of night. Thus arousing the fear of God, fear sin as though the flame of eternal fire is stealthily approaching you.

Tuesday
II Peter 2:9–22; Mark 13:14–23

If any man shall say to you, Lo, here is Christ; or, lo, He is there; believe him not (Mark 13:21). Christ the Lord, our Savior, having established upon earth the Holy Church, is well pleased to abide in it as its Head, Enlivener, and Ruler. Christ is here, in our Orthodox Church, and He is not in any other church. Do not search for Him elsewhere, for you will not find Him. Therefore, if someone from a non-Orthodox assemblage comes to you and begins to suggest that they have Christ—do not believe it. If someone says to you, "We have an apostolic community, and we have Christ," do not believe them. The Church founded by the Apostles abides on the earth—it is the Orthodox Church, and Christ is in it. A community established only yesterday cannot be apostolic, and Christ is not in it. If you hear someone saying, "Christ is speaking in me," while he shuns the [Orthodox] Church, does not want to know its pastors, and is not sanctified by the Sacraments, do not believe him. Christ is not in him; rather another spirit is in him, one that appropriates the name of Christ in order to divert people from Christ the Lord and from His Holy Church. Neither believe anyone who suggests to you even some small thing alien to the [Orthodox] Church. Recognize all such people to be instruments of seducing spirits and lying preachers of falsehoods.

Wednesday
II Peter 3:1–18; Mark 13:24–31

The day of the Lord will come as a thief in the night (II Peter 3:10). A thief in the night sneaks up when he is not expected. So will the day of the Lord also come when it is not expected. But when the One Who is coming is not expected, no preparations are made for meeting Him. Lest we allow such negligence, the

Lord commanded: *Watch: for ye know not what hour your Lord doth come* (Matt. 24:42). Meanwhile, what are we doing? Are we watching? Are we waiting? We must confess that we are not. Some at least await death, but scarcely anyone awaits the day of the Lord. And it is as if they are right. Our fathers and forefathers waited, but the day did not come. Since we do not see anything, why should we think that it will come in our days? Thus, we do not think and do not wait. It would not be a wonder if, with such a disposition as ours, the day of the Lord were to fall upon us like a thief. We shall be like the inhabitants of a city which the governor of the province promised to visit on that day or the next. They waited for him an hour, waited another hour, waited a day, and then said, "I suppose he's not coming," and went home. But as soon as they departed and gave themselves over to sleep—he appeared. It will be the same with us. Whether we are waiting or not, the day of the Lord will come, and it will come without warning. For the Lord said: *Heaven and earth shall pass away: but My words shall not pass away* (Mark 13:31). But is it not better to wait, lest we be taken unawares? For we will pay for it.

THURSDAY
I John 1:8–2:6; Mark 13:31–14:2

What the Apostle directed us toward yesterday, the Gospel now openly suggests to us: *Take ye heed, watch and pray: for ye know not when the time is.... Watch ye therefore ... lest coming suddenly He find you sleeping* (Mark 13:33, 35–36). It is necessary to wait and every instant to keep in mind that the Lord is about to appear and shine like lightning from one end of the universe to the other. It is thought by some that it is possible to replace this waiting upon the Lord with waiting for death. This is good, or at least this should be done. But awaiting the coming of the Lord is one thing, and awaiting death another. They lead to different thoughts and to different feelings, born under the impact of these different thoughts. Await the day of the Lord, when all will end in an irrevocable decision. After our death, time will still continue in an undecided state; but the day of the Lord will assign everything for eternal ages, and it will be sealed, so you cannot expect any changes. "I have been waiting," you say. So wait longer, and continue to wait. "But this," you say, "will poison all my joys." It will not poison your joys; it will only drive away from your everyday life those joys that are illegitimately so called. You will still rejoice, but only in the Lord. It is possible to wait for the Lord with this joy; and if the Lord finds you in this joy, He will not call you to account, but will praise you.

FRIDAY
I John 2:7–17; Mark 14:3–9

The world passeth away, and the lust thereof (I John 2:17). Who does not see this? Everything around us passes away—things, people, events; and we ourselves are passing away. Worldly lust also passes; we scarcely taste the sweetness of its satisfaction before both the lust and the sweetness disappear. We chase after something else, and it is the same; we chase after a third thing—again the same. Nothing stands still; everything comes and goes. What? Is there really nothing constant? There is, says the Apostle: *He that doeth the will of God abideth for ever* (I John 2:17). How does the world, which is so transient, endure? Because God desires that the world endure. The will of God is the world's unshakable and indestructible foundation. It is the same among people—whosoever begins to stand firmly in God's will is made steadfast and firm at once. One's thoughts are restless when chasing after something transient. But as soon as one comes to his senses and returns to the path of the will of God, his thoughts and intentions begin to settle down. When at last one succeeds in acquiring the habit for such a way of life, everything he has, both within and without, comes into quiet harmony and serene order. Having begun here, this deep peace and imperturbable serenity will pass over to the next life as well, and there it will abide unto the ages. Amidst the general transience of things around us, what is not transient, but rather constant within us, is to walk in the will of God.

SATURDAY
II Tim. 3:1–9; Luke 20:45–21:4

Who are those *having a form of godliness, but denying the power thereof?* (II Tim. 3:5). Who are those others, *ever learning, and never able to come to the knowledge of the truth?* (II Tim. 3:7). The former are those who maintain all the external routines in which a godly life is manifested, but who do not have a strong enough will to maintain their inner dispositions as true godliness demands. They go to church and stand there readily, but they do not make the effort to stand with their mind before God continuously and to reverently fall down before Him. Having prayed a bit, they release the reins of the control of their mind, and it soars, circling over the entire world. As a result, they are outwardly located in church, but according to their inner state they are not there; only the form of godliness remains in them, while its power is not there. With them everything else [in the spiritual life] can be thought about in the same way.

The latter are those who, having entered the realm of faith, do nothing but invent questions: "What is this? What is that? Why this way? Why that way?" They are people suffering from empty inquisitiveness. They do not chase after the truth, but only ask and ask. Having found the answer to their questions, they do not dwell on them for long, but soon feel the necessity to look for another answer. And so they whirl about day and night, questioning and questioning, and are never fully satisfied with what they learn. Some people chase after pleasures, but these chase after the satisfaction of their inquisitiveness.

Sunday of the Prodigal Son
I Cor. 6:12–20; Luke 15:11–32

The Sunday of the Prodigal Son says so much to us! It speaks about our peace and abundance in the house of the Heavenly Father, about our mad departure from the Father's guardianship to unbridled freedom, about the richness of the heritage given us despite our disobedience, about its reckless waste on all sorts of indecencies, and about our utter impoverishment as a result. But then it talks also about how one recovers his senses and, coming to himself, decides to return to his greatly merciful Father. It talks about how he returns, how he is received lovingly and is restored to his first state. Who will not find this lesson profitable? If you abide in your Father's house, do not strive for freedom. You see how a similar experience ended! If you have run away and are squandering all, stop this quickly. If you have already squandered everything and are living in poverty, resolve quickly to return—and then, return. There every lenience and the former love and prosperity await you. This last step is the most necessary one. But there is no point in enlarging upon this. All has been said concisely and clearly. Come to your senses, resolve to return, arise and hasten to the Father. His embrace is open and ready to receive you.

Monday
I John 2:18–3:10; Mark 11:1–11

Yesterday the parable about the Prodigal Son invited us to return from dissipation to the good path. Now the Holy Apostle John inspires us for this, giving us the assurance that if we do this, then when the Lord appears we will be like Him. What can compare with such a dignity? I should think that upon hearing this, you would be filled with a desire to attain this for yourself. It is a good and most necessary thing! Do not put off undertaking that through which it is attained. Read further: *Every man that hath this hope in Him, purifies himself, even as He is pure* (I John 3:3). Is there anything within you in need of purifying? Of course—no small amount will be found. Make haste: for where the Lord is, nothing that defiles shall enter in (cf. Apoc. 21:27). Do not be taken aback by the difficulty of this matter. The Lord Himself will be your Helper in all things. Simply desire it wholeheartedly and turn to the Lord for His much-needed help. His grace-filled power will merge with your effort, and things will go easily and successfully. As there is no sin that can overcome the mercy of God, so there is no moral uncleanness that can resist the grace-filled power that consumes it. Only on your part, let there be a lack of desire for this uncleanness, an earnest effort to repulse it, and your recourse in faith to the Lord.

Tuesday
I John 3:11–20; Mark 14:10–42

St. Peter fervently insisted that he would not reject the Lord; but when it came down to it, he denied Him, and three times, no less. Such is our weakness! Do not rely upon yourself, and when you enter into the midst of enemies, place all your hope of overcoming them in the Lord. For this purpose a fall was allowed to this great man—so that afterwards no one would dare on his own to do something good or to overcome some enemy, either internal or external. You must hope in the Lord, but not stop trying. Help from the Lord joins our efforts, and thus makes them powerful. If these efforts are not there, God's help has nowhere to descend, and it will not descend. But again, if you are filled with self-reliance, and consequently you have no need for help and seek no help—again, God's help will not descend. How is it to descend when it is considered unnecessary? Neither, in this case, is there anything with which to receive it. It is received by the heart. The heart opens up to receive it through a feeling of need. So both the former and the latter are needed. Say, "Help, O God!" But don't just lie around.

WEDNESDAY
I John 3:21–4:6; Mark 14:43–15:1

If help is needed, ask. "I asked," you say, "and it was not given." But then why is it given to others? With the Lord there is no respect of persons, that He would give to one, and not give to another, without any reason. He is ready to give to all—for He loves to give. If He does not give to someone, the reason is not in Him, but in the one asking help. Among such reasons can be some that we cannot even guess. But there exist known reasons, visible to everyone. St. John points out one of these reasons (and is it not the chief reason?) to be the absence of confidence, and the absence of confidence comes from condemnation by the heart or the conscience. *Beloved,* he says, *if our heart condemn us not, then have we confidence toward God. And whatsoever we ask, we receive of Him, because we keep His commandments, and do those things that are pleasing in His sight* (I John 3:21). There is nothing more to add to these words. Everything is clear in and of itself. What master will help an unfaithful servant, a squanderer and profligate? Will the Lord really indulge us when we do not want to please Him and fulfill His commandments, if we only start praying when an extreme need arises?

THURSDAY
I John 4:20–5:21; Mark 15:1–15

This is the victory that overcometh the world, even our Faith (I John 5:4)—the Christian Faith. To overcome the world—what does this mean? Not to exterminate all those who love the world, or to annihilate and destroy all which is loved by the world. It

THOUGHTS FOR EACH DAY OF THE YEAR

means rather that while living amidst those who love the world and moving amidst customs loved by the world, we should live as ones alien to everyone and everything. As soon as you have rejected the world and everything worldly, you have by this very action overcome the world. But what teaches you to reject the world and what gives you strength for this? Our [Orthodox] Faith. It discloses the destructiveness of the delusions of the world and inspires the desire to free oneself of their nets. Then, when one resolves to break these bonds, when one repents and approaches the Mysteries of renewal—Baptism or Repentance—faith allows him to mystically feel the sweetness of a life opposed to the world, a sweetness with which all the pleasures of the world cannot in any way enter into comparison. As a result, a loathing for everything worldly dwells in the heart, which is actually victory over the world. But in this mystical action, as a result of which loathing for the world is born, the power to steadfastly abide in this loathing and alienation from the world is also granted; and this is a decisive and lasting victory.

Friday
II John 1:1–13; Mark 15:22–25, 33–41

St. John the Theologian writes: *Many deceivers are entered into the world, who confess not that Jesus Christ is come in the flesh* (II John 1:7). Such it was in his time, whereas now deceivers enter the world who confess that Christ is come in the flesh, but who nevertheless are "deceivers and antichrists" (cf. II John 1:7). This began more openly in the time of Arius and continues to this day. However, the ancient deceivers stumbled more in the dogma about the person of Jesus Christ our Savior, whereas from the time of Luther they began to stumble in the teaching about salvation in Him. How many such "teachers" have there been? Among us there have appeared "deceivers and antichrists," who say "believe and it is enough"; nothing more is needed—neither the Church, nor the Sacraments, nor the priesthood. These too begin their deception starting with Christ the Lord and salvation in Him. But since they do not interpret these correctly, they are antichrists, and subject to condemnation. Beware of them. *Whosoever transgresseth, and abideth not in the doctrine of Christ hath not God* (II John 1:9). These people do not have Him, because they do not have the doctrine of Christ. This doctrine is in the Church, and they have separated themselves from the Church. Only those who follow the Church have the doctrine of Christ and abide in it. They therefore have both Christ, the Son of God, and God the Father. But the others do not, although they keep saying that they do. Do not receive them, neither bid them Godspeed (cf. II John 1:10).

SATURDAY (COMMEMORATION OF THE DEAD)
I Thess. 4:13–17; John 5:24–30

Now the Holy Church directs our attention beyond the borders of our present life, to our fathers and brothers who have passed on from here. The Church hopes, by reminding us of their state (which we ourselves shall not escape), to prepare us to spend Cheese-fare Week properly, as well as Great Lent, which follows. Let us listen to our mother, the Church; and commemorating our fathers and brothers, let us take care to prepare ourselves for our passing over to the other world. Let us bring to mind our sins and bemoan them, setting out in the future to keep ourselves pure from any defilement. For nothing unclean will enter the Kingdom of God, and at the Judgment no one unclean will be justified. After death you cannot expect purification. You will remain as you are when you cross over. You must prepare your cleansing here. Let us hurry, for who can predict how long one will live? Life could be cut off this very hour. How can we appear unclean in the other world? With what eyes will we look at our fathers and brothers who will meet us? How will we answer their questions: "What is this that is wrong in you? What is this? And what is this?" What shame will cover us! Let us hasten to set right all that is out of order, to appear at least in a somewhat tolerable and bearable state in the other world.

SUNDAY OF THE LAST JUDGMENT (MEATFARE SUNDAY)
I Cor. 8:8–9:2; Matt. 25:31–46

The Dread Judgment! The Judge comes in the clouds, surrounded by a countless multitude of bodiless heavenly powers. Trumpets sound to all the ends of the earth and raise up the dead. The risen regiments pour into the preordained place, to the throne of the Judge, having a foreboding of what verdict will sound in their ears. For everyone's works are written on the brow of their nature, and their very appearance will correspond to their deeds and morals. The division of those on His right hand and those on His left is accomplished in and of itself.

At last all has been determined. Deep silence falls. In another instant, the decisive verdict of the Judge is heard: to some, "Come," to the others, "Depart." "Have mercy on us, O Lord, have mercy on us! May Thy mercy, O Lord, be upon us!" they shall say, but then it will already be too late to plead. We need to take the trouble now to wash away the unfavorable marks written upon our nature. At the Judgment, we may be ready to pour out rivers of tears in order to wash ourselves, but this would do us no good then. Let us weep now—if not rivers of tears, then at least streams; if not streams, then at least drops. If we cannot find even this much, then let us become contrite in heart, and confess our sins to the Lord, begging Him to forgive them, and promising not to offend Him any more through the violation of His commandments. Then, let us be zealous to faithfully fulfill this promise.

MONDAY
III John 1:1–14; Luke 19:29–40, 22:7–39

What does it mean *to walk in truth* (III John 1:4)? It means to accept truth in your heart, to abide in such thoughts and feelings as the truth requires. In this way, it is the truth that God is everywhere and sees everything. He who accepts this truth with his heart and begins to keep himself both inwardly and outwardly as if God Himself is before him and is seeing everything within him, is walking in this truth. It is true that God contains all, and that without Him we cannot do anything successfully. He who accepts this with his heart and turns in prayer to God for help in whatever he does, accepting whatever happens to him as being from the hand of the Lord, is walking in this truth. It is true that death could steal us away at any hour, and that immediately after death comes the [particular] Judgment. He who accepts this truth with his heart and begins to live as if he were about to die this minute and appear before the Judgment of God, is walking in this truth. So it is concerning every other truth.

THE MEETING OF THE LORD
TUESDAY
Heb. 7:7–17; Luke 2:22–40

At this Meeting, the Lord is surrounded on one side by Symeon—righteousness which awaits salvation, but not of itself; and by Anna—a life of strict fasting and prayer, made alive by faith; and on the other side by essential, comprehensive, and steadfast purity—Joseph the Betrothed. Transfer all of these spiritual attitudes to your heart and you will meet the Lord—not as One Who is being carried to you, but as One Who comes to you Himself. You will take Him into the embrace of your heart, and you will sing a hymn which will pass throughout the heavens and gladden all the angels and saints.

WEDNESDAY
Joel 2:12–26; 3:12–21

Now therefore, saith the Lord your God, turn to Me with all your heart, and with fasting, and with weeping, and with lamentation and rend your hearts, and not your garments, and turn to the Lord your God: for He is merciful and compassionate, long-suffering, and plenteous in mercy.... Sound the trumpet in Sion, sanctify a fast, proclaim a solemn service.... Let the bridegroom go forth of his chamber, and the bride out of her closet.... Let the priests that minister to the Lord weep, and say, Spare Thy people, O Lord (Joel 2:12–17). Who now hearkens unto this voice, resounding in the Church? If on the city squares a thunderous voice should resound from heaven, saying, "Spare yourselves, O people, so that the Lord will spare you!"—perhaps someone would hear it and awake from his ecstasy of pleasures, lusts, and wine. The priests do not cease to plead, "Spare us, O Lord!" But from the Lord comes the just yet terrible answer, "I will not spare, for there are none seeking to be spared." All are standing with their backs to the Lord; they have turned from Him and forgotten Him.

THURSDAY
Jude 1:11–25; Luke 23:1–34, 44–56

Woe, proclaims the Holy Apostle Jude, to them who conduct themselves in a corrupt way in society, who without fear fatten themselves at feasts, who froth in their own shame, walk after their own lusts, speak great swelling words, and separate themselves from the unity of the Faith. Woe! For behold, the Lord will come with ten thousands of His holy angels to execute judgment upon all, and to expose all that are ungodly in all their ungodly works which their ungodliness has committed (cf. Jude 1:14–15).

FRIDAY
Zach. 8:7–17, 19–23

So will I save you, and ye shall be a blessing, promises the Lord through the prophet Zachariah (Zach. 8:13). But under what condition? Under the condition that every man will speak the truth to his neighbor, that men will righteously sort out their affairs amongst themselves, that men will not remember wrongs in their hearts against their neighbor, that they will love no false oath, and will love truth and peace. If these conditions are met, says the Lord, *they shall be to Me a people, and I will be to them a God, in truth and in righteousness* (Zach. 8:8), and His blessing shall spread among them. Then all strangers shall hear and say, "Let us go speedily to them to pray before the Lord, for we have heard that the Lord is with them (cf. Zach. 8:21–23). *And many peoples and many nations shall come to seek earnestly the face of the Lord Almighty* (Zach. 8:22).

Thus did the high moral purity of the first Christians attract people and nations to the Lord. Those who live always according to the spirit of Christ are, without the use of words, the best preachers of Christ and the most convincing apostles of Christianity.

SATURDAY OF THE HOLY FATHERS
Gal. 5:22–6:2; Matt. 11:27–30

They that are Christ's have crucified the flesh with the affections and lusts (Gal. 5:24). Nowadays, this order of things has been perverted: people crucify the flesh, but not together with the affections and lusts—rather by means of affections and lusts. How people now torture their bodies with overeating, drunkenness, lustful deeds, dancing, and merry-making! The most heartless master does not torture his lazy animal this way. If we were to give our flesh freedom and reason, its first word would be against its mistress, the soul—that the soul has unlawfully interfered in the flesh's affairs, brought in passions alien to it, and tortured it by carrying out these passions in the flesh. Our body's needs are essentially simple and passionless. Look at the animals: they do not overeat, they do not sleep in excess, and having satisfied their fleshly needs at the proper time, they remain calm for the entire year. Only the soul, which has forgotten its better inclinations, has by its intemperance developed out of the body's basic needs a multitude of unnatural inclinations, which are unnatural for the body as well. However, in order to cut off, in every possible way, the fleshly passions from the soul which it has grafted onto itself, it is necessary to crucify the flesh. This can be done only by not giving it its fill of what is necessary, or by meeting its needs to a far lesser degree than what it demands.

FORGIVENESS (CHEESEFARE) SUNDAY
Rom. 13:11–14:4; Matt. 6:14–21

For if ye forgive men their trespasses, your Heavenly Father will also forgive you; but if ye forgive not men their trespasses, neither will your Father forgive your trespasses (Matt. 6:14–15). What a simple and handy means of salvation! Your trespasses are forgiven under the condition that you forgive your neighbor's trespasses against you. This means that you are in your own hands. Force yourself to pass from agitated feelings toward your brother to truly peaceful feelings—and that is all. The day of forgiveness—what a great, heavenly day of God this is! If all of us used it as we ought, this day would make Christian societies into heavenly societies, and the earth would merge with heaven.

MONDAY (FIRST WEEK OF LENT)
Is. 1:1–20; Gen. 1:1–13; Prov. 1:1–20

"The Fast has come, the mother of chastity."[8] What was the time before this day? A time of fornication.[9] The soul has fornicated with all that struck its eye as pleasant—both with people and with things and, more fully, with sinful passions. Everyone has his own passion which he pleases in every way. It is time to put an end to this. May each of you comprehend your Delilah, who binds you and hands you over to evil enemies, and abandon her. Then you will be given more than Samson was given: Not only shall your hair grow but so also shall good thoughts; and not only shall your strength return but so also your strength of will. Your eyes shall also open, your mind shall have sight, and it shall see the Lord, yourself, and everything around you in the proper light. Behold, now is the favorable time! Behold, now is the day of salvation!

TUESDAY
Is. 1:19–2:3; Gen. 1:14–23; Prov. 1:20–33

The readings offered are about the creation, the original state before the fall, and the promise of salvation in our Lord Jesus Christ. Take heed and learn! Now is the time for your re-creation. Embrace the Lord, and He will give you light which will enlighten your sinful darkness; He will set a firmament amidst your restless thoughts and the desires of your sin-loving heart—the good intention to firmly and steadfastly serve Him. He will establish the dry land and the sea, and will give everything its place within you. Then you will begin to bring forth first herbs, grasses, and trees—the firstfruits

---

[8] From the first aposticha verse in Matins on the first day of Great Lent.—ED.

[9] The word translated here as "fornication," *bluzhdeniye,* has a double meaning in Russian, both of fornication and of roaming.—TRANS.

of the virtues, and then living creatures—perfect spiritual and God-pleasing works; until at last the image and likeness of God is restored in you, as you were created in the beginning. All of this will the Lord create for you in these six days of spiritual creation, which is your preparation for Holy Communion,[10] if you will pass this time with attention, reverence, and contrition of heart.

WEDNESDAY
Is. 2:3–11; Gen. 1:24–2:3; Prov. 2:1–22

Thou shalt call to wisdom, and utter thy voice for understanding; and if thou shalt seek it as silver, and search diligently for it as for treasures; then shalt thou understand the fear of the Lord, and find the knowledge of God (Prov. 2:3–5). The root of a God-pleasing life is fear of the Lord. When it comes, then, as a creative force, it will restructure everything within you and re-create in you a beautiful order—a spiritual cosmos. How can you acquire the fear of God? It is in you, only it is smothered. Resurrect it. Give voice to your mind, and open your heart to accept the influence of truth. Until now, your mind was not given a voice; it was enslaved, and did not dare to speak sensibly. Let it now speak. It will begin to speak about God's omnipotence, which upholds you and could abandon you at any instant; about God's omnipresence and omniscience, which sees everything within you and is angered with you for all that is bad within you; about God's justice, which is ready to punish you now, but is restrained until the [foreordained] time by His mercy;

[10] In St. Theophan's time it was a widespread custom in Russia for people to spend the first week of Great Lent preparing to receive Holy Communion on Saturday. This preparation, in Russian called *goveniye*, involves fasting, attending Divine services, reading prayers (including Canons, Akathists, etc.), doing prostrations, and engaging in other spiritual activities, instead of going to work. On the Friday of the first week of Lent, people would go to Confession. Thus, when St. Theophan mentions the "six days of spiritual creation," he refers to these first six days of Lent: five days of preparation, and Holy Communion on Saturday.—TRANS.

about death, which at every instant is ready to catch you and give you over to judgment and retribution. Listen and bring your heart to a feeling of these truths. Awaken this feeling—and the fear of God will come together with it. This is the dawn of life.

THURSDAY

Is. 2:11–22; Gen. 2:4–19; Prov. 3:1–18

Fear God, and depart from all evil (Prov. 3:7). Set this as the goal of your preparation for Holy Communion, so that at the end of this preparation the fear of God will dwell in you, and a firm intention to avoid every evil will take root, even if you should have to lose everything, including your life, in order to acquire this. Do not limit yourself to an external routine of preparation alone, but focus in particular on yourself. Enter within yourself and examine your views, as to whether they are in agreement in all things with the true word of God. Examine your inclinations and dispositions, as to whether they are what the Lord demands of you in the Gospels. Examine your whole life, as to whether it agrees with God's commandments in every way. Bemoan and hate whatever is offensive to God, and set in your mind never to do it again. If you do this, you will be most wise; but you would be most unwise not to do this.

FRIDAY

Is. 3:1–14; Gen. 2:20–3:20; Prov. 3: 19–34

The Lord resists the proud; but He gives grace to the humble (Prov. 3:34). Particularly remember these words when you go to Confession. Nothing binds your tongue to keep it from saying, "I am a sinner," as does pride. Humble yourself before the Lord, do not spare yourself, do not fear the face of man. Reveal your shame for it to be washed; show your wounds for them to be healed; tell of all your unrighteousness, that you may be justified. The more merciless you are with yourself, the more compassion the Lord will show toward you, and you will leave with a sweet feeling of forgiveness. This is that grace of our Lord Jesus Christ, given by Him to those who humble themselves through sincere confession of their sins.

SATURDAY
Heb. 1:1–12; Mark 2:23–3:5

We have approached the chalice of the Lord, we have been at the Lord's Supper. Glory to Thee, O God! Glory to Thee, O God! Glory to Thee, O God! Now is the great day of the Lord! The most glorious celebration in heaven! There is no city, village, or house where there are not people receiving Holy Communion. Across the breadth of Russia, throughout the south and east, so many people clothed in the white garments of justification have tasted of the Divine life and have most sincerely united themselves with the Lord! The Lord's Body, the Body of the Church, has been renewed, and has been clothed in the glory belonging to it, hidden from the eyes of man but visible to the eyes of angels. The angels worshiped the Firstborn when He was brought to the world in His power; now they have worshiped Him because the world has been brought again to Him. They have worshiped Him and sung out: *Thy throne, O God, is for ever and ever: the scepter of Thy Kingdom is a scepter of righteousness* (Ps. 44:7).

FIRST SUNDAY OF LENT
Heb. 11:24–26, 32–12:2; John 1:43–51

The Sunday of Orthodoxy.[11] Do not forget the right word[12] which

---

[11] The first Sunday of Great Lent is called the "Sunday of Orthodoxy," on which is celebrated the victory of Orthodoxy over the Iconoclast heresy and the restoration of the veneration of icons.—TRANS.

[12] The "right word" is a reference to the meaning of the word "Orthodox," which is literally "rightly glorifying."—TRANS.

you spoke to God, renewing your covenant with Him, but which you broke through your negligence. Remember how and why you broke it and try to avoid being unfaithful again. Pretty words are not glorious; faithfulness is glorious. Is it not glorious to have a covenant with a king? How much more glorious it is to have a covenant with the King of kings! But this glory becomes your disgrace if you are not faithful to this covenant. How many great people have been glorified since the beginning of the world! And all of them have been glorified for their faithfulness, in which they stood firm, regardless of great misfortunes and sorrows as a result of this faithfulness. They *had trial of cruel mockings and scourgings, yea, moreover of bonds and imprisonment: They were stoned, they were sawn asunder, were tempted, were slain with the sword: they wandered about in sheepskins and goatskins; being destitute, afflicted, tormented (of whom the world was not worthy): they wandered in deserts, and in mountains, and in dens and caves of the earth.... Wherefore, seeing we are compassed about with so great a cloud of witnesses ... let us run with patience the race that is set before us, looking unto Jesus the Author and Finisher of our faith* (Heb. 11:36–38, 12:1–2).

MONDAY (SECOND WEEK OF LENT)
Is. 4:2–6, 5:1–7; Gen. 3:21–4:7; Prov. 3:34–4:22

Keep thine heart with the utmost care; for out of these are the issues of life (Prov. 4:23). Having prepared, confessed, and received the Holy Mysteries, a Christian renews within himself the grace-filled springs which were opened in him through holy Baptism, and which were later so many times obstructed by carelessness and falls, and so many times cleansed by repentance. Now these springs have been cleansed once again after the most recent falls. Let us preserve them, at least from this point onward, from renewed obstruction as a result of thoughtlessness, distraction, and negligence concerning those actions which maintain the springs' purity and proper flow of waters. Let us continue fasting, not give liberty to our feelings, not cease fervent prayers and tears, not forget works of love; let us seek to hear the word of God and, most of all, seek to converse with the Lord, Who is within us. Through this conversation we shall uphold the fear of God and zeal to please Him within ourselves, for in this lies the source of our spiritual life.

TUESDAY
Is. 5:7–16; Gen. 4:8–15; Prov. 5:1–15

And Cain said to the Lord God, My crime is too great for me to be forgiven (Gen. 4:13). Was it possible to talk like this before the countenance of God, Who is of course strict in righteousness but is always ready to have mercy upon a sinner who truly repents? Envy obscured sensible thoughts, deliberate transgression hardened his heart and, behold, Cain rudely replied to God Himself: *Am I my brother's keeper?* (Gen. 4:9). God wanted to soften his stony heart with the hammer of His strict judgment; but Cain did not give in and, locked in his coarseness, he committed himself to the lot which he had prepared for himself through his envy and murder. What is amazing is that after this he lived like anyone else: he had children, established a household, and maintained earthly relations. Yet the mark of his being an outcast and of his despair continued to lie upon him. Thus this is an inner matter, which takes place in the conscience. It proceeds from the realization of one's relationship to God, under the influence of burdensome passions, sinful habits, and deeds. Let people heed this now especially! But along with this let people resurrect their belief that there is no sin that can overcome God's mercy; however, both time and work are needed to soften the heart. Truly, there is either salvation or ruin!

WEDNESDAY

Is. 5:16–25; Gen. 4:16–26; Prov. 5:15–6:3

When Moses and Aaron began to intercede before Pharaoh to let their people go, the answer to this was increased work for the oppressed Israelites, to the point that they raised an outcry against their intercessors: *Ye have made our savor abominable before Pharaoh* (Ex. 5:21). This is exactly what the soul of a repentant sinner experiences. When the fear of God and one's conscience—the inner Moses and Aaron—begin to inspire a soul to finally rise up onto its feet and shake off the yoke of sinful slavery, joy passes through all of its members. But the enemy does not sleep. He heaps mountains of mental obstacles, such as thoughts that sin is insurmountable, and he brings in fear from all sides: fear for one's prosperity, for external relationships, for one's influence, even for one's life. It even happens that one stops, having only just begun. Be inspired, brother! *The Lord of hosts shall be exalted in judgment, and the holy God shall be glorified in righteousness* (Is. 5:16). God is stronger than the enemy. Cry out to Him, and you will hear the same thing that Moses heard then: *Now thou shalt see what I will do to Pharaoh* (Ex. 6:1).

The enemy does not have power over a soul; he can only frighten it with illusory terrors. Do not give in. Endure and go forward courageously, saying to yourself: I will not give in, even unto death, and I will go bravely wherever the Lord calls me, with the spirit of repentance which now acts in me.

THURSDAY

Is. 6:1–12; Gen. 5:1–24; Prov. 6:3–20

Give not sleep to thine eyes, nor slumber with thine eyelids; that thou mayest deliver thyself as a doe out of the toils, and as a bird out of a snare (Prov. 6:4–5). Everyone who in his heart has set out now, before the face of the Lord, to live according to His commandments, should take this rule as his guide. He must not give sleep to his eyes—not these outer eyes, but the inner eyes of his mind—that they might gaze into his heart and faithfully observe all that occurs there, and thus he who is zealous will be able to find the enemy's snares and avoid danger from them. The heart now becomes an arena for struggle against the enemy. There the enemy unceasingly sows his own [seed], which is in turn reflected in one's thoughts. Such thoughts, however, are not always outrageously bad, but are for the most part disguised by false goodness and correctness. The chain of all thoughts is just like an intricate net! He who heedlessly sets out after them will not escape entanglement and, consequently, the danger of a fall. This is why, brother, you must keep the eye of your mind sharp-sighted by means of strict attention toward everything that occurs in you and around you. Take note of what your relentless "advisor" proposes to you on the left side and investigate the reason it was proposed to you and where it will lead, and you will never fall into his snares. Only, do not forget that attentiveness alone is not effective. It must be joined with abstinence, wakefulness, and unceasing prayer to the Lord. Combine all these, and it will be difficult to catch you.

Friday
Is. 7:1–14; Gen. 5:32–6:8; Prov. 6:20–7:1

My Spirit shall certainly not remain among these men forever, because they are flesh (Gen. 6:3). Man has two opposing forces within him, but his consciousness is one—the human personality. The characteristics of this personality are determined by his inclinations. If he sides with the spirit, he is spiritual;[13] if he

---

13 What St. Theophan calls man's "spirit," *dukh* in Russian, corresponds to the Greek *nous* (also translated as "mind" or "intellect"): the highest part of the human soul, and the faculty by which man knows God and enters into communion with Him. In the words of St. John Damascene, "The soul does

sides with the flesh, he is fleshly. The spirit does not disappear altogether even from the fleshly, but it is enslaved and has no voice. It becomes yoked and serves the flesh like a slave serves its mistress, inventing all sorts of pleasures for it. Similarly, the flesh does not disappear from the spiritual, but it submits to the spirit and serves it. It loses its natural rights for food through fasting, its rights for sleep through vigil, for rest through continuous labor and weariness, for pleasing the senses through seclusion and silence. Where the flesh reigns, God does not abide, for His organ of communication with man is the spirit, which is not given its due priority in the flesh. God's approach is felt for the first time when the spirit begins to claim its own through the operation of the fear of God and of one's conscience. When one's consciousness and freedom are also aligned with them, then God communicates with man and begins to dwell in him. From that moment begins the inspiration of the soul, of the flesh, and of the entire inner and outer man, while God becomes all in all in him. By becoming spiritual, man is made Divine. What a marvelous benefit, and how little it is remembered, valued, and sought after!

SATURDAY

Heb. 3:12–16; Mark 1:35–44

He went out, and departed into a solitary place, and there prayed (Mark 1:35). The Lord prays as a man, or, it is better to say, as the One Who is incarnate in human nature. His prayer is intercessory

---

not have the *nous* as something distinct from itself, but as its purest part, for as the eye is to the body, so is the *nous* to the soul" (*On the Orthodox Faith* 2.12, in *St. John of Damascus: Writings,* Fathers of the Church, vol. 37 [New York: Fathers of the Church, Inc., 1958], p. 236). According to St. Diodochus of Photiki, the *nous* dwells "in the depths of the soul" (*On Spiritual Knowledge and Discrimination* 79, in *The Philokalia,* vol. 1 [London: Faber and Faber, 1979], p. 280).—ED.

for us, and at the same time it is a model and example for us. The Apostle Paul teaches that the Spirit prays in those who have accepted the Spirit. Of course, He [the Spirit of God] does not pray of Himself, but by stirring prayerful aspirations for God in the human spirit. Behold true prayer—prayer which uplifts the spirit. But this is prayer at its highest stage. Those who seek cleansing and sanctification will find that the path to such prayer is through great labor in prayer. Solitude and nighttime are the most appropriate circumstances for this labor. The labor itself is a multitude of prostrations with heartfelt sighs. It is toil and more toil, driving away all laziness. The Lord will have pity on you and give you the spirit of prayer, which will start to work in you, just as breathing works in your body. Begin! Behold, now is the favorable time.

SECOND SUNDAY OF LENT
Heb. 1:10–2:3; Mark 2:1–12

I am the door: by Me if any man enter in, he shall be saved (John 10:9). The Lord says the same in another place: *No man cometh unto the Father, but by Me* (John 14:6). He even more succinctly confirms this when he says: *Without Me ye can do nothing* (John 15:5). A Christian is a person who is wholly in Christ and whose every good quality is from Christ. His justification is by Christ, and his body is also of Christ. He who is being saved is being saved because he is clothed in Christ. The Father is accessible to him only when he is in this state. We have fallen away from God and are therefore subject to His wrath. Only when we draw near in Christ, for Christ's sake, does God's judgment recede and His mercy reach out to us and accept us as we draw near. The seal of Christ is imprinted on the entire nature of a Christian, and he who carries this seal will walk through the valley of the shadow of death and fear no evil (cf. Ps. 22:4).

In order to become this way we have the Sacraments—

Baptism, and Communion—for which Confession acts as a mediator for those who sin after Baptism. But this is from the Lord. We must do our part to cultivate a spirit of acceptance: faith which confesses, "I am lost and can be saved only by the Lord Jesus Christ"; love which fervently strives to devote all to the Lord and Savior, sparing nothing; hope that does not hope in itself, but only in its assurance that the Lord will not abandon us and will help us in every way, both internally and externally throughout all of our life, until our hope takes us to the place where He Himself abides.

MONDAY (THIRD WEEK OF LENT)
Is. 8:13–9:7; Gen. 6:9–22; Prov. 8:1–21

The fear of the Lord hates unrighteousness (Prov. 8:13); and if it hates unrighteousness, it will drive it away; if it drives it away, the soul will be cleansed of it, and will thus appear righteous before the Lord. This is everything that we now seek with such effort. Thus, restore the fear of God in yourself and maintain it, and you will possess the most powerful means for self-healing. The fear of the Lord will not allow you to sin, and it will compel you to do every good thing on every possible occasion. Then you will fulfill the commandment: *Turn away from evil, and do good* (Ps. 33:14), which the prophet gives to those seeking true life. How can one attain fear of God? *Seek, and ye shall find* (Matt. 7:7). We cannot say in this regard, "Do this," or "Do that"; the fear of God is a spiritual feeling, secretly conceived in a heart that is turning to God. Reflection helps, and the effort to have this feeling helps; but in fact it is given by the Lord. Search it out as a gift and it will be given to you. When it is given, then obey it without contradicting, and it will correct all your unrighteousness.

Tuesday
Is. 9:9–10:4; Gen. 7:1–5; Prov. 8:32–9:11

Wisdom,[14] God the Word, *has built a house for herself*—the holy Church—and in it *she has ... prepared her table* (the word of God and the Holy Mysteries, especially the Mystery of [Christ's] Body and Blood). And *she has sent forth her servants*, the Holy Apostles and their successors, to call everyone to herself for the supper (Prov. 9:1–3). Many have already been called, but the summons still continues. So let the whole house be filled. The feast continues unceasingly. Glory be to God, Who is so merciful toward us! Let us all go! Let us enter in, let no one remain outside the door. During these days of the Fast the summons is particularly

---

[14] In the book of Proverbs, "wisdom" refers in some places to human wisdom, and in others to Divine Wisdom. In the first verses of Proverbs chapter 9 quoted above, the Fathers of the Church have seen "wisdom" as a personification of the Son of God, through Whom the economy of salvation has been effected. (See the quotations of St. Hippolytus, St. Gregory of Nyssa, St. John Chrysostom, St. Ambrose of Milan, Blessed Augustine, St. Cyprian of Carthage, St. Gregory the Dialogist. St. Leo the Great, and St. Bede the Venerable, in *Ancient Christian Commentary on Scripture, Old Testament,* vol. 9, ed. J. Robert Wright [Downers Grove, Ill.: InterVarsity Press, 2005], pp. 72–75.) As Fr. Michael Pomazansky explains, in these verses the wise Solomon "is prophetically exalted in thought to the prefiguration of the *New Testament economy of God* which is to be revealed in the preaching of the Savior of the world, in the salvation of the world and of mankind, and in the creation of the New Testament Church" (Pomazansky, *Orthodox Dogmatic Theology,* 3rd ed., Platina, Calif.: St. Herman of Alaska Brotherhood, 2005, pp. 370–71). It is important to note that the personification of "wisdom" here, as in other places in the book of Proverbs, must not be taken in a literal sense—as modern-day "sophiologists" have done in interpreting "wisdom" as the feminine aspect of God or as a Feminine Being on the boundary between the God and the world—but rather figuratively, in accordance with the parabolic and metaphorical nature of the book. As it is said at the beginning of Proverbs, in reading this book *the man of understanding will gain direction, and will understand a parable, and a dark speech, the sayings of the wise also, and riddles* (Prov. 1:6).—Ed.

intensified, and the spiritual supper is particularly abundant. This makes it all the more inexcusable to be deprived of this supper. Let all carve in their memory the following words of Wisdom: *They that sin against Me act wickedly against their own souls* (Prov. 8:36); and so have pity upon yourself.

WEDNESDAY
Is. 10:12–20; Gen. 7:6–9; Prov. 9:12–18

It is remarkable how Wisdom calls to herself the foolish: *Whoso is foolish, let him turn aside to Me* (Prov. 9:4). Accordingly, the clever are barred from entering into the house of Wisdom, or the Holy Church. One must lay aside every kind of cleverness at the very entrance of this house. On the other hand, if all wisdom and knowledge are to be found within the house of Wisdom, then outside this House, outside the Holy Church, there is only foolishness, ignorance, and blindness. How wondrous is that which God has established! When you enter the Church, put aside your own mind, and you will become truly wise; cast away your self-centered activity, and you will become truly active; renounce your own self, and you will truly become master over yourself. Ah, if only the world could grasp this wisdom! But this is hidden from it. Not understanding the wisdom of God, the world clamors against it, and the world keeps these senseless sensible ones in their blindness.

THURSDAY
Is. 11:10–12:2; Gen. 7:11–8:3; Prov. 10:1–22

By a multitude of words thou shalt not escape sin (Prov. 10:19). Christians who are attentive to themselves call all the senses the windows of the soul; if these windows are opened, all the inner warmth will leave. But the widest opening, the most spacious doorway that releases this warmth copiously, is a tongue given freedom to speak as much and whatever it wants. A multitude of words causes the same degree of harm to attentiveness and inner harmony as is inflicted by all of the senses together, for talkativeness touches upon the objects of all the senses and forces a soul to see without seeing, to hear without hearing, to touch without touching. What daydreaming is inwardly, a multitude of words is outwardly; but the latter is more ruinous, for it is real and, therefore, makes a deeper impression. Furthermore, it is closely connected with self-opinion, impudence, and self-will—those destroyers of inner harmony which are like a tempest, leaving lack of feeling and blindness in their wake. After all this, how can one escape sin in the presence of a multitude of words?

FRIDAY

Is. 13:2–13; Gen. 8:4–21; Prov. 10:31–11:12

Ungodliness encounters unjust dealing (Prov. 11: 5).[15] Impiety is an incorrect relationship with God, or complete forgetfulness of God, to which also belongs unbelief in the existence of God and in His Providence for creatures. Some souls, being oppressed by wicked thoughts like these, but desiring, nevertheless, to be respectable individuals, resolve, "I will be upright, honest, and humane, not occupying myself with whether there is something higher than me which observes me, has expectations of me, and is able to demand an account." And what is the result? The blessing of God—which they do not seek—does not abide with them, and their affairs do not prosper. Their conscience daily reminds them about their works either of unrighteousness, dishonesty, or inhumanity. They only manage to make a show of righteousness before other people in order to justify themselves, sharply fending off accusation, and falsely interpreting facts as needed. He whose conscience is

---

[15] The Slavonic for Proverbs 11:5 reads: *The impious shall fall by his own impiety.*—TRANS.

inwardly blameless has no need of self-justification. Those who are not attentive to themselves allow this inner discord to slip out. Those who are attentive control it with difficulty. Oh, when will one such person conscientiously look at this discord, and discern where it comes from and how to set it right? He could then both set himself right and direct others toward the proper harmony.

SATURDAY
Heb. 10:32–38; Mark 2:14–17

I came not to call the righteous, but sinners to repentance (Mark 2:17). Through the mouth of Wisdom the Lord called the foolish to Himself (cf. Prov. 9:4). He Himself, sojourning upon the earth, called sinners. Neither the proud "clever ones" nor the self-willed righteous ones have a place with Him. Let intellectual and moral infirmity rejoice! Let proud intelligence and practicality step aside! Total weakness that acknowledges itself as such and hastens with faith to the Lord, Who heals the weak and fills the impoverished, will become strong both intellectually and morally, but will continue to acknowledge both its intellectual poverty and evil inclinations. The power of God, under this unprepossessing cover and made perfect in weakness, invisibly creates a different person who is mentally and morally bright. This brightness is often manifest here, but it is always manifest there, in heaven. Behold what is hidden from the wise and prudent and is revealed only to babes (cf. Matt. 11:25)!

THIRD SUNDAY OF LENT
Heb. 4:14–5:6; Mark 8:34–9:1

Whosoever will come after Me, let him deny himself, and take up his cross, and follow Me (Mark 8:34). It is impossible to follow the Lord as a cross-bearer without a cross, and everyone who follows Him unfailingly goes with a cross. What is this cross? It consists of all sorts of inconveniences, burdens, and sorrows—weighing heavily both internally and externally—along the path of the conscientious fulfillment of the commandments of the Lord, in a life according to the spirit of His instructions and requirements. Such a cross is so much a part of a Christian that wherever there is a Christian, there is this cross, and where there is no such cross, there is no Christian. Abundant privileges and a life of pleasure do not suit a true Christian. His task is to cleanse and reform himself. He is like a sick person who needs cauterization or amputation; how can this be without pain? He wants to tear himself away from the captivity of a strong enemy, but how can this be without struggle and wounds? He must walk counter to all the practices that surround him, but how can he sustain this without inconvenience and constraint? Rejoice as you feel the cross upon yourself, for it is a sign that you are following the Lord on the path of salvation which leads to heaven. Endure a bit. The end and the crowns are just around the corner!

Monday (Fourth week of Lent)
Is. 14:24–32; Gen. 8:21–9:7; Prov. 11:19–12:6

The Apostle Paul says that the Israelites, crossing the sea, were baptized in it (cf. I Cor. 10:2). Such a baptism served for them as a division between Egypt and themselves. Peter the Apostle adds: *The like figure whereunto even baptism doth also now save us* (I Peter 3:21). Our Baptism saves us and serves as a dividing wall between the dark, satanic realm of sin and the world, and the brightness of life in Christ. One who is baptized cuts himself off from all earthly hopes and supports, and lives in this age as if in a desert, not tied to anything. His heart is not on the earth—it is totally in that age. All that is here touches him in passing, so that having a wife, he is as though he had none; buying, he is as though possessing nothing. In general, he uses the world as though he did not use it (cf. I Cor. 7:30).

TUESDAY
Is. 25:1–9; Gen. 9:8–17; Prov. 12:8–22

Baptism according to Apostle Peter is *the answer of a good conscience toward God* (I Peter 3:21). He who has been baptized gives a vow to live the rest of his time according to a pure conscience, according to the whole breadth of the Lord's commandments, accepted in his conscience. Moral purity is a characteristic of one who is baptized. The Apostle Paul compares the brightness of this life with the brightness of the resurrected Lord. *That like as Christ was raised up from the dead by the glory of the Father, even so we also should walk in newness of life* (Rom. 6:4). In Baptism, the old sin-loving man dies and a new man arises, zealous to do good works. *Likewise reckon ye also yourselves*, ye who are baptized, *to be dead indeed unto sin but alive unto God through Jesus Christ our Lord. Let not sin therefore reign in your mortal body, that ye should obey it in the lusts thereof. Neither yield ye your members as instruments of unrighteousness unto sin: but yield yourselves unto God, as those that are alive from the dead, and your members as instruments of righteousness unto God. For sin shall not have dominion over you* (Rom. 6:11–14).

WEDNESDAY
Is. 26:21–27:9; Gen. 9:18–10:1; Prov. 12:23–13:9

Baptism (*kreshcheniye*) in the Russian language sounds like cross (*krest*). This is a fortunate consonance, for although the visible action of Baptism is submersion, its essence is a co-crucifixion with Christ on the inner, spiritual cross. The Apostle Paul says: *Our old man is crucified with Him* in Baptism (Rom. 6:6). This is not some sort of mechanical act, but a moral change, or a revolution of thoughts, goals, desires, and sympathies. Before, all of these were stained with self-pleasing; now all are selflessly dedicated to God, in Christ Jesus, by the grace of the Holy Spirit. [If you were baptized as an infant] you will say, "I didn't understand that when I was baptized." Now you understand; set it in your conscience to carry out the meaning of Baptism, for your Baptism is indelible. Even at the Judgment its seal will be visible either for you or against you.

THURSDAY
Is. 28:14–22; Gen. 10:32–11:9; Prov. 13:20–14:6

He that spares the rod hates his son: but he that loves, carefully chastens him (Prov. 13:24). Leave the children aside—let us work on ourselves. For each of us this means the following: do not spare yourself, chasten yourself earnestly. Self-pity is the root of all our stumblings into sin. He who does not indulge himself is always steadfast in good. Most of all you must keep your flesh, that slow-witted slave, in the strictest discipline. When you exhaust the flesh, it is humble; but give it only a small privilege, and already it begins to show its claws and to rage with passion-loving eyes. But what is amazing is that, no matter what is said, everyone stands up for the flesh, and invents all sorts of pleasing things for it. Even science, it seems, would not move forward without this. What sort of science can this be?

FRIDAY
Is. 29:13–23; Gen. 12:1–7; Prov. 14:15–26

The Lord had said unto Abraham: Get thee out of thy country, and from thy kindred, and from thy father's house, unto a land that I will show thee (Gen. 12:1). This is an explicit image for the change of heart which occurs in true believers, when they sincerely take upon themselves their cross and follow Christ. They leave their father—selfishness—crucifying it through self-denial. They leave their kindred—their personal sinful leanings, passions, and habits—crucifying them through the resolution to follow unswervingly and in all things the passion-slaying commandments of the Lord. They leave their country—the entire sinful realm, the world with all of its demands, crucifying it with the resolution to be alien to it—although for this it might be necessary not only to endure loss of property and social status, but even to endure death itself.

SATURDAY
Heb. 6:9–12; Mark 7:31–37

Flesh and blood cannot inherit the Kingdom of God (I Cor. 15:50). Consequently, to receive the Kingdom it is necessary to become fleshless and bloodless; that is, to become steadfast in such a disposition of life that it is as if blood and flesh did not exist. This is attained by a complete renunciation of deeds that come from flesh and blood. *Now the works of the flesh are manifest, which are these: Adultery, fornication, uncleanness, lasciviousness, idolatry, witchcraft, hatred, variance, emulations, wrath, strife, seditions, heresies, envyings, murders, drunkenness, revelings, and such like.* Having listed all of these, the Apostle adds: *I tell you before, as I have also told you in time past, that they which do such things shall not inherit the Kingdom of God* (Gal. 5:19–21). *He that hath ears to hear, let him hear* (Matt. 11:15)!

FOURTH SUNDAY OF LENT
Heb. 6:13–20; Mark 9:17–31

In His talk about the Beatitudes, the Lord depicts a heavenly heart (Matt. 5:1–12). It contains humility, weeping and contrition, meekness and angerlessness, complete love of righteousness, perfect mercifulness, purity of heart, love of peace and peacemaking, and the suffering of misfortunes, false accusations, and persecution for the sake of the Christian Faith and life. If you want heaven, be like this, and even here on earth you will have a foretaste of heaven, into which you will enter after death—prepared, like a preordained heir.

Monday (Fifth week of Lent)
Is. 37:33–38:6; Gen. 13:12–18; Prov. 14:27–15:4

The eyes of the Lord behold both the evil and the good in every place (Prov. 15:3). Oh, if only rational creatures would always keep this in mind! Then not only would they not dare to commit excesses openly and to give themselves over to dissoluteness of the flesh, but neither would they inwardly, in their thoughts and in the movements of their heart, allow anything unpleasing to God. They would then stand like soldiers at the front before the king, with all attention and strictness toward themselves, that they not be found ignorant of their orders, nor be subject to the king's wrath and punishment. The orders given to rational creatures are the commandments of God, which determine the proper form of their thoughts, and how their feelings and dispositions ought to be.

Tuesday
Is. 40:18–31; Gen. 15:1–15; Prov. 15:7–19

Hell and destruction are manifest to the Lord; how shall not also be the hearts of men? (Prov. 15:11). But the sinner keeps thinking that no one sees him. Concealing himself from human eyes, in the darkness of night or in a deserted place, he supposes that he is not noticed by anyone. But God's eye has seen everything; the sinner's guardian angel and conscience were witnesses. At some time you will stand at the Judgment: then all that is hidden will be laid bare: uncompromising witnesses will be present—and you shall be speechless. The verdict will not be subject to appeal. There is only one way to prevent this ultimate inevitability: repentance.

The door to repentance is open. Hurry to enter, before the hour strikes. When? You do not know. But it will put an end both to your sins and to any hope of pardon.

WEDNESDAY
Is. 41:4–14; Gen. 17:1–9; Prov. 15:20–16:9

The thoughts of the wise are ways of life, that he may turn aside and escape from hell (Prov. 15:24). It is well known to all that hell exists, and that anyone can end up there as a result of his deeds. But not all remember this, or live such a well ordered life that they are clearly trying to avoid hell. They live without thinking about it, saying, "Maybe ... maybe we will somehow not end up in hell." Where is our reason? In earthly affairs one might get away with "maybe," but in such a decisive affair which, once accomplished, will abide unto the ages of ages unchanged, "maybe" reveals lack of reason to the utmost degree. Do not pride yourself, O Reason, on your reasonableness, when you do not remember this and do not suggest to us thoughts of life: how to avoid hell and be saved.

THURSDAY
Is. 42:5–16; Gen. 18:20–33; Prov. 16:17–17:17

Pride goes before destruction, and folly before a fall (Prov. 16:18). Therefore, do not allow evil thoughts to come in, and there will be no falls. And yet, what are people most careless about? About their thoughts. They allow them to seethe as much and however they like, not even thinking to subdue them or to direct them to rational pursuits. Meanwhile, within this inner turmoil the enemy approaches, places evil in the heart, seduces it, and inclines it toward evil. And the person, not noticing this himself, is ready for evil. It remains for him either to carry out the evil that is fixed to his heart or to struggle against it. But this is our sorrow: almost no one takes on the struggle, while all are led to evil as if bound.

FRIDAY
Is. 45:11–17; Gen. 22:1–18; Prov. 17:17–18:5

The souls of the righteous are in the hand of God (Wisdom 3:1). But in whose hand are the souls of sinners? The Savior told the Apostles that Satan seeks to sift them like wheat (cf. Luke 22:31), that is, he seeks to knock them from the right path, to take them into his hands and do with them as he pleases. That is why everyone who turns away from the Lord is in the hands of Satan, and he sifts them and casts them wherever he desires. Due to this the heads of sinners are constantly spinning, because the enemy, dragging them here and there, does not give them a chance to come to their senses. As soon as the enemy notices that someone is starting to have second thoughts, he starts to shake him even more strongly, so that his head again becomes clouded and his thoughts become scattered.

SATURDAY
Heb. 9: 24–28; Mark 8: 27–31

The Lord asked the Apostles Whom they thought He was. In the person of the Holy Apostle Peter, they answered, *Thou art the Christ* (Mark 8:29). This confession did not ripen suddenly, but once it ripened, it settled in the depths of his heart and became the source of his guidance. It was overshadowed by the death of the Lord but not shaken, and being resurrected in even greater power by the Resurrection, it directed the Apostles for their entire lives to preach to the whole world. There is a moment for each believer, when he utters with all his strength, "Thou art the Christ, my Lord and Savior. Thou art my salvation, my light, my strength, my comfort, my hope and eternal life." Then there is accomplished that through which the believer cries with the Apostle: "Who shall separate me from the love of Christ?" (cf. Rom. 8:35), and like him he begins to pursue all that is pleasing to Christ the Lord, until he comes unto the measure of His stature (cf. Eph. 4:13).

FIFTH SUNDAY OF LENT
Heb. 9:11–14; Mark 10:32–45

The sinful woman, upon hearing that the Savior was in the house of Simon, came there with an alabaster box of ointment. Standing behind the Lord, by His feet, she began to weep and washed His feet with her tears, then wiped them with her hair, kissed them, and anointed them with myrrh (cf. Luke 7:36–39). She did not say anything; she only acted, and through her actions revealed a most tender love for the Lord. Because of this it was spoken of her: *Her sins, which are many, are forgiven; for she loved much* (Luke 7:47). Oh, when will we talk less and act more, and through our actions witness our love for the Lord? You might say, "If He were here I would be ready now to do everything for Him." But He is here, invisible in His person, but visible in all Christians, most of all in the needy. Anoint the invisible Lord with loving prayer of the heart and mind, and for His sake do everything possible for the needy, and you will be doing this for God.

MONDAY (SIXTH WEEK OF LENT)
Is. 48:17–49:4; Gen. 27:1–41; Prov. 19:16–25

Thus says the Lord: *I am thy God, I have shown thee how thou shouldest find the way wherein thou shouldest walk. And if thou hadst hearkened to My commandments, then would thy peace have been like a river, and thy righteousness as a wave of the sea. Thy seed also would have been as the sand, and the offspring of thy belly as the dust of the ground: neither now shalt thou by any means be utterly destroyed, neither shall thy name perish before Me.* Under what condition should all this come to pass? *Go forth of Babylon* (Is. 48:17–20).

Babylon is an image of all-around sinfulness. Abandon sin

and turn to the Lord with all your heart. He will not remember your transgressions, and will consign all of your unrighteousness to oblivion. You will enter again into His mercy—and then you need only to walk the way which He will teach you, and your inner peace will be like a river; the good thoughts of your heart, like the sand; and the fruits of your good works, like the dust of the ground.

TUESDAY
Is. 49:6–10; Gen. 31:3–16; Prov. 21:3–21

He that stops his ears from hearing the poor, himself also shall cry, and there shall be none to hear him (Prov. 21:13). And we often marvel—why does God not listen to our prayers? Here is the reason! Because there surely have been instances when we have stopped our ears from hearing the entreaties of the needy; so the Lord does not hear us either. It is no great woe if a prayer about something temporal is not heard; but how woeful if the Lord will not listen to us when we begin to pray to Him for the forgiveness of our sins. He will not listen if the cry to Him of those whom we have scorned is stronger than our prayers. We must hurry to avert this extreme misfortune, according to the example of Zacchaeus, whose wise decision caused the Lord to say, *This day is salvation come to this house* (Luke 19:9).

WEDNESDAY
Is. 58:1–11; Gen. 43:26–31; Prov. 21:23–22:4

Cry aloud, says the Lord to the Holy Prophet Isaiah, *and spare not* convicting the transgressions of My people. What did the people do? *They seek Me day by day ... and desire to draw nigh to God* (Is. 58:1–2). But is there really a sin in this? Indeed, they ought to do this. Yes, they ought to, but the fact is that they do not do this as they ought. They hope to be successful in their seeking through fasting alone, not caring for works of righteousness and love.

"Fasting is pleasing to Me," says the Lord, "but only such fasting whereby people, in humbling their body, forgive offenses, forgive debts, feed the hungry, bring the outcast to their house, and clothe the naked. When all of this is done together with fasting, then you will succeed in seeking Me and approaching Me; *then shall thy light break forth as the morning ... and the glory of God shall compass thee. Then shalt thou cry, and God shall hearken to thee; while thou art yet speaking He will say, Behold, I am here ... and thy God shall be with thee continually* (Is. 58:8–9, 11).

THURSDAY
Is. 65:8–16; Gen. 46:1–7; Prov. 23:15–24:5

Hear, my son, and be wise, and rightly direct the thoughts of thine heart (Prov. 23:19). Out of the heart continually proceed thoughts, which sometimes are good, but more often are evil. The evil ones should not be followed at all, but even the good ones should not always be carried out. It happens that even thoughts which are good in and of themselves in reality are inappropriate, due to circumstances. This is why it is prescribed to be attentive to oneself, to keep an eye on all that proceeds out of the heart—to reject the evil, consider what is good, and fulfill only what proves to be truly good. But best of all would be to totally imprison the heart, so that nothing leaves it and nothing enters it without the permission of the mind; so that the mind would come first in all things, determining the movements of the heart. But the mind is this way only when it is the mind of Christ. Thus, unite with Christ in mind and heart and everything within you will be in good working order.

FRIDAY
Is. 66:10–24; Gen. 49:33–50:26; Prov. 31:8–31

The holy forty days of Great Lent have come to an end! Now

each of you, sit and calculate the result—what was there in the beginning and what is there now? There was trading, so what are the gains? Is there at least a small profit? We have stepped into the arena: so, did we run, and having run, did we achieve what we expected? A struggle was declared: so, did we arm ourselves, did we fight? And, having fought, did we fall or did we conquer? Attentive and vigilant fasters, having labored with contrite and humbled hearts, cannot but rejoice upon looking back. However, for us who are careless and flesh-pleasing, concerned only with fleshly comforts and things that please us, there is always only shame. But even this is lacking. Some take a beating but feel no pain, because they have a copper forehead and an iron neck.

LAZARUS SATURDAY
Heb. 12:28–13:8; John 11:1–45

If one has Martha's love of labor—all manner of good works, and Mary's sitting at Jesus' feet—an attentive and warm appeal to the Lord with all his heart, then the Lord Himself will come to him and resurrect his Lazarus—his spirit, and will release him from all his emotional and fleshly bonds. Then a truly new life will begin in him, bodiless in the body and unearthly on the earth. It will be a true resurrection in the spirit before the future resurrection, which will include the body.

PALM SUNDAY
Phil. 4:4–9; John 12:1–18

Who did not meet the Lord when He triumphantly entered Jerusalem as a king; and who did not cry out then, *Hosanna to the Son of David!* (Matt. 21:15)? But only four days passed, and the same crowd cried with the same tongues, *Crucify Him, crucify Him!* (John 19:6). An amazing change! But why should we be surprised? Do we not do the very same thing when, upon receiving the Holy Mysteries of the Body and Blood of the Lord, we barely leave the church before forgetting everything—both our reverence and God's mercy toward us? We give ourselves over as before to self-pleasing deeds—at first small and then also large. Perhaps even before four days have passed, although we do not cry, "Crucify Him!" we will crucify the Lord within ourselves. The Lord sees all of this, and endures it.

Glory to Thy long-suffering, O Lord!

GREAT MONDAY
Matt. 24:3–35

The Lord goes to His voluntary Passion. We must accompany Him. This is the duty of anyone who confesses that he has become who he is now by the power of Christ's Passion: the duty of anyone who hopes to receive something which is so great and glorious that it could not even enter one's mind. How must one accompany Him? Through reflection and sympathy. Follow the suffering Lord in thought; and through your reflections extract such impressions as could strike your heart and bring it to feel the sufferings that were borne by the Lord. In order to better accomplish this, you must make yourself suffer through perceptible lessening of food and sleep, and an increase in the labor of standing and kneeling. Fulfill all that the Holy Church does, and you will be a good traveling companion of the Lord to His sufferings.

GREAT TUESDAY
Matt. 24:36–26:2

Now the people, the priests, and the Jewish authorities have heard the word of the Lord in the temple for the last time. This word is all-embracing; it embraces all the past, present, and future. Through the question about John [the Baptist], the Lord gives the understanding that He is the true Messiah. Through the parable about the two sons, He suggests that the Israelites will be rejected and that in their place the Gentiles will be called. Through the parable about the husbandmen He tells them that destruction awaits those who are cast out. Through the parable about the marriage of the king's son He teaches that even among those who come to Him not all will be worthy, and there will be found those whom He will rightly cast into outer darkness. Through His answers to the questions about tribute to Caesar and about the first commandment, as well as in His accusatory speech, He defines the characteristic features of a life of salvation. Finally, to His disciples separately, He predicts the destruction of Jerusalem and reveals the mystery of His Second Coming. It was enough to attentively listen to all of this to be convinced that He is the true Savior of the world—the Christ—and to submit to His commandments and teaching. Even now, reading the Gospel chapters about all that happened on this day[16] is the most effective way to revitalize our faith in the Lord; and by renewing the Christian's awareness of what he must be and what to expect, the reading will enkindle his zeal and inspire him to confess the Lord not only with his tongue, but also through works.

GREAT WEDNESDAY
Matt. 26:6–16

The Lord was silent on Wednesday and Thursday until Thursday evening, so that at that time He could pour forth words with His disciples and to His disciples—words not like anything in any writings, not only of human origin but also Divine. Now, as the Church points out, we hear from the Lord's mouth that [the disciples] should not hinder His anointing with myrrh, for this served as a preparation for His death. Before His eyes was only death—the final mystery of His coming to earth for our

---

[16] That is, two days before Judas' betrayal.—ED.

salvation. Let us also immerse ourselves in deep contemplation of this mystery-filled death, to draw from it good hope for the salvation of our souls, which are burdened by many sins, and which do not know how to obtain peace from the weariness of our awakened conscience, and from the knowledge of the righteousness of God's Judgment, which is dread and impartial.

ANNUNCIATION
GREAT THURSDAY
I Cor. 11:23–32; Matt. 26:1–20; John 13:3–17;
Matt. 26:21–39; Luke 22:43–45; Matt. 26:40–27:2
For Annunciation: Heb. 2:11–18; Luke 1:24–38

The Annunciation and the establishment of the Mystery of the Body and Blood of Christ. What a combination! We partake of the true Body and the true Blood of Christ—the very ones which in the Incarnation were taken from the most spotless blood of the Most Pure Virgin Theotokos. In such a manner, in the Incarnation, accomplished at the hour of the Annunciation, the foundation for the Mystery of the Body and Blood was set. And now this is brought to remembrance for all Christians, so that, remembering this, they might honor the Most Holy Theotokos as their true mother, not as a mere supplicant and intercessor, but as the nourisher of all. Children are nourished by the milk of their mother; but we are nourished by the Body and Blood of Christ, which are from the Most Holy Virgin Theotokos. Being nourished thus, in essence we drink milk from her breasts.

GREAT FRIDAY
Ex. 33:11–23; Job 42:12–16; Is. 52:13–54:1; I Cor. 1:18–2:2;
Matt. 27:1–38; Luke 23:39–43; Matt. 27:39–54;
John 19:31–37; Matt. 27:55–61

The Crucifixion of Christ the Lord and the Synaxis of Archangel

Gabriel! Another consoling combination! Gabriel proclaims beforehand the birth of the Forerunner; Gabriel brings good tidings to the Virgin; it was he, very likely, who proclaimed the joy of the birth of the Savior; none other than he proclaimed the Resurrection of Christ the Lord to the women. Therefore Gabriel is the herald and bearer of every joy. The Crucifixion of Christ is the joy and gladness of all sinners. A sinner, coming to a feeling of his sinfulness and of the all-righteous truth of God, has nowhere to take shelter, except under the shadow of the Cross. Here he accepts the assurance that he has no forgiveness while he stands alone before God with his sins and even with his tears over them. The only salvation for him is in the Lord's death on the Cross. On the Cross the handwriting of all sins was torn up (cf. Col 2:14). And everyone who accepts this with complete faith is made a participant in this mystery of forgiveness. As this faith ripens, confidence of forgiveness ripens as well, and also comfort from the feeling of entering into the state of forgiveness for all ages. The Cross is a source of joy, because a sinner with faith imbibes from it the joy of forgiveness. In this sense, it is in its own way an archangel, bringing good tidings of joy.

GREAT SATURDAY
Rom 6:3–11; Matt. 28:1–20

The Lord sleeps bodily in the tomb; in soul He has descended into hell and preached salvation to the souls there. The Old Testament saints were not in heaven, although they abode in the consoling faith that they would be brought there as soon as the Promised One came to earth, since they had lived by faith in Him. There also the Forerunner foretold His coming. When the Lord descended, all who believed cleaved to Him and were lifted up by Him into heaven. But even that heaven is only the threshold of the true Paradise which will be revealed after the general resurrection and Judgment. Although all of the New Testament saints are also blessed in heaven, they await an even more perfect bliss in the age to come, with a new heaven and new earth (cf. Apoc. 21:1), when God will be all in all (cf. I Cor. 15:28).

THE BRIGHT RESURRECTION OF CHRIST
Acts 1:1–8; John 1:1–17

Pascha, the Lord's Pascha! The Lord has led us from death to life by means of His Resurrection. And "the angels in heaven hymn" this Resurrection, having seen in the countenance of the Lord and Redeemer the brightness of the deified human nature in the glory foreordained for it. All who truly believe in Him and cleave to Him with all their soul are changed into His image by the power of His Resurrection. Glory, O Lord, to Thy most glorious Resurrection! The angels hymn, rejoicing with us and foreseeing the filling of their assembly. Vouchsafe us also with pure hearts, O Lord, to glorify Thee resurrected, seeing in Thy Resurrection the cutting off of our consuming decay, the sowing of a most bright new life, and the dawn of future eternal glory, into which Thou hast gone before us by Thy Resurrection for our sake. The tongues not only of men but also of angels have insufficient strength to express Thine unspeakable mercy toward us, O most gloriously resurrected Lord!

BRIGHT MONDAY
Acts 1:12–17, 21–26; John 1:18–28

When the angel announced the good tidings of the Lord's Incarnation, he said: *Hail, thou that are highly favored!* (Luke 1:28).[17] Proclaiming to the shepherds the birth of Christ the Savior, he also said: *Behold, I bring you good tidings of great joy*

---

[17] An English translation of the Slavonic reads: *Rejoice, thou who art full of grace.*—TRANS.

(Luke 2:10). But when proclaiming the Lord's Resurrection to the women, the angel only said: *He is not here, but is risen* (Luke 24:6)! He does not add "rejoice," for joy would fill their hearts on its own, as soon as the assurance came that the Lord in truth was risen. At that time this assurance was tangible: the angel prepared it, and the Lord in His appearing completed it. And everyone's joy was inexhaustibly full! Now our churches, houses, and squares are arrayed in the garments of rejoicing, and everyone is caught up in a general stream of joy. Now turn your thoughts a little away from the externals and, gathering them in your heart, raise up the truth of the Resurrection, in all of its breadth, depth, and height, so that your rejoicing may be more than external. Bear out that spirit of joy like a spring of bright water, gushing from the bosom of the earth.

Bright Tuesday
Acts 2:14–21; Luke 24:12–35

At that time the Jews attempted to darken the light of Christ's Resurrection with the mist of a lie: *His disciples stole Him* (Matt. 28:13). It was easy to overcome such pettiness, and the truth triumphed. But until now the enemy has not ceased to cloud the Sun of Resurrection, hoping to overshadow it. Let no one be troubled! What can be expected from the father of lies other than lies? He taught many of his minions to write entire books against the Resurrection. This written mist is also dissipated by books. Do not pick up a bad book, and you will not be beclouded by it; but if you should accidentally come upon such a book, take up a good book as an antidote, and you will refresh your head and breast. There is another mist that comes from the enemy—in our thoughts. But this can also be immediately dissipated, like smoke in the wind, through sensible Christian discernment. Review with discernment everything that has been accomplished, and you will see as clear as day that it would have been impossible for all of it to happen except through the power of Christ's Resurrection. This conviction will then be a firm stronghold from which you will easily repel and strike down the enemies of the truth.

BRIGHT WEDNESDAY
Acts 2:22–36; John 1:35–51

The mind can prove the truth of the Resurrection through reason based on the Scripture, and a non-believer cannot but admit the power of its arguments, as long as a sense of truth is not yet dead in him. A believer does not need proof, because the Church of God is filled with the light of the Resurrection. Both of these indicators of truth are faithful and convincing. But counter-reasoning can spring up and contradict the mind's reason, and faith can be trampled and shaken by perplexities and doubts coming from without and arising within. Is there no invincible wall around the truth of the Resurrection? There is. It will occur when the power of the Resurrection, received at Baptism, begins to be actively revealed, as it purges the corruption of soul and body and establishes within them the beginnings of a new life. He who experiences this will walk in the light of the Resurrection, and anyone speaking against the truth of the Resurrection will seem to him insane, like a person saying in the daytime that it is night.

BRIGHT THURSDAY
Acts 2:38–43; John 3:1–15

Beneficial is the work of those who, using sound reason, crush the enormous lie mustered against the truth of the Resurrection. Read and arm yourself with these thoughts; meanwhile, do not be too lazy to allow more and more space for the power of Christ's Resurrection to enter into you. The more you do this, the more you will breathe the air of the Resurrection, and you will become quite safe from all the darts of the enemy directed against this truth. You ask, what is needed for this? Nothing special: be the way you ought to be, according to the vow you made at holy Baptism, which is our resurrection. Did you spit on Satan and all his works? Then continue to preserve yourself thus in relation to him. Did you unite yourself with Christ? Then abide with Him. The works of darkness and light are obvious. Flee from the former and be assiduous with the latter. But do this without any compromises, even the smallest, so that the norm of your life might become the following: there is no communion of light with darkness, or of Christ with Belial (cf. II Cor. 6:15).

Bright Friday
Acts 3:1–8; John 2:12–22

There are certain individuals whom the Holy Fathers praise for their Christian lives, for they rose from the dead before the general resurrection. What is the secret of such a life? They mastered the characteristic features of a life according to the resurrection, as they are shown in the word of God, and made them their own inner qualities. The future life is devoid of all that is fleshly: there men do not marry, nor are women given in marriage; they will not nourish themselves with dead food, and they will receive a spiritual body. Thus, whoever lives estranged from all fleshly things receives in himself, or returns to himself, elements of the future life according to the resurrection. Reach the point that all fleshly things within you die, and you will be resurrected before the future resurrection. The Apostle indicates the path to this when he says: *Walk in the Spirit, and ye shall not fulfill the lust of the flesh* (Gal. 5:16). And he attests that through this path it is surely possible to attain what is awaited: *He that soweth to the Spirit,* he says, *shall of the Spirit reap life everlasting* (Gal. 6:8).

BRIGHT SATURDAY
Acts 3:11–16; John 3:22–33

We have two lives, one fleshly and one spiritual. Our spirit is as though buried in our flesh. Once it begins to extract itself— coming to life by God's grace—from its intertwining with the flesh, and begins to appear in its spiritual purity, then it will be resurrected, or it will resurrect itself piece by piece. When it wholly tears itself out of this binding, then it comes forth as if from the tomb, in a renewed life. In this manner the spirit becomes separate, alive, and active; whereas the tomb of the flesh is separate, dead, and inactive, though both are in the same person. This is the mystery of which the Apostle speaks: *Where the Spirit of the Lord is, there is liberty* (II Cor. 3:17). This is liberty from the decay which surrounds our incorruptible spirit, or from passions which corrupt our nature. This spirit, entering into the freedom of the children of God, is like a beautifully colored butterfly, fluttering away from its cocoon. Behold its rainbow coloring: *love, joy, peace, long-suffering, gentleness, goodness, faith, meekness, temperance* (Gal. 5:22). Is it possible for such a beauty of perfection not to arouse in us a desire to emulate it?

THOMAS SUNDAY
Acts 5:12–20; John 20:19–31

My Lord and my God! (John 20:28) cries the Holy Apostle Thomas. Do you feel the strength with which he has grasped the Lord, and how tightly he is holding onto Him? A drowning man grasps the plank on which he hopes to be saved in the same way. We will add that whoever does not have the Lord like this for himself and does not keep himself this way in relation to the Lord does not yet believe in the Lord as he should. We say, "Savior and Lord," meaning that He is the Savior of all; but Thomas says "*my*

Savior and Lord." He who says, "my Savior" feels his own salvation proceeding from Him. The feeling of salvation is closely related to the feeling of perishing, out of which the Savior pulls whomever He saves. For a man who is life-loving by nature and who knows that he cannot save himself, the feeling that he is perishing forces him to seek the Savior. When he finds Him and feels the power of salvation proceeding from Him, he grasps Him tightly and does not want to be torn from Him, though he be deprived of life itself for this. In the spiritual life of a Christian such events are not only imagined in the mind, but experienced in actuality. Then, both his faith and his union with Christ become firm, like life and death. Only such a person can sincerely cry, "Who shall separate me?" (cf. Rom. 8:35).

MONDAY
Acts 3:19–26; John 2:1–11

Repent ye therefore, and be converted, that your sins may be blotted out, when the times of refreshing shall come from the presence of the Lord (Acts 3:19). Thus spoke the Holy Apostle Peter to the Jews who crucified the Lord, comforting them that they did it out of ignorance. But we are crucifying the Lord within ourselves for a second time, not out of ignorance, but through our sins. The Most Merciful One receives us, too, when we repent and turn to Him with all our heart. We did this during Great Lent. Each came running to the Lord with tears of repentance over his sins. The more sincerely one did this, the more strongly he felt the refreshment of forgiveness proceeding from the face of the Lord, through the hand and the word of absolution of God's priest. Now what is left for us to do? To be on guard against new falls, that we not fall again into the guilt of crucifying the Lord. The Apostle says that heaven has only received the Lord Jesus until the times of the restitution of all things (cf. Acts 3:21). Then He will come again and set forth judgment. With what eyes will those who pierced His side look upon Him? Indeed, we too will have to stand in their ranks if we stop bringing forth fruits of repentance and return to our old ways.

TUESDAY
Acts 4:1–10; John 3:16–21

He that believeth not in the Son of God is condemned already (John 3:18). For what? For the fact that when light is all around, he remains in darkness, due to his love for it. Love of darkness and hatred of the light make him entirely to blame, even without his determining where the truth lies; for he who has sincere love for the truth will be led by this love from the darkness of deception to the light of truth. One example is the Holy Apostle Paul. He was a sincere lover of truth, devoted with all his soul to what he considered to be true, without any self-interest. Therefore, as soon as he was shown that the truth lay not in what he considered to be true, at that very moment he cast aside the old—which proved to be untrue—and cleaved with all his heart to the new, which was tangibly proven to be the truth. The same occurs with every sincere lover of truth. The truth of Christ is clear as day: seek and ye shall find. Help from above is always ready for the sincere seeker. Therefore, if someone remains in the darkness of unbelief, it is only due to his love for that darkness, and for this he is already condemned.

WEDNESDAY
Acts 4:13–22; John 5:17–24

Whether it be right in the sight of God to hearken unto you more than unto God, judge ye. For we cannot but speak the things which we have seen and heard (Acts 4:19–20). Thus spoke the Holy Apostles Peter and John to the authorities when the latter forbade them to speak about the resurrected Lord Jesus, after they had healed a man lame from childhood by His name. They did not fear threats, for the obviousness of the truth did not allow them to be silent: "We have seen and heard," they said, "and our hands have handled," as St. John later added (cf. I John 1:1). They are eyewitnesses. According to the principles of human knowledge, eyewitnesses are the first reliable witnesses of the truth. In this regard, there is not a single field of human knowledge that has similar witnesses. Eighteen and a half centuries have passed since that time, and the power of their testimony has not diminished at all, and consequently the obviousness of the truth testified by them has not diminished. If people fall away into faithlessness—and now there are very many who are falling away—they fall away for no reason other than a lack of good sense. They do not want to examine things and are carried away by phantoms, to which the delusion of a depraved heart willingly imparts some probability. Poor souls! They are perishing, fancying that they have landed at last on the right track, and they rejoice especially that they have entered this track first and become leaders for others. But it is no great joy to sit *in the seat of the pestilent* (Ps. 1:1).

THURSDAY
Acts 4:23–31; John 5:24–30

And they shall come forth: they that have done good, unto the resurrection of life; and they that have done evil, unto the resurrection of damnation (John 5:29). This is how everything ends! As each river flows into its own sea, so the flow of each of our lives comes, at last, to a place in accordance with its nature. Those who will be resurrected unto life will also be at the Judgment; but the Judgment will only seal their justification and the fact that they are appointed to life, while the others will be resurrected only to hear their condemnation to eternal death. Their life and death are characterized even now—because some perform living works, while others perform dead and deadening works. Living works are those which are done according to the commandments, with joy of spirit, unto the glory of God. Dead works are those which are done in opposition to the commandments, with forgetfulness of God, to please oneself and one's passions. Dead works are all those which, although in form they may not oppose the commandments, are done without any thought about God and eternal salvation, according to some aspect of self-love. God is life; only what contains part of Him is alive. And so whoever has only dead and deadening works is bound directly for death, and on the last day will come out into the condemnation of death; but whoever has all living works is bound for eternal life, and on the last day will come and receive it.

FRIDAY
Acts 5:1–11; John 5:30–6:2

Why did Ananias and Sapphira sin so badly? Because they forgot that God sees their deeds and thoughts. If they had kept in mind that God sees everything both outward and inward more clearly than any person sees, themselves included, it would not have entered their minds to lie in such a way before the Apostles. This is the cause of all our sins and sinful plans. We contrive to conceal everything from the gaze of man, and think that everything is fine. People seem not to see anything and assume we are in good shape, but this does not change our essential nothingness. Knowing this, let each of you repeat to yourself: "Why does Satan fill my heart to lie before the face of God?" (cf. Acts 5:3). God's eyes, which are brighter than the sun, see into the innermost recesses of the heart; neither night, nor sea, nor cave are concealed from Him. Remember this and so arrange your inward and outward behavior, even if no one sees it. If the All-seeing One were alien to us, it would be possible to regard His omniscience indifferently. But He is Judge, and He often pronounces His judgment, by virtue of His Omniscience, sooner than we expect. It could be that He has already pronounced judgment upon us the very moment we think to hide ourselves and our sins with a dark lie, saying, "God doesn't see!"

SATURDAY
Acts 5:21–33; John 6:14–27

What Peter and John first said to the authorities was later said by all the Apostles: *We ought to obey God rather than men. The God of our fathers raised up Jesus, Whom ye slew and hanged on a tree. Him hath God exalted with His right hand to be a Prince and a Savior, for to give repentance to Israel, and forgiveness of sins. And we are His witnesses of these things; and so is also the Holy Spirit, Whom God hath given to them that obey Him* (Acts 5:29–32). What sincerity, fullness, precision, and clarity of confession! God arranged in such a way for the Crucified to be our Savior through the forgiveness of sins in repentance. The witnesses are the Apostles as observers, and the Holy Spirit, manifestly acting in the Apostles and in all believers. The same witnesses are powerful even unto our own days. What the Holy Apostles say is the same as if we ourselves saw and heard it with our eyes and ears. And the Spirit of grace acts uninterruptedly in the Holy Church in miracle-working, in the conversion of sinners, and, especially, in the transformation of those earnestly working for the Lord, in their sanctification and in filling them with evident grace-filled gifts. These gifts give great power to their sanctification, and these together are powerful in forming a firm conviction of the truth of Christ in all truth-loving souls. Thanks be to the God of truth, Who has revealed His truth to us so clearly!

SUNDAY OF THE MYRRH-BEARING WOMEN
Acts 6:1–7; Mark 15:43–16:8

The tireless women! They would not give sleep to their eyes nor slumber to their eyelids (cf. Ps. 131:4) until they found their Beloved! But the men as it were dragged their feet: they went to the tomb, saw it empty, and remained in confusion about what it could mean, because they did not see Him. Does this mean that they had less love than the women? No, here was a reasoning love which feared making a mistake due to the high price of this love and its object. When they too saw and touched Him, then each of them, not with his tongue, like Thomas, but with his heart confessed: *My Lord and my God!* (John 20:28), and no longer could anything separate them from the Lord. The Myrrh-bearers and the Apostles are an image of the two sides of our life: feeling and reasoning. Without feeling life is not life. Without reasoning life is blind—it offers little sound fruit, and much is wasted. We must combine both. Let feeling go forward and arouse; let reason determine the time, place, method, and, in general, the practical arrangement of what the heart suggests for us to do. Within, the heart comes first, but in practical application, reason comes first. When the feelings become educated in discerning good and evil, then perhaps it will be possible to rely on the heart alone. Just as shoots, flowers, and fruits grow from a living tree, so then will goodness alone begin to emerge from the heart, and will be rationally merged into the course of our life.

MONDAY
Acts 6:8–7:5, 47–60; John 4:46–54

St. Stephen says: *The most High dwelleth not in temples made with hands.... What house will ye build Me? saith the Lord, or, what is the place of My rest?* (Acts 7:48–49). Only the temple in the heart, not made with hands, can contain God, as the Lord said: *If a man love Me, he will keep My words: and My Father will love him, and We will come unto him, and make Our abode with him* (John 14:23). How this is accomplished is unfathomable to us, but it is true because it is obvious that then *it is God Who worketh in you both to will and to do of His good pleasure* (Phil. 2:13). Do not deliberate about it, just give your heart to the Lord, and He Himself will make of it a temple for Himself—but give it unsparingly. If there are parts which are not given, then an integral temple cannot be made from the heart, for one thing will be decayed, another broken—and what will result, if anything results, will be a temple with holes or without a roof, or without doors. It is not possible to live in such a temple: the Lord will not dwell in it. It will only seem that it is a temple, but in reality it will just be a pile of material.

TUESDAY
Acts 8:5–17; John 6:27–33

Then Simon himself believed also: and when he was baptized, he continued with Philip (Acts 8:13). He both believed and was baptized, but nothing came of him. One must think that there was something not quite right in the formation of his faith. Sincere faith is the renunciation of your mind. You must bare your mind and present it to faith as a clean slate, so that faith might inscribe itself on the mind as it is, without any admixture of alien phrases and statutes. When one's former beliefs remain in the mind, then a mixture occurs after the tenets of the Faith are written there. The consciousness will be confused between the mind's sophism and the operations of faith. Simon was therefore a model for all heretics, and such are all who enter the realm of faith with their own sophistries—both then and now. They are confused in faith and nothing comes of them other than harm: for themselves, when they remain silent; for others, when this confusion is not kept within themselves alone, but breaks out, due to their thirst to be teachers. Hence there always turns out to be a party of people more or less in error about the Faith, with a wretched surety of their infallibility, and with a dangerous drive to remake everyone their own way.

WEDNESDAY
Acts 8:18–25; John 6:35–39

St. Peter says to Simon: *Thou hast neither part nor lot in this matter: for thy heart is not right in the sight of God. Repent therefore of this thy wickedness, and pray God, if perhaps the thought of thine heart may be forgiven thee* (Acts 8:21–22). Thou hast no part.... But Simon did not even begin to think that he had gone so far astray. Outwardly he had not done anything outrageous; only his thinking was wrong—so wrong, that the Apostle was uncertain as to whether it would be forgiven him even if he repented and entreated God. That is how important the heart's disposition is, and the thoughts that proceed from it according to this disposition! Judging by this, a person may be one way on the outside, and completely different on the inside. Only God sees this inner state, and those to whom the Spirit of God, Who tries all hearts, reveals it. With what fear and trembling must we work out our salvation! And how sincerely and zealously must we pray to God: *Create in me a clean heart, O God; and renew a right spirit within me* (Ps. 50:10). Then, at the Judgment, something terrible and amazing will happen. The Lord will say: *I know you not* (Matt. 25:12) to those who not only were sure of their own godliness, but who also appeared godly to everyone else. What remains for us to do? Only to cry out: "Thou who knowest all things, save us, O Lord!" As Thou knowest, grant a saving formation to our heart!

THURSDAY
Acts 8:26–39; John 6:40–44

St. Philip asked the eunuch: *Understandest thou what thou readest?* He replied, *How can I, except some man should guide me?* (Acts 8:31). How often those who read the word of God and the writings of the Fathers experience the same thing! What is read will not fit into our head; the mind cannot hear or grasp it, as if it were something foreign to it, about topics of an unknown realm. This is why an interpreter is needed who is familiar with the meaning of the words. St. Philip had the same Spirit that had given those prophecies, and so it was not difficult for him to interpret what the eunuch found hard to understand. It is the same for us now: we must find a person who stands on such a level of life and knowledge as is touched upon by the Scripture which is difficult for us, and he will interpret it without difficulty, because each level has its own spiritual field of vision. He who stands on a lower level does not see everything that he who stands on the higher sees—he can only guess about it. If it happens that the Scripture which is incomprehensible for us touches upon subjects of the higher level, but the interpreter we encounter stands on the lower level, he cannot explain it as he should, and will apply everything to his own field of vision, and it will remain for us as dark as before. One must marvel at how people undertake to interpret Scriptural topics while being totally foreign to the realm of these subjects. It does not turn out as it should, but they do not forget to become puffed up over their own interpretations.

Friday
Acts 8:40–9:19; John 6:48–54

St. Paul at first defended the Old Testament observances as zealously as he did because he was sincerely certain that it was the unalterable will of God that these observances remain unchanged. He was not zealous because it was the Faith of his fathers, but because in being zealous he was offering service to God. In this lay the spirit of his life—to devote himself to God and direct all his energy toward things pleasing to Him. Thus, in order to bring about his conversion, or to make him stand for the New Testament order of things rather than that of the Old

Testament, it was sufficient to tangibly show him that God no longer wanted the Old Testament but rather the New, and that He transferred all of His goodwill from the former to the latter. The Lord's appearance to him on the road accomplished this. There it became clear to him that he was not directing his zeal where he ought, that he was not pleasing God by acting as he did, but was acting contrary to His will. This vision of the state of things, with the help of God's grace, immediately changed his strivings, and he cried out: *Lord, what wilt Thou have me to do?* (Acts 9:6). And from that moment he directed all of his zeal toward what was shown to him, and he did not forget this event for his entire life, but thankfully remembering it, stirred up his zeal with it—not sparing anything to work for his Lord and Savior. This is how all people act who have sincerely turned to the Lord.

SATURDAY
Acts 9:20–31; John 15:17–16:2

When St. Paul began to preach in Damascus, all were amazed, saying: *Is not this he that destroyed them which called on this name?* (Acts 9:21). Is it not always this way? Those close to someone who converts from unbelief to belief, or from sin to virtue, marvel over what has happened with this person. He did everything our way and now suddenly everything has changed: his words and his gaze, his step and his thoughts are not the same, and his undertakings are different, and the places where he goes are different. It is as if one were walking toward the west, and then suddenly turned around to the east. These two lives are contradictory and mutually exclusive. He who wants to combine them, or to make a whole life with part from the one and part from the other, will waste both time and effort with no success. What can these lives have in common? Only those who do not understand things can say, "Why does it have to be so drastic?"

Sunday of the Paralytic
Acts 9:32–42; John 5:1–15

Behold, thou art made whole: sin no more, lest a worse thing come unto thee (John 5:14). Sin does not strike only the soul, but the body as well. In some cases this is exceedingly obvious; in others, although it is not as obvious, the truth remains the truth: that all the illnesses of the body always stem from sins. A sin is committed in the soul and directly makes it sick; but since the life of the body comes from the soul, then the life coming from a sick soul is, of course, not healthy. The mere fact that sin brings darkness and sorrow must act unfavorably on bodily health. But when you remember that it separates man from God, the Source of life, and places man in disharmony with all laws acting in himself and in nature, then one must marvel how a sinner remains alive after sinning. This is the mercy of God, Who awaits repentance and conversion. Consequently, a sick person must rush first of all to be cleansed of sins and make peace with God in his conscience. This paves the way for the beneficial action of medicine. They say that there was one distinguished doctor who would not begin treatment until the patient had confessed and received the Holy Mysteries; and the more serious the disease, the more urgently he insisted upon this.

Monday
Acts 10:1–16; John 6:56–69

When the Lord presented His teaching about the Mystery of His Body and Blood, setting it forth as a necessary condition for contact with Himself and as a source of true life, then *many of His disciples went back, and walked no more with Him* (John 6:66). Such an act of God's boundless mercy toward us seemed too miraculous to them, and their disinclination toward the miraculous tore them from the Lord. The Lord saw this, and although He was prepared to be crucified for the salvation of every person, He did not consider it possible to diminish or annul the miracle. It is so crucial in the economy of our salvation! Albeit with regret, He allowed them to depart from Him into the darkness of unbelief and destruction, and said to them and to the chosen twelve as well, *Will ye also go away?* (John 6:67). This showed that He was ready to let them go also, if they could not yield before that which was miraculous. So it is that to flee from the miraculous is to flee from the Lord and Savior; and one who turns away from the miraculous is as one who is perishing. May those who are horrified by even the mention of the miraculous heed this! Even they will come across a miracle which they will not be able to thwart: death, and after death, judgment. But whether this inability to thwart it will serve them unto salvation, only God knows.

TUESDAY
Acts 10:21–33; John 7:1–13

The world cannot hate you; but Me it hateth, because I testify of it, that the works thereof are evil (John 7:7). The Lord did not say this to His disciples; to His disciples He foretold later that the world would hate and persecute them also, because He had taken them out of the world. Therefore, take note of what the world hates, and you will learn where Christ's portion is. The world rebels most strongly against what is of Christ, what is closest to Him, and what is most conformable to His Spirit. This is an external indicator, but for those who live externally this is enough. The world does not act on its own, but is kindled in its works by its prince—Satan, whose works the Lord destroyed and continues to destroy in believers and through believers. He cannot do anything to the Lord directly; this is why he directs his anger upon those who believe in Him, so that in frustrating them he will frustrate the Lord. He does not act directly in this, but through his agencies, which constitute the world. This does not mean that he is strong; do not fear him, but rather be bold, for the Lord has overcome the world and the prince thereof. Satan is in no condition to do anything to one who does not himself yield.

Mid-Pentecost
Wednesday
Acts 14:6–18; John 7:14–30

On Mid-Pentecost a cry is heard from the Lord: *If any man thirst, let him come unto Me, and drink* (John 7:37). If that is the case, then let us all go to Him. Whoever thirsts for anything, as long as it is not contrary to the Spirit of the Lord, will find satisfaction without fail. You who thirst for knowledge, go to the Lord, for He is the only Light that truly enlightens every man. You who thirst for cleansing from sins and the soothing of the burning of your conscience, go to the Lord, for He has lifted up the sins of the whole world upon the tree (cf. I Peter 2:24) and torn up their handwriting (cf. Col. 2:14). You who thirst for peace of heart, go to the Lord, for He is the Treasure, the possession of which will make you forget all deprivations and despise all goods in order to possess Him alone. You who need strength—He has every strength. If it is glory—He has glory on high. If it is freedom—He is the giver of true freedom. He will resolve all of our uncertainties, break the bonds of the passions, disperse all sorrows and grieving, enable us to overcome all the impediments, temptations, and snares of the enemy, and will smooth out the path of our spiritual life. Let us all go to the Lord!

Thursday
Acts 10:34–43; John 8:12–20

I am the Light of the world: he that followeth Me shall not walk in darkness, but shall have the light of life (John 8:12), says the Lord.

Consequently, he who turns away from the Lord turns away from the light and is headed into darkness, and therefore he is a true obscurantist.[18] You know what the teaching of Christ demands. As soon as someone puts forth thoughts contrary to this teaching, do not fear calling him an obscurantist, for this is his real name. The Lord teaches that God is One in Essence and three in Person—this is a ray of the supernatural light of truth. Whoever preaches the contrary leads people into darkness from the light, and he is an obscurantist. The Lord teaches that God is Tri-hypostatic; and having created the world by His Word, He guides it through His Providence. This is the Divine light which illuminates the gloomy paths of our life, but not with an earthly, comforting light. He who preaches contrary to this leads people into dreary darkness—he is an obscurantist. The Lord teaches that God created man according to His image and likeness and set him to live in Paradise. When man sinned, God righteously drove him out of Paradise to live on this earth, which is full of sorrows and want. However, He was not angered with him unto the end, but it was His good pleasure to arrange salvation for him through the death on the Cross of the incarnate Only Begotten Son of God—and this is the spiritual light, illuminating the moral gloom that enshrouds our souls. He who preaches contrary to this leads people into darkness and is an obscurantist. The Lord teaches: believe, and upon receiving the power of grace in the Divine Mysteries, live according to His commandments, and you will be saved—this is the only way for the light of God to enter us and enlighten us. He who teaches something to the contrary wants to keep us in darkness and therefore is an obscurantist. The Lord teaches: enter in at the narrow gate of a strict life of self-denial; this is the only path to the light. Whoever is traveling the broad path of pleasing himself

---

[18] During St. Theophan's time there was already much talk among "progressive" people about Christian "obscurantism." The Orthodox faithful were often accused of "obscuring" the enlightenment of more progressive groups; thus they were called obscurantists or reactionaries.—TRANS.

is headed into darkness, and is an obscurantist. The Lord teaches: remember the last things: death, judgment, hell, and heaven. This is a light that illuminates our future. Whoever teaches that death is the end of all casts darkness over our fate, and is thus an obscurantist. Lovers of the light! Learn by this to distinguish where the darkness is, and depart from it.

FRIDAY
Acts 10:44–11:10; John 8:21–30

They asked the Lord: *Who art Thou?* He answered: *Even the same ... from the beginning* (John 8:25). He is in front, behind Him are the Holy Apostles, and behind the Apostles are the pastors and teachers and the entire Church of Christ. Judge now who are the true avant-garde. Although so many have followed them for such a long time and continue to follow them, they have not ceased to be in front, for they continue to be in front, while others continue to follow them. Thus for us Christians there already is an avant-garde; and if someone attempts to push new people to the fore—it is obvious that they must be understood as being an avant-garde heading in the opposite direction, that is, on the path which leads to the bottom of hell. There is nothing to add to this. Be warned—for who is his own enemy? Try only to understand this in a real way; hold firmly to the known truth of Christ, and let the others repeat what they want.

SATURDAY
Acts 12:1–11; John 8:31–42

The Lord said: *If the Son therefore shall make you free, ye shall be free indeed* (John 8:36). Here is where freedom is! The mind is bound with bonds of ignorance, delusions, superstitions, and uncertainties. It struggles, but cannot get away from them. Cleave to the Lord, and He will enlighten your darkness and dissolve all the bonds in which your mind languishes. The passions bind the will and do not give it space in which to act. It struggles like one bound hand and foot, and cannot get away. But cleave to the Lord and He will give you the strength of Samson, and will dissolve all the bonds of untruth that bind you. Constant worries surround the heart and give it no peace. But cleave to the Lord, and He will soothe you. Then, at peace, and seeing everything around you clearly, you will walk with the Lord without hindrance or stumbling through the gloom and darkness of this life, to the all-blessed, complete joy and spaciousness of eternity.

SUNDAY OF THE SAMARITAN WOMAN
Acts 11:19–26, 29–30; John 4:5–42

The Samaritan woman's fellow citizens said to her after two days with the Savior in their midst: *Now we believe not because of thy saying: for we have heard Him ourselves, and know that this is indeed the Christ, the Savior of the world* (John 4:42). It happens this way with everyone. At first they are called to the Lord by an external word or, as for many now, simply by birth. But when they taste in practice what it is to live in the Lord, they no longer cleave to the Lord through their external affiliation with Christian society, but through their inner union with Him. It is necessary for all who are born in Christian societies to make this a law for themselves, that is, to not limit themselves to mere external affiliation with the Lord, but to seek to unite with Him inwardly, that they may always bear witness within themselves that they are standing in the truth. Why is this necessary? It is necessary to embody within oneself the truth of Christ. The truth of Christ is a restoration of what is fallen. Thus, put off the old man, which is corrupt according to deceitful lusts, and put on the new man, which is created after God in righteousness and true holiness (cf. Eph. 4:22–24), and you will know within yourself that the Lord Jesus Christ is in truth the Savior not only of the world but of you personally.

Monday
Acts 12:12–17; John 8:42–51

What means, do you think, did the Lord use to explain to the Jews the reason for their not believing in Him? The means He used was to tell them the truth. *And because I tell you the truth, ye believe Me not* (John 8:45). The lie, as it is said, turned into their flesh and blood, and made them incapable of receiving the truth. Why do people not believe today? For the same reason—the Lord speaks the truth, and therefore they do not believe. But how can this be? Are they not all learned, and do they not talk only about the truth? They have many words, but no works. The weaving of their schemes is like the spinning of a spider's web, but they do not notice the flimsiness of it. The principles of their systems are groundless, and their conclusions cannot be proved, but they are satisfied with them nevertheless. There is now such a demand for hypotheses that it seems that they alone make up the entire content of their minds, and this is reputed to be solid education. They apply the fog of their dreams to the few facts they have procured, and in this fog these facts appear in a totally different way than what they are in reality. Nevertheless, this is all reputed to be the sphere of immutable truth. So their mind has gone rotten, and its taste has been ruined! How can it contain the truth? And so they do not believe the Lord, Who speaks only the truth.

Tuesday
Acts 12:25–13:12; John 8:51–59

The Jews became angry with the Lord because of His accusation, and picked up stones *to cast at Him*. But the Lord went *through the midst of them, and so passed by* (John 8:59). They did nothing to the Lord, but they destroyed themselves, for the consequence of their unbelief was the terrible sentence of the Lord: *Behold, your house is left unto you desolate* (Matt. 23:38), and also: *Let us go hence* (John 14:31). And the Lord passed to another place and chose other peoples for His habitation, instead of the beloved Israel. Even now, insignificant people, in the self-delusion of a proud mind which does not contain the truth of Christ, take up stones of opposition to the Lord and cast them at Him. They do not harm Him, because He is the Lord, and His truth is the immutable truth; they only destroy themselves. The Lord goes by, leaving such people in their vain wisdom, which spins them around the way a whirlwind spins loose specks of dust. But when an entire nation is carried away with false wisdom, then the entire nation is left to its fate, as was the case with the Jews. Understand, O ye nations, and submit yourselves to the Lord!

WEDNESDAY
Acts 13:13–24; John 6:5–14

The disciples told the Lord to send the multitude away so they could buy themselves food in the villages; but the Lord said to them, *They need not depart; give ye them to eat* (Matt. 14:16). This preceded the miracle of feeding the five thousand men, along with women and children, with five loaves of bread and two fishes. Such an event, which had particular significance in the life of the Lord, offers also the following lesson. The multitude is an image of humanity, hungering and thirsting after the truth. When the Lord said to the Apostles, *Give ye them to eat*, He was indicating to them in advance their future ministry to the human race—to feed it with the truth. The Apostles did this for their times; in subsequent times they passed this service on to the pastors who succeeded them. The Lord's words extend to the present pastors as well: *Give ye them to eat*. And the pastors should keep this obligation in their conscience—to feed the people with the truth. There should be unceasing preaching of the word of God in church. What sort of pastors are silent pastors?

And yet they are often silent—silent beyond measure. But one cannot say that this occurs from a lack of faith in their heart. It is just their misunderstanding, a bad habit. Nevertheless, this is no justification.

THURSDAY
Acts 14:20–27; John 9:39–10:9

And Jesus said, For judgment I am come into this world, that they which see not might see; and that they which see might be made blind (John 9:39). They who could not see were the simple people who believed the Lord in simplicity of heart, while they who saw were the scribes and learned men of that time, who due to their pride of mind did not believe and held back the people. Our clever ones think that they see, and this is why they are alienated from that faith in the Lord which those who are simple in heart and mind firmly hold to. Therefore, according to the truth of the Lord, they are blind, whereas the people see. They are exactly like those birds which can see at night, but not during the day. The truth of Christ is dark for them, whereas what is contrary to this truth—falsehood—to them seems clear: here they are in their element. This is so obvious, but nevertheless they are ready to ask, *Are we blind also?* (John 9:40). There is nothing to hide—you are blind. But since it is your own fault that you are blind, the sin of blindness and the inability to see the light lies upon you. You can see, but you do not want to, because you have come to love a deceptive, yet seductive lie.

FRIDAY
Acts 15:5–34; John 10:17–28

Ye believe not, because ye are not of My sheep, says the Lord to the unbelieving Jews. *My sheep hear My voice, and I know them, and they follow Me* (John 10:26–7). Unbelievers are not of Christ's fold. At that time, the unbelievers were those who had not yet entered into the fold; but now the unbelievers are all those who have fallen away from the Faith or who lag behind the flock of Christ. The Lord is the Shepherd: all of His sheep go after Him, following His teaching and fulfilling His holy commandments. Sinners are sheep that are sick and weak, but still plod along together with the fold. But those who have lost faith are those who have totally fallen behind, and have been abandoned to be eaten by wild beasts. These are the ones who are truly left behind. They are not of Christ's fold and they do not hear His voice. He does not know them because they do not let themselves be known, as the woman with the issue of blood did. And at the Judgment it will be said to them: *I know you not ... depart* (Luke 13:27).

SATURDAY

Acts 15:35–41; John 10:27–38

Though ye believe not Me, believe the works, says the Lord (John 10:38). The works of the Lord were obvious to all, and He could point to them openly. They are the healing of various diseases, the driving out of demons, power over nature, knowledge of the thoughts of the heart, prophesying of the future, power in one's word, and dominion over souls. All of these clearly proved that Jesus Christ was from God, and that His word was the truth. Other works were added to these for us: His glorious death, Resurrection and Ascension, the descent of the Holy Spirit, the foundation of the Church, the marvelous spiritual gifts in believers, the triumph over the pagans, and the grace-filled power which to this day has not ceased to act in the Church of God. All of these are the works of the Lord. To any unbeliever one can say: If you do not believe the word, believe these works, which loudly witness to the Divinity of our Lord Jesus Christ; and having come to belief, accept His entire truth. But how did those Jews answer the Lord at that time? *They sought again to take*

Him (John 10:39). What do today's unbelievers do? They sit and weave lie onto lie, not in order to "take" the Lord—for this is not according to their strength—but to "take" those who are simple in faith and cannot unravel their sly weavings.

SUNDAY OF THE BLIND MAN
Acts 16:16–34; John 9:1–38

Simplicity of faith argues with crafty unbelief. Faith, coming to the blind man who received sight, enlightened his mind's eyes, and he clearly saw the truth. See how everything was logical for him. They asked him: What do you say of Him who gave you sight? *He is a prophet* (John 9:17), he responded, that is, a messenger of God clothed in miracle-working power. An indisputably true conclusion! But learned erudition does not want to see this truth and seeks to evade its consequences. However, this being impossible, it approaches unlearned simplicity with the suggestion: *Give God the praise: we know that this Man is a sinner* (John 9:24). Simplicity of faith does not know how to connect these concepts—sinfulness and miracle-working—and expresses this openly: *Whether He be a sinner or no, I know not: one thing I know, that, whereas I was blind, now I see* (John 9:25). What can one say against such deduction? But the logic of the unbelievers is obstinate, and even in the face of the obvious it is not ashamed to affirm that it does not know where He who opened the blind man's eyes is from. *Why herein is a marvelous thing*, the sensible logic of faith says to them, *that ye know not from whence He is, and yet He hath opened mine eyes. Now we know that God heareth not sinners: but if any man be a worshipper of God, and doeth His will, him He heareth. Since the world began was it not heard that any man opened the eyes of one that was born blind. If this man were not of God, He could do nothing* (John 9:30–33). It would seem as though after this nothing remained other than to bow down before the power of such a conclusion. But learned erudition

could not stand the sensible logic of faith, and drove it away....
Go now and prove the truth of the Faith to those whose mind
has been corrupted with obstinate unbelief. The unbelievers of
all times are cut from the same cloth.

MONDAY
Acts 17:1–15; John 11:47–57

What do we? for this man doeth many miracles (John 11:47).
Jewish erudition found the Savior to be guilty. And in our
days, German erudition[19] finds what is supernatural to be out
of place in the Gospels of Christ: everything is good, only this
[the miraculous] just won't work. These two ways of thinking
meet in the final analysis. Jewish erudition decided: *It is expedient
that one man should die* (John 11:50), and that the rest might
not perish, while German erudition states: We will eliminate the
supernatural to preserve all the other Gospel truths. And what
came of this? The Jews destroyed their own nation, while the
Germans have lost all Christian truths, and are now left with
almost nothing. The Lord is the Cornerstone of the house of
salvation; similarly, faith in the supernatural is the cornerstone of
the entire building of God-inspired truth. The Savior Himself, in
His Person, is the crown of the supernatural, and in the Church
He is its inexhaustible Source. He who touches this point is
touching the apple of God's eye.

TUESDAY
Acts 17:19–28; John 12:19–36

*Except a corn of wheat fall into the ground and die, it abideth alone:
but if it die, it bringeth forth much fruit* (John 12:24). And so, if

---

[19] By "German erudition" St. Theophan is referring here to the German
philosophy and Biblical scholarship of his time.—ED.

you want to be fruitful, die. Die in a real way, bearing always the feeling in your heart that you have already died. Just as a dead man does not respond to anything surrounding him, so do the same: if they praise you, be silent; if they rebuke you, be silent; if you make a profit, be silent; if you are full, be silent; or if you are hungry, be silent. Be this way to all external things and inwardly abide in the place where all the dead abide—in the other life—before the all-righteous face of God, preparing to hear the final sentence. You may say, "What fruit can come if everything is dying?" No, nothing will die. Rather, energy will appear—and what energy! You will say to yourself, "I have but one minute remaining. The verdict is coming right now; let me hurry to do something." And you'll do it. Keep this up every minute.

WEDNESDAY
Acts 18:22–28; John 12:36–47

O Lord, who has believed our report? (Is. 53:1), the Prophet Isaiah laments in astonishment. Now it would be fitting to cry out, "Who now sincerely believes Thy word, O Lord?" Almost everyone has become slack. The tongues of many are silent about their faith, while it is rare to find a heart that has not turned in the other direction. What is the reason for this? Interest in unbelief has begun to be felt; the need for unbelief has developed, for protecting interests of the heart which do not agree with faith. Here is the root of evil. Reason is not the adversary of faith, but a corrupt heart is. Reason is only guilty here in that it submits to the heart and begins to philosophize, not according to the foundations of truth, but according to the desires of the heart. Furthermore, powerful arguments for the truth seem worthless to the mind, and some trifling argument against the truth becomes a whole mountain. In general, confusion comes into the mental realm, blinding the mind, which does not and cannot see, no matter how you push it.

Ascension
Thursday
Acts 1:1–12; Luke 24:36–53

St. Paul expresses the power of the Lord's Ascension in this manner: *When He ascended up on high, He led captivity captive, and gave gifts unto men* (Eph. 4:8). Having satisfied God's righteousness, the Lord opened for us all the treasures of God's goodness. This is indeed a capturing or taking of spoils after victory. The beginning of the distribution of these spoils to people is the descent of the Holy Spirit, Who, having descended, always abides in the Church and gives everyone what he needs, receiving all from that captive captivity (cf. Eph 4:8). Let everyone come and take. But prepare for yourself a repository for that treasure, which is a pure heart; have hands with which to take it, which is unreflecting faith. Then step forth, searching hopefully and praying relentlessly.

Friday
Acts 19:1–8; John 14:1–11

If ye had known Me, ye should have known My Father also (John 14:7). Therefore, deists[20] do not know God, in spite of the fact that they bear His name (Deus=God, whence comes the word "deist"), and reason eloquently about Him. There is no true God without the Son and the Holy Spirit. He who believes in God but

---

[20] Deism is the belief that a Supreme Being created the universe and its laws, but afterwards refrained from interfering with the operation of those laws and from intervening in human affairs. A belief system based on human reason without reference to revelation, deism denies the doctrine of the Holy Trinity as well as prophecy and miracles. It became popular in Western Europe during the so-called Age of Enlightenment, and attracted adherents in Russia during the eighteenth and nineteenth centuries, particularly among the upper classes.—Ed.

does not confess Him as the Father of the Son, does not believe in a god that is the true God, but in some personal invention. The true God gave us His Son; He gave men *power to become the sons of God* (John 1:12); He loves them, and hears each of their prayers, for the sake of the Son. That is why he who has the Son has the Father; and he who does not have the Son, does not have the Father. No one comes to the Father except through the Son, and no one receives anything from the Father except through the Son. Apart from the Son there is no path to the true God, and he who dreams of inventing Him is deluded.

SATURDAY
Acts 20:7–12; John 14:10–21

And whatsoever ye shall ask of the Father *in My name, that will I do* (John 14:13). What a consoling promise! But how few make use of it! People rarely keep this in mind. There are people who do not understand this at all, and do not accept it. Why is this so? Because they do not love the Lord and do not fulfill His commandments. This unfaithfulness of the heart toward the Lord cuts off any boldness to petition the Lord, just as a lazy servant does not dare ask something of his masters, for he knows that he does not deserve any mercy. The established prayers are read in their usual course, and they contain very great petitions; but they are merely read, and this, as we well know, is far from prayer and petitioning. We cannot stand with true prayer before the Lord and extend our petitions to Him until our conscience is clear before Him.

SUNDAY OF THE HOLY FATHERS OF THE FIRST ECUMENICAL COUNCIL
Acts 20:16–18, 28–36; John 17:1–13

Arius began to deny the Divinity of the Son of God and His

co-essentiality with God the Father. The entire Church rose up against him; all believers, from all ends of the earth, unanimously confessed that the Lord Jesus Christ is the Only Begotten Son of God, true God of true God; begotten, not made, of one essence with the Father. Someone might think that this enthusiasm for unity was by chance, but this faith was then tried by fire when the authorities and powerful of this world began to side with the Arians. Neither fire, nor sword, nor persecution could extinguish this faith, and it was immediately found in every place among everyone, as soon as the pressure from external powers ceased. This means that it makes up the heart of the Church and the essence of its confession. Glory be to the Lord, Who preserves this faith within us! For, as long as it exists, we are still Christians, though we may not live as such. If it ceases to exist, that would be the end of Christianity.

MONDAY
Acts 21:8–14; John 14:27–15:7

The Lord Jesus Christ is the vine, a grape tree; Christians are branches and shoots. We cleave to Him through faith and bear fruit through a life according to faith. The Heavenly Father is the husbandman who watches over this tree. Any branch which does not bring forth fruit—that is, whoever believes but does not live according to faith—the Lord cuts off. But He purges those which bring forth fruit—that is, those who not only believe, but are also zealous to live according to faith. These the Lord helps in every way to become rich in good works, which are the fruits of faith. Let each person arrange his life according to this law of God's action upon us, firmly remembering that without the Lord one can do nothing. Run to Him with every need. May His sweetest and most holy name be ever impressed upon your mind, heart, and tongue.

TUESDAY
Acts 21:26–32; John 16:2–13

When He, the Spirit of truth, is come, He will guide you into all truth
(John 16:13). Why is this source of knowledge not mentioned in
books of rhetoric? It is not surprising that this point is not found
in pagan books of rhetoric, but why is it not found in Christian
ones? Can it be that when a Christian begins to philosophize
he ought to cease being a Christian and forget all the true and
unquestionable promises which were given to him? People often
explain how to see and hear; they also teach well enough how to
make generalizations and inductions from what is seen and heard.
But when the time comes to unravel the meaning of it all, here
the nursling of logic is left to the devices of his own guesswork.
Why not suggest to him: "You have the revelations of the Spirit
of truth—follow them"? They resolve the meaning of all existence
and events in an indisputable manner, for they proceed from God,
in Whom lies the source of existence itself. Has all the guessing
multiplied so greatly that now all books (about God's world) are
filled only with guesses precisely because no one remembers to
make that suggestion? It would be all right if these books were
at least a little worthwhile, but it is clear at first glance that they
are but the fruit of a childish imagination.

WEDNESDAY
Acts 23:1–11; John 16:15–23

The Lord said to the Holy Apostles before His sufferings: *A little
while, and ye shall not see Me: and again, a little while, and ye shall
see Me* (John 16:16). The Lord's sufferings and death so struck the
Holy Apostles that the eyes of their minds became dim, and they
no longer saw the Lord as the Lord. The light was hidden, and
they sat in a bitter and wearisome darkness. The light of Christ's

Resurrection dispersed this darkness, and they again saw the Lord. The Lord Himself explained His words thus: *Ye shall weep,* He said, *and lament, but the world shall rejoice; and ye shall be sorrowful, but your sorrow shall be turned into joy* (John 16:20). It is said that every soul experiences a similar defeat on the way to perfection. Universal darkness covers it, and it does not know where to go; but the Lord comes, and changes its sorrow into joy. This is truly as necessary as it is for a woman to suffer before a man is born of her into the world. Can we not conclude from this that he who has not experienced this has not yet given birth to a real Christian within himself?

THURSDAY
Acts 25:13–19; John 16:23–33

Verily, verily, I say unto you, Whatsoever ye shall ask the Father in My name, He will give it you (John 16:23) the Lord said, even confirming the point: *Verily, verily, I say unto you.* What a shame for us that we do not know how to make use of such a true promise! And it would be good if this only caused us shame, otherwise a shadow would be cast over the promise itself, as though it were too great and impossible. No, the guilt lies entirely on us, mainly because we recognize that we are not faithful servants of Christ, and our conscience does not allow us to expect mercy from the Lord. In addition, it happens that when someone starts asking God about something, he does it with a divided soul. He mentions that thing in his prayer once or twice, as if in passing, and then drops it, and says later, "God does not hear." No, when asking for something in particular, one must be persistent and indefatigable in prayer, like the widow who forced even the heartless judge to satisfy her petition by simply not giving him any peace. When true men of prayer ask for something in prayer, they unite it with fasting, vigil, all sorts of deprivation, and charity. Furthermore, they ask not for a day or two, but for months and years, and thus they receive what they ask for. Imitate them, if you desire to have success in prayer.

FRIDAY
Acts 27:1–44; John 17:18–26

As thou, Father, art in Me, and I in Thee, that they also may be one in Us.... I in them, and Thou in Me (John 17:21–23). This is the golden chain that ties us with Divinity! We have fallen away and a Mediator has arisen, Who is one with God the Father and has become one with us. Becoming one with Him we are united in Him, and through Him with God the Father. Glory to Thy boundless mercy toward us, O Tri-hypostatic God, Who was well pleased to establish for us such a bright path to deification! The Lord raises us up high; do not refuse His good gift. Confess His mercy and praise His unspeakable goodness! You think it humble to refuse such a height, but you are actually revealing crude ingratitude and carelessness toward a lofty gift. Know that there is no middle ground—it is all or nothing. If you do not want this loftiness, you will remain outside in bitter abasement, both temporally and eternally.

SATURDAY OF THE DEAD
Acts 28:1–31; John 21:15–25

No one is lazy in commemorating his own [reposed] parents, but it is also necessary to commemorate all Orthodox Christians—and not only on this day, but at all times, in every prayer. We ourselves will be there [among the reposed], and will need this prayer as a poor person needs a piece of bread and a glass of water. Remember that prayer for the reposed is strong through its communality, in that it comes from the entire Church. The Church breathes prayer. Just as it is in nature, when during pregnancy a mother breathes and the strength she receives from this breath passes on to her child, so also in a grace-filled way the Church breathes a prayer which is shared by all, and the power of the prayer passes on to the reposed, who are held in the bosom of the Church, which is made up of the living and the dead, the militant and the triumphant. Do not be slothful about zealously commemorating all of our departed fathers and brothers whenever you pray. It will be your alms for them.

SUNDAY OF HOLY PENTECOST
Acts 2:1–11; John 7:37–52; 8:12

The economy of our salvation has been accomplished! The operations of all the Persons of the Most Holy Trinity have henceforth come into effect to accomplish it. That which God the Father willed, the Son of God has fulfilled in Himself, and the Holy Spirit has now descended in order to impart it to the faithful. For our salvation is *according to the foreknowledge of God the Father, through sanctification of the Spirit, unto obedience and sprinkling of the Blood of Jesus Christ* (I Peter 1:2). For this reason we are *baptized in the name of the Father, and of the Son, and of the Holy Spirit*, obliged to observe all things whatsoever He has commanded us (cf. Matt. 28:19–20). Those who do not confess the Most Holy Trinity cannot participate in the saving action of Its Persons and thus receive salvation. Glory to the Father and to the Son and to the Holy Spirit, the Trinity one in essence and undivided, Who granteth us to confess It! O Father Almighty and Word and Spirit, one Nature united in three Persons, transcendent and most Divine! Into Thee have we been baptized, and Thee shall we bless throughout all ages.

MONDAY
Eph. 5:9–19; Matt. 18:10–20

Comforting His disciples, the Lord said that it would be better for them if He ascended to heaven for, having ascended, in place of Himself He would send the Comforter—the Spirit. The Holy Spirit has descended and abides in the Church, accomplishing in each believer the work of Christ. Each Christian is a communicant of the Spirit. This is something so necessary, that in fact whoever does not have the Spirit is not of Christ. Look closely at yourself—is the Spirit of grace within you? For He does not remain in everyone; He can depart. Here are the signs of His presence: first, He finds a spirit of repentance and teaches a Christian to turn to God and correct his life; the spirit of repentance, accomplishing its work, passes the Christian on to a spirit of holiness and purity. This is succeeded, at last, by a spirit of sonship. The characteristic of the first is work-loving zeal; the characteristic of the second is warmth and a sweet burning of the heart; the characteristic of the third is the feeling of sonship whereby the heart sighs to God: *Abba, Father!* (Mk. 14:36). Examine which of these levels you are on. If you are not on any of them, take care for yourself.

TUESDAY
Rom. 1:1–7, 13–17; Matt. 4:25–5:13

After the Lord's Baptism, when the Spirit had descended upon Him in the form of a dove, He was led into the wilderness to be tempted. Such is the path common to all. St. Isaac the Syrian notes in one place that as soon as you taste grace-filled consolation or receive some gift from the Lord, expect temptations. Temptations conceal the brightness of grace from one's own eyes, and they usually corrode every good through self-opinion and self-exultation. These temptations are sometimes outward, such as sorrows and humiliation, and sometimes inward, such as passionate thoughts, which are purposely set loose like unchained beasts. Therefore, we must pay heed to ourselves and strictly sort out what occurs with us and in us, to see why it is happening, and what it obliges us to do.

Wednesday
Rom. 1:18–27; Matt. 5:20–26

Except your righteousness shall exceed the righteousness of the scribes and Pharisees, ye shall in no case enter into the Kingdom of Heaven (Matt. 5:20). Characteristic of the scribes is knowledge of the law without concern for life according to the law. Characteristic of the Pharisees is correctness of outward behavior without particular concern for correctness of thoughts and feelings in the heart. Both attitudes are condemned to remain outside of the Kingdom of Heaven. Let everyone receive the lesson he needs from this. If you want to learn the Gospel law, do so—but in a way that enables you to establish your life according to this knowledge. Try to be correct in your behavior, but keep your inner feelings and dispositions correct at the same time. If you have gained some knowledge, do not stop there, but go further and understand the demands such knowledge makes of you—then act appropriately. Let your behavior show that your feelings and dispositions are not the result of externals, but that your external behavior proceeds from your feelings and dispositions, and actually expresses them. If you establish yourself this way, you will be higher than the scribes and Pharisees, and the doors of the Kingdom will not be closed to you.

Thursday
Rom. 1:28–2:9; Matt. 5:27–32

Whosoever looketh on a woman to lust after her hath committed adultery with her already (Matt. 5:28). Living in society, one cannot help looking at women. What to do? A man does not commit adultery simply by looking at a woman, but by looking at her with lust. Look if you must, but keep your heart on a leash. Look with the eyes of a child—purely, without any evil thoughts.

One must love women as well, for they are not excluded from the commandment about love of neighbor—but with love that is pure, which bears the soul and the spiritual aspect in mind. Just as in Christianity there is neither male nor female before God, so it is in the mutual relations of Christians. But this is very difficult, you will say. Yes, it does not happen without a struggle, but struggle presupposes a lack of desire for evil. This lack of desire is imputed as purity by the merciful Lord.

FRIDAY
Rom. 2:14–29; Matt. 5:33–41

But I say unto you, That ye resist not evil (Matt. 5:39); in other words, allow yourself to be a victim of human selfishness and malice. But how can one live like that? Do not worry. He Who gave this commandment is our Provider and Guardian. When you desire to live like this—not to resist any evil—with complete faith, with your whole soul, the Lord Himself will arrange a life for you which is not only bearable, but joyful. Furthermore, resistance can in fact irritate an aggressor even more and motivate him to invent new troubles, whereas a yielding demeanor disarms him and humbles him. Thus, if you just suffer the first onslaught of malice, people will take pity on you and leave you alone, while resistance and revenge kindle malice, which is passed on from the individual to his family, and then from generation to generation.

SATURDAY
Rom. 1:7–12; Matt. 5:42–48

Love your enemies, bless them that curse you, do good to them that hate you, and pray for them which despitefully use you, and persecute you (Matt. 5:44). There is no one on earth without love. People love their parents and relatives, their benefactors and protectors.

But the feeling of love toward parents, relatives, protectors, and benefactors is natural, forming in the heart on its own. That is why the Lord does not give it value. Real Christian love is proved by our relationship with our enemies. Not only should slight and incidental annoyances not extinguish our love for others—neither should attacks and persecutions, misfortunes and deprivations, intentionally and maliciously inflicted. We must not only bless people [that inflict these upon us], but also do good to them and pray for them. See whether you have such a disposition toward your enemies, and judge by this whether you have Christian love, without which there is no salvation.

SUNDAY OF ALL SAINTS
Heb. 11:33–12:2; Matt. 10:32–33, 37–38; 19:27–30

The Holy Church commemorates saints every day. However, because there have been God-pleasers who struggled in obscurity and were not revealed to the Holy Church, the Church has established a day on which we glorify all those who have pleased God throughout the ages, so that not one might be left unglorified by the Church. The Church established that this be done immediately after the Feast of the Descent of the Holy Spirit, since it is by the grace of the Holy Spirit that all the saints have been made and continue to be made. The grace of the Holy Spirit brings repentance and the forgiveness of sins. It leads one into battle against the passions and lusts, and crowns this labor with purity and passionlessness. And thus a new creature appears, fit for a new heaven and a new earth. Let us be zealous to follow the saints of God. Today's Gospel reading teaches us how to do this: it demands fearless confession of faith in the Lord and preferential love for Him, the raising of the cross of self-denial, and heartfelt renunciation of everything. Let us place a beginning according to these instructions.

MONDAY
Rom. 2:28–3:18; Matt. 6:31–34; 7:9–11

Take no thought (Matt. 6:31). Then how is one to live? We have to eat, drink, and wear clothes. But the Savior does not say, "Do nothing," but rather, *Take no thought.* Do not weary yourself with cares that consume you both day and night and give you not a moment of peace. Such care is a sinful disease. It shows that a man is relying upon himself and has forgotten God, that he has lost hope in God's Providence, that he wants to arrange everything for himself solely by his own efforts and to procure all that is necessary and preserve what he has procured by his own means. He has become chained in his heart to his property, and thinks to rest upon it as though it were a solid foundation. Love of possessions has bound him, and he thinks only of how to get more into his hands. This mammon has replaced God for him. By all means, work—but do not weary yourself with evil cares. Expect every success from God and commit your lot into His hands. Accept all that you obtain as a gift from the Lord's hand, and wait with the firm hope that He will continue His generous giving. Know that if God so desires, a rich man can lose all he has in one minute. All is decay and dust. Is it worthwhile wearying yourself for this? So, take no thought!

TUESDAY
Rom. 4:4–12; Matt. 7:15–21

Beware of false prophets (Matt. 7:15). From the beginning of Christianity to this day, there has not been a time when this warning has not been applicable. The Lord did not indicate exactly which false prophets to beware of, for how could they be identified? They change like fashions and are continually generating more like them. They always appear in sheep's clothing, with a likeness of goodwill in their works and a mirage of truth in their speech. In our time their clothing is sewn of progress, civilization, education, freedom of thought and deed, a personal conviction which does not allow for faith, and things like that. All of this is a deceptive cloak. Therefore, if you come across this show of clothing, do not be hasty to open your ears to the words of "prophets" dressed in such clothes. Examine closely whether there is a wolf concealed under this sheep's clothing. Know that the Lord is the only motivator toward true perfection, the sole softener of hearts and morals, the sole educator, the sole giver of freedom and filler of the heart with a sense of the truth, which forms a conviction so strong that nothing in the world has the power to shake it. Therefore, as soon as you perceive in the talk of these new "prophets" some shadow of contradiction of the teaching of the Lord, know that they are predatory wolves, and turn away from them.

WEDNESDAY
Rom. 4:13–25; Matt. 7:21–23

Not everyone that saith unto Me, Lord, Lord, shall enter into the Kingdom of Heaven; but he that doeth the will of My Father Who is in heaven (Matt. 7:21). You will not be saved through prayer alone; you must unite prayer to the fulfillment of the will of God—all that each person is responsible for according to his calling and way of life. And prayer should have as its primary object the petition that God not let us depart from His holy will in any way. Conversely, he who is zealous to fulfill God's will in all things has boldness in prayer before God and greater access to His throne. Moreover, prayer that is not accompanied by walking in God's will is often not true, sober, and heartfelt prayer, but only outward reading, during which one's moral dysfunction is concealed by a multitude of words like a fog, while the thoughts are actually disorderly and wandering. Both [prayer and the fulfillment of God's will] must be made orderly through piety, and then there will be fruit.

THURSDAY
Rom. 5:10–16; Matt. 8:23–27

They set off for the other side of the sea. The Lord was sleeping. A tempest arose and everyone was terrified, but they forgot that the Lord was with them and that thus there was nothing to fear. This also happens in the earthly and spiritual course of life. When a tempest of misfortunes or passions arises we usually become worried to the point of paralysis and think that this is normal. But the Lord sends us a lesson: *O ye of little faith!* (Matt. 8:26). And justly! It is impossible not to notice what is happening, but it is possible to maintain a wise calmness. First and foremost, see what the Lord wants of you, and submit humbly to His strong hand. Do not rush about, do not become frenzied. Then arouse your faith that the Lord is with you, and fall at His feet in prayer. Do not cry, "I am perishing!" but with devotion call out, "Lord! If Thou wilt—Thou canst do all things. Not my will, but Thy will be done." Believe that this is how you will safely escape the tempest that has arisen.

FRIDAY
Rom. 5:17–6:2; Matt. 9:14–17

The Lord was asked why His disciples did not fast. He answered that the time had not yet come for them. Then in a parable he showed that, in general, the strictness of outer asceticism must correspond to the renewal of the inner powers of the spirit. First kindle the spirit of fervor, and then take on austerities; for then there will be a new inner power capable of enduring them profitably. If you take them on without first having this fervor, either because you were impressed by the example of others or because you wanted to make a show of your own asceticism, then it will bring no profit. You will sustain this austerity for a bit, and then you will weaken and drop it. And you will be worse off than before. Austerity without the inner spirit is like a patch of new linen on an old garment, or new wine in old wineskins. The patch will fall off and the rent made even worse; and the wine will burst the wineskin, and the wine will be lost, and the wineskin ruined (cf. Mark 2:22; Luke 5:37). This, by the way, does not mean that austerity is bad, but only suggests that one must begin it in the proper order. The need for it must come from within, so that it might satisfy the heart, and not just press from the outside like a weight.

SATURDAY
Rom. 3:19–26; Matt. 7:1–8

Judge not, that ye be not judged (Matt. 7:1). What a disease—gossip and judging others! Everyone knows that this is a sin; nevertheless, there is nothing more common in our words than judgment of others. One says, "Do not count it as judging, O Lord," but continues judging to the end. Another justifies himself by saying that any reasonable person must have an opinion about what is going on, and in his gossip he tries to be coolly reasonable; but even a simple ear cannot help but discern a high-minded and gloating judgment of others in his words. Meanwhile, the sentence of the Lord for this sin is stern and resolute; he who judges others will not be justified. What should one do? How can one avoid misfortune? A decisive remedy against judging others consists in this: to consider yourself condemned. He who feels himself condemned will have no time to judge others. His only words will be, "Lord, have mercy! Lord, forgive my transgressions!"

SECOND SUNDAY AFTER PENTECOST
Rom. 2:10–16; Matt. 4:18–23

The Lord called Peter and Andrew, and, leaving all, they immediately followed Him. He called James and John, and they also immediately left all and followed the Lord. Why did they follow Him so quickly and willingly? Because they saw something better. Such is the law that we have in our soul, that once it has tasted and known what is better, it is repulsed by what is worse and abandons it. Here is accomplished the same thing that the Lord later described in His parable about the treasure hid in a field, and about the pearl of great price. The treasure and the pearl are faith in the Lord and communion with Him, according to the strength of one's faith. We have already been named possessors of this in Baptism. Why do we value this treasure so little and thus exchange it for barren ground? Because we were not brought up to cultivate a taste for this treasure, and it becomes foreign to our heart. Our heart does not know this better thing. It only knows that there is the bad, the very bad, and the not so bad, and bases its outlook upon this assessment. Here is the entire reason why the Lord calls some and they come, while we, the chosen ones, run from Him.

MONDAY
Rom. 7:1–13; Matt. 9:36–10:8

Sending the Holy Apostles to preach, the Lord commanded them to call everyone, saying, *The Kingdom of Heaven is at hand* (Matt. 10:7), that is, the Kingdom has come—go toward it. What ought we to preach? We should cry to all, "Sons of the Kingdom! Don't run from the Kingdom into bondage and slavery"—for they are in fact running. Some are captivated by freedom of mind. They say, "We don't want the bonds of faith and the oppression of authority, even Divine authority; we'll figure things out and make up our minds for ourselves." So they have made up their minds. They have built fables in which there is more childishness than in the mythology of the Greeks—and they magnify themselves.... Others are enticed by the broad path of the passions. They say, "We don't want to know positive commandments or the demands of conscience—this is all abstract: we need tangible naturalness." And they have gone after it. What has come of it? They have bowed down before dumb beasts. Has not the theory that man originated from animals arisen from this moral fall? This is where they have gone! And everyone runs from the Lord, everyone runs....

TUESDAY
Rom. 7:14–8:2; Matt. 10:9–15

The Lord also said to the Apostles that if a city does not receive them, and will not hear their words, then *it shall be more tolerable for the land of Sodom and Gomorrah in the Day of Judgment, than for that city* (Matt. 10:15). And what will happen to us for our refusal to hear the words of Divine revelation? It will be immeasurably intolerable for us. To disbelieve the truth of God after so many tangible proofs is the same as reviling the Holy Spirit and blaspheming. And yet we are not afraid. The Spiritists console one person: "What judgment? We just have to be born one more time." The scientists explain to another: "Whom is there to judge? Everything is made of atoms; they'll fly apart and that will be the end of everything." But, friends, the hour of death is coming; these dreams will fly apart like phantoms, and we will all be faced with inexorable reality. What then? What wretched times we live in! The enemy has contrived to destroy our souls. He knows that fear of death and judgment is the strongest means for sobering up a soul, and so he makes every attempt to drive this away, and he succeeds. But extinguish the fear of death, and fear of God will disappear. And without the fear of God, the conscience becomes mute. The soul becomes empty—it becomes a waterless cloud, carried about by every wind of teaching and every fit of the passions.

WEDNESDAY
Rom. 8:2–13; Matt. 10:16–22

He that endureth to the end shall be saved (Matt. 10:22). Do we have anything to endure? In this no one is lacking. Everyone's arena of endurance is vast, and therefore our salvation is at hand. Endure everything to the end and you will be saved. However, you must endure skillfully—otherwise, you may not gain anything by your endurance. First of all, keep the holy Faith and lead an irreproachable life according to the Faith. Immediately cleanse with repentance every sin that occurs. Second, accept everything that you must endure as from the hands of God, remembering firmly that nothing happens without God's will. Third, give sincere thanks to God for everything, believing that everything which proceeds from the Lord is sent by Him for the good of our souls. Thank Him for sorrows and for consolations. Fourth, love sorrow for the sake of its great salvific power and cultivate within yourself a thirst for it as for a drink which, although bitter, is healing. Fifth, keep in your thoughts that when misfortune comes, you cannot throw it off like a tight-fitting garment; you must bear it. Whether in a Christian way or in a non-Christian way, you cannot avoid bearing it; so it is better to bear it in a Christian way. Complaining will not deliver you from misfortune, but only make it heavier; whereas humble submission to God's Providence and a good attitude relieve the burden of misfortunes. Sixth, realize that you deserve even greater misfortune. Recognize that if the Lord wanted to deal with you as you rightly deserve, would He have sent you such a small misfortune? Seventh, above all, pray, and the merciful Lord will give you strength of spirit. With such strength, when others marvel at your misfortunes, they will seem like nothing to you.

THURSDAY
Rom. 8:22–27; Matt. 10:23–31

There is nothing covered, that shall not be revealed; and hid, that shall not be known (Matt. 10:26). Consequently, no matter how we hide ourselves in our sins now, it is of no use to us at all. The time will come—and is it far off?—when all will come to light. What should we do? Do not hide. If you have sinned, go and reveal your sin to your spiritual father. When you receive absolution, the sin vanishes, as if it had never existed. Nothing will have to be revealed and shown later. If you hide the sin and do not repent, you will retain it within yourself, and there will be something to be brought to light at the proper time unto your accusation. God has revealed all of this to us in advance, so that while still here we will manage to disarm His righteous and terrible judgment upon us sinners.

FRIDAY
Rom. 9:6–19; Matt. 10:32–36, 11:1

Whosoever therefore shall confess Me before men, him will I confess also before My Father which is in heaven (Matt. 10:32). Is it hard to confess the Lord? It is not hard at all. How hard is it to say, when necessary, that our Lord Jesus Christ is the Only Begotten Son of God, and God, Who for our sake came to earth, became incarnate of the Holy Spirit and the Virgin Mary and became man, was crucified, suffered, was buried, arose on the third day, ascended into the heavens and sits at the right hand of God the Father, and again will come to judge the living and the dead—Who sent the Holy Spirit upon the Holy Apostles, who through His power established on the earth the Holy Church, which, teaching the truth and sanctifying through the Mysteries, leads all of its faithful children to the Heavenly Kingdom along a sure path? We repeat all of this every time we hear and read the Symbol of Faith. Thus, imprint these truths in your heart and be ready, not fearing any person, to show that one must believe in this way and in no other in order to be saved, preparing also to endure whatever comes to you as a result of this. Bar the lips of false teachers of Christianity with the word of truth, and you will receive what has been promised by the Lord. Confess Him as God and Savior before men, and He will confess before God the Father that you are His faithful follower and confessor.

SATURDAY
Rom. 3:28–4:3; Matt. 7:24–8:4

Today's Gospel reading says that one who hears the sayings of the Lord and does them is like one who builds a house upon a rock; but one who hears them and does not do them is like one who builds a house upon sand. Everyone should learn this by heart and repeat it often; the truth contained in it is graphically clear and anyone can understand it. Everyone has had many experiences of this. Take your thoughts, for example. While you are thinking about something, they are unstable and restless, but when you write them down, they become solid and fixed. An undertaking is unsure and its details can change many times before it is begun; yet any further considerations cease once you have set it in motion. In this manner, moral rules are alien to us; they are outside of us and unstable before they are fulfilled. But once we fulfill them, they enter within, settle in the heart and form the basis of our character—good or evil. *See then that ye walk circumspectly* (Eph. 5:15).

THIRD SUNDAY AFTER PENTECOST
Rom. 5:1–10; Matt. 6:22–33

If therefore thine eye be single[21] *thy whole body shall be full of light. But if thine eye be evil, thy whole body shall be full of darkness* (Matt. 6:22–23). Here the mind is called the eye, and the entire composition of the soul is called the body. Thus, when the mind is simple, the soul is bright; but when the mind is evil, the soul is dark. What are a simple mind and an evil mind? A simple mind is one which accepts the word of God as it is written, and is convinced beyond a doubt that all is indeed as is written. It has no deceit, no wavering or hesitation. An evil mind is one which approaches the word of God with slyness, artful disputing, and questioning. It cannot believe directly, but subjects the word of God to its sophistry. It approaches the word not as a disciple, but as a judge and critic, to test something stated there, and then either scoffs at it or says in a haughty manner, "Yes, not bad." Such a mind has no firm tenets, because it clearly does not believe the word of God, and its own philosophizing is always unstable—today one way, tomorrow another. Hence, it has only wavering, confusion, and questions without answers. Everything is out of place with it, and it walks in the dark, fumbling along its way. A simple mind sees everything clearly: everything in it has a definite character, determined by the word of God. That is why everything in it has its place, and it knows exactly how to behave with relation to things—it walks along open, visible roads, with complete assurance that they lead to the true goal.

---

[21] An English translation of the Slavonic is *If thine eye be simple.*— TRANS.

Monday
Rom. 9:18–33; Matt. 11:2–15

The Kingdom of Heaven suffereth violence, and the violent take it by force (Matt. 11:12). The Kingdom suffereth violence—that is, it is attained with violence, with labor, force, and difficult spiritual struggles. Therefore, only those who lead a labor-filled ascetic life attain it. Thus, every sort of comfort is renounced along the path to the Kingdom. Pleasures of all types distance us from the Kingdom. But these days we have concern only for pleasures—sometimes emotional, but more often fleshly: to eat, drink, have fun, make merry, and luxuriate in everything. We have said to the Kingdom, "I beg you to excuse me," although there is a feast in the Kingdom—a royal feast—one so sumptuous that we could not even conceive of it, because we do not have the taste for it. What is considered sweet there is bitter to us, what is pleasant there is repulsive to us, what gladdens one there is a burden for us. We have gone totally separate ways. And the Kingdom, together with the violent who take it by force, withdraws from us. We are glad about this, and are even ready to drive them away more quickly. Indeed, we have already started talking about it, but the evil one has not yet managed to arrange this.

Tuesday
Rom. 10:11–11:2; Matt. 11:16–20

The Lord says that we who do not hear the Gospel are like those to whom merry songs are sung, but who do not dance; to whom sad songs are sung, but who do not cry—nothing can be done with them. We are promised the Heavenly Kingdom, most bright and joyous, but we are unmoved, as though someone else were being spoken to. We are threatened with impartial judgment and unending torments, but we are not alarmed, as if we did not hear.

Downtrodden, we have lost all feeling of true self-preservation. We move as ones being led directly to destruction, and have not a care for our destiny. We have lost heart and given ourselves over to carelessness—let what happens, happen! Such is our state! Is this not why suicides are so frequent? It is the fruit of modern teachings and views on man and his significance! There is progress for you! There is enlightenment! It would be better to be totally ignorant, but save your soul with fear of God than, having attained the title of an enlightened person, to perish unto the ages, never thinking for your entire life about what will happen after death. Not a single jot shall pass from the word of God, which describes both the Heavenly Kingdom and hell—all will be as it is written. Let everyone take this to heart as something that touches you personally; and take care for yourself, with all your strength, as long as there is time left.

WEDNESDAY
Rom. 11:2–12; Matt. 11:20–26

The Lord showed many signs in Capernaum, Bethsaida, and Chorazin, yet the number of those who believed did not correspond to the power of the signs. That is why He severely denounced those cities and sentenced them: in the Day of Judgment it shall be more tolerable for Tyre and Sidon, Sodom and Gomorrah, than for these cities. We need to judge ourselves according to such a model. How many signs has the Lord shown to Russia, saving it from the most powerful enemies and subduing peoples under it! How many treasures has He granted it, pouring out unceasing signs—in the holy relics and miracle-working icons scattered throughout all of Russia! And yet in our days Russians are starting to turn aside from the Faith: one group is falling into total unbelief, another group is falling away into Protestantism, a third group is secretly weaving their own beliefs, thinking to combine Spiritism and theological ravings with Divine revelation.

Evil is growing; evil beliefs and unbelief are raising their head, while faith and Orthodoxy are weakening. Will we not come to our senses? We will end up like the French, for instance, or others.... But if that happens, how do you think it will be for us on the Day of Judgment, after God has shown so many mercies to us? O Lord! Have mercy and save Orthodox Russia from Thy righteous threatening which stands before us!

THURSDAY
Rom. 11:13–24; Matt. 11:27–30

Come unto Me, all ye that labor and are heavy laden, and I will give you rest (Matt. 11:28). O Divine, O dear, O sweetest voice of Thine! Let us all follow the Lord, Who calls us! But first we must experience something difficult and burdensome for us. We must experience that we have many sins, and that these sins are grave. From this is born the need to seek relief. Faith will then show us that our only refuge is in the Lord and Savior, and our steps will direct themselves toward Him. A soul desiring to be saved from sins knows what to say to the Lord: "Take my heavy, sinful burden from me, and I will take Thine easy yoke." And this is it how it happens: the Lord forgives one's sins, and his soul begins to walk in His commandments. The commandments are the yoke, and sins are the burden. But comparing the two, the soul finds that the yoke of the commandments is as light as a feather, while the burden of sins is as heavy as a mountain. Let us not fear readily accepting the Lord's easy yoke and His light burden. In no other way can we find rest unto our souls.

FRIDAY
Rom. 11:25–36; Matt. 12:1–8

If ye had known what this meaneth, I will have mercy, and not sacrifice, ye would not have condemned the guiltless (Matt. 12:7).

Therefore, in order to be saved from the sin of condemnation, we must obtain a merciful heart. Not only does a merciful heart not condemn a seeming infringement of the law, but neither does it condemn an obvious one. Instead of judgment it feels pity, and it would sooner weep than reproach. Truly the sin of condemnation is the fruit of an unmerciful, malicious heart that takes delight in debasing its neighbor, in blackening its neighbor's name, in trampling his honor underfoot. This is a murderous affair, and is done in the spirit of the one who is a murderer from the beginning (cf. John 8:44). Here there occurs much slander as well, which comes from the same source, for that is why the devil is the devil—he is a slanderer, spreading slander everywhere. Hasten to arouse pity in yourself every time the evil urge to condemn comes over you. Then turn in prayer to the Lord with a compassionate heart, that He might have mercy upon all of us, not only upon the one whom we wanted to condemn, but upon us as well—perhaps even more so upon us—and the evil urge will die.

SATURDAY
Rom. 6:11–17; Matt. 8:14–23

To one of those who wanted to follow the Lord, He said: *The Son of man hath not where to lay his head* (Matt. 8:20). To another who wanted first to bury his father, He said, "Leave the dead; others will bury him, but you follow Me" (cf. Matt. 8:21). This means that he who wants to follow the Lord should not expect any comfort on earth after following Him, but only deprivations, needs, and sorrows. And it means that worldly cares, even the most legitimate, are not compatible with following Him. It is necessary to decisively renounce everything, so that nothing attaches you to the earth, and then to condemn yourself to every kind of suffering or cross. Having thus prepared yourself, follow the Lord. This is the direct will of the Lord! But whom is this commandment for—only the Apostles or all Christians? Let everyone figure it out himself. Deny yourself and take up the cross. Was this said to everyone? Love the Lord more than father and mother, brothers and sisters, wife and children—was this said to everyone? The conclusion is clear. What should we do? One time the Apostles posed the same question to the Lord, and He answered them: *The things which are impossible with men are possible with God* (Luke 18:27).

FOURTH SUNDAY AFTER PENTECOST
Rom. 6:18–23; Matt. 8:5–13

What faith the centurion has! The Lord Himself marveled. The essence of this faith is that he confessed the Lord to be the God of all things, the all-powerful Sovereign and Master of all that exists. For this reason he beseeched: *Speak the word only, and my servant shall be healed* (Matt. 8:8). "I believe that everything is under Thine authority and everything obeys Thy slightest beckoning." The Lord requires the same faith of us as well. He who has this faith knows no lack, and whatsoever he asks, he receives. Thus has the Lord Himself promised. Oh, when will we have such faith, if only a little? But this faith is a gift; we must ask for it as well, and ask for it with faith. Let us ask for it, with a feeling of need for it. Let us ask for it continually and fervently, at the same time aiding its unfolding within us through corresponding thoughts, and most of all by submitting to God's commandments.

MONDAY
Rom. 12:4–5, 15–21; Matt. 12:9–13

It is lawful to do well on the sabbath days (Matt. 12:12). After healing the man with a withered hand in the synagogue on the Sabbath, the Lord said this as a reproach to the Pharisees, who took the commandment about the Sabbath rest so far that they even measured the number of steps they could walk on that day. But since it is not possible to do good works without movement, they would sooner have agreed to neglect good works than to allow any extra movement. The Savior denounced them for this time and again, because the Sabbath required rest from worldly cares and not from works of piety and brotherly love. In Christianity, instead of the Sabbath, Sunday is celebrated with the same goal: rest from all worldly affairs and the devotion of that day solely to God's works. Christian sobriety has never reached the point of pharisaic pettiness concerning not doing things on Sunday. However, the permissible allowance for doing things on this day has been set far beyond the proper limits. Not doing things kept the Pharisees from performing good works, whereas the things which Christians allow themselves are what lead them away from good works. On the eve of Sunday they go to the theater and then to some other entertainment. In the morning they oversleep and there is no time to go to church. There are several visits, then lunch, and in the evening again entertainment. Thus all their time is relegated to the belly and to pleasing the other senses, and there is no time even to remember God and good works.

TUESDAY
Rom. 14:9–18; Matt. 12:14–16, 22–30

He that is not with Me is against Me; and he that gathereth not with Me scattereth abroad (Matt. 12:30). Who is with the Lord? He who lives and acts in His spirit; he who allows himself neither thoughts, nor feelings, nor desires, nor intentions, nor words, nor deeds which would be displeasing to the Lord and in opposition to His revealed commandments and decrees. He who lives and acts otherwise is not with the Lord and consequently does not gather, but scatters. What does he scatter? Not only energy and time, but also what he gathers. For example, someone who gathers riches not with the Lord amasses only riches, not sharing with others, while depriving himself even of necessary things. Someone else gathers riches and spends a part on his own luxurious lifestyle, a part on donations made out of vainglory, and saves a part for his heirs. In the other world he will appear with nothing—and there he will be the poorest of the poor. On the other hand, someone who gathers riches with the Lord passes on what is gathered unto eternal treasuries through the hands of the poor and needy. When such a person dies, he will find that in the next world all his riches are intact, not scattered, although he spent them throughout his life. The same applies to the gathering of knowledge. Here scattering is even more obvious, because it can be seen how one who philosophizes, but not in the Lord, gathers a seeming mountain of knowledge, but it is no more than rubbish—a phantom of the truth, but not the truth. Such people not only lack knowledge, but even lose human sense. They become delirious, like those who are asleep. Read the systems of the materialists,[22] and you will see that this is so.

WEDNESDAY

Rom. 15:7–16; Matt. 12:38–45

In every person who lives unrepentant in sin, there lives a demon, as if in a house, who takes charge over everything within him. When by the grace of God such a sinner comes to contrition over his sins, repents, and ceases to sin—the demon is cast out from him. At first the demon does not disturb the one who has repented because, in the beginning, there is much fervor within him which burns demons like fire and repulses them like an arrow. But then, when fervor begins to grow cold, the demon approaches from afar with its suggestions, throws in memories about former pleasures, and calls the person to them. If the penitent does not take care, his sympathy will soon pass to a desire for sin. If he does not come to his senses and return to his former state of soberness, a fall is not

---

[22] Materialism is the philosophy that nothing exists except matter, and that all phenomena (including consciousness) are the result of material interactions.—ED.

far off. The inclination for sin and the decision to commit it are born from desire—the inner sin is ready, and the outward sin is only waiting for a convenient occasion. When an occasion presents itself, the sin will be accomplished. Then the demon will enter again and begin to drive a person from sin to sin even faster than before. The Lord illustrated this with the story about the return of the demon into the clean, swept house (cf. Matt. 12:45).

THURSDAY
Rom. 15:17–29; Matt. 12:46–13:3

For whosoever shall do the will of My Father Who is in heaven, the same is My brother, and sister, and mother (Matt. 12:50). By this the Lord gives us to understand that the spiritual kinship which He came to plant and raise up on the earth is not the same as fleshly kinship; although in the form of its relationships, the spiritual is identical to the fleshly. The spiritual also contains fathers and mothers—they are those who give birth to people with the word of truth, or the Gospel, as the Apostle Paul says. And it contains also brothers and sisters—those who are born spiritually from the same person and grow in one spirit. The bond between [spiritual] relatives is founded on the action of grace. It is not external, not superficial, but it is as deep and alive as the fleshly bond, only it has its place in another, much higher and more important sphere. This is why it predominates over the fleshly and, when necessary, offers the fleshly as a sacrifice to its spiritual interests without regret, in full certainty that this sacrifice is pleasing to God and is required by Him.

FRIDAY
Rom. 16:1–16; Matt. 13:4–9

The parable about the sower depicts the various relationships of souls toward the word of God. In the first group stand those who do not heed the word at all. They hear, but what is heard does not enter into their soul; it lies on its surface, like the seed by the wayside. The word does not fit within them because they have another way of thinking, other principles, other tastes. That is why it soon disappears from memory and is forgotten, as though it had not been heard at all. In the second group are those who hear the word willingly and receive it quickly, but do not want to bear any labor to fulfill it. Therefore, they delight in the word—especially its promises—until a sacrifice is required. As soon as the necessity arises to sacrifice something for faithfulness to the word, they betray it, renouncing both the word and its promises, in order to cater to their attachments. In the third group are those who receive the word and begin to live according to it, but then give themselves over too much to the cares and sorrows of the world, to earthly concerns which suppress all the good undertakings which had just formed under the influence of the word of God. In the fourth group are those who receive the word with full faith and resolve to live according to its requirements, with a readiness for all sacrifices and labor, and who do not allow their heart to be tied to anything earthly. Each of you, sit and decide which of these groups you belong to.

Saturday
Rom. 8:14–21; Matt. 9:9–13

When someone, by his fear of God and the demands of his conscience, already has an awakened thirst for spiritual things, he possesses a certain sense that enables him to understand the meaning of words relating to the spiritual realm, although they might be clothed in the form of a parable. For such people, a parable does not hide the truth, but rather reveals it even more clearly. But he who does not have this inward disposition does not understand anything when he hears about spiritual subjects in the form of parables. Even if one were to offer him a word on these subjects that was not in the form of a parable, he would only understand the words but not comprehend the essence of the matter. It would go against all of his notions and seem to him to be an absurdity, which he would not hesitate to mock. This is precisely why the Lord spoke to the people in parables. Whoever is spiritually inclined will understand a parable, whereas someone with no such inclinations will not understand no matter what you say. *Because they seeing see not; and hearing they hear not, neither do they understand.... For this people's heart is waxed gross* (Matt. 13:13, 15). Meanwhile, the parable does not deprive of needed instruction those who are capable of seeing the hidden truth: *For whosoever hath, to him shall be given, and he shall have more abundance* (Matt.13:12).

Fifth Sunday after Pentecost
Rom. 10:1–10; Matt. 8:28–9:1

The Gadarenes saw the Lord's wondrous miracle when He cast out a legion of demons, and yet the whole city came out and besought the Lord *that He would depart out of their coasts* (Matt. 8:34). We do not observe them regarding the Lord with hostility, but neither do we observe any faith in them. They are seized with a sort of indeterminate fear, and as a result they asked Him, "Pass us by, wherever Thou desirest—only do not touch us." This is a real image of the kind of people who live peacefully on their estates. An order of things has formed around them which is not unfavorable; they are used to it, and have neither thoughts about nor the need for changing or abolishing anything, and they fear to make a new step. They feel, however, that should a command come down from above, the fear of God and their conscience would force them to renounce the old and accept something new. Therefore, they strive to avoid any circumstance which might lead them to such beliefs, so that they might continue living quietly in their old habits, pleading ignorance. These are the sort of people who are afraid to read the Gospels and patristic books, or to discuss spiritual matters. They fear that if their conscience is thereby disturbed, it might wake up and start forcing them to abandon what they have and take up something else.

MONDAY
Rom. 16:17–24; Matt. 13:10–23

Why do many people not understand discussions about spiritual things? It is due to a thickening of their heart. When their heart is full of attachments to earthly things, it grows coarse, as is said: *He grew fat, he became thick and broad* (Deut. 32:15). In this state it gravitates downward like a heavy weight, dragging and chaining the entire soul to the earth, along with the mind. Then, continually churning in its circle of low objects, it becomes low in its thought and cannot soar up on high, like a bird weighed down with food. Churning there, it does not see the heavenly, and its entire disposition is against it. Heaven is an alien country to these people. Such a person has nothing within the totality of his understanding and experience to which he could relate the heavenly, that he might be able to see it, if only *through a glass, darkly* (I Cor. 13:12). That is why he will not try to discuss it, nor does he wish to listen to others discussing it, and he will not pick up any books written about it. Is this not why you will often find any number of secular magazines in people's homes, but not a single spiritual periodical or book—not even the Gospels?

TUESDAY
I Cor. 1:1–9; Matt. 13:24–30

The good seed was sown, but the enemy came and sowed tares among the wheat. The tares in the Church are heresies and schisms, while in each of us they are bad thoughts, feelings, desires, and passions. A person accepts the good seed of the word of God, decides to live in a holy way, and begins to live in this way. When such a person falls asleep, that is, when his attention toward himself weakens, then the enemy of salvation comes and places evil ideas in him which, if not rejected at the start, ripen into desires and dispositions, introducing their own spheres of activity, which mix themselves in with good works, feelings, and thoughts. In this way both remain together until the harvest. This harvest is repentance. The Lord sends the angels—a feeling of contrition and the fear of God—and they come in like a sickle, then burn up all the tares in the fire of painful self-condemnation. Pure wheat remains in the granary of the heart, to the joy of the man, the angels, and the Most Good God worshiped in Trinity.

WEDNESDAY
I Cor. 2:9–3:8; Matt. 13:31–36

The Kingdom is like a grain of mustard seed and leaven. A small grain of mustard seed grows up into a large bush; leaven penetrates a whole lump of dough and makes it leavened. Here, on the one hand, is an image of the Church, which in the beginning consisted only of the Apostles and a few other people. It then spread and became more numerous, penetrating all of humanity. On the other hand, it is an image of the spiritual life revealed in every person. Its first seed is the intention and determination to be saved through pleasing God in accordance with faith in the Lord and Savior. This determination, no matter how firm, is like a tiny speck. In the beginning it embraces only one's consciousness and activities. Then, from this, all of the activity of a spiritual life develops. Its movement and strength multiply and mature within its own self, and it begins to penetrate all the powers of the soul—the mind, will, and feelings—then fills them with itself, leavens them according to its spirit, and penetrates the entire constitution of the human nature—body, soul, and spirit—in which it was engendered.

THURSDAY
I Cor. 3:18–23; Matt. 13:36–43

And they (those who commit offenses and iniquity) shall be cast *into a furnace of fire: there shall be wailing and gnashing of teeth. Then shall the righteous shine forth as the sun in the Kingdom of their Father* (Matt. 13:42–43). Thus will be carried out the division of good and evil, light and darkness. Now is the period of time in which they are mixed. It pleased the Lord to arrange that the freedom of creatures should grow and be strengthened in good through the struggle against evil. Evil is allowed, both in connection with inward freedom and from outside of a person. It does not determine anything, it only tempts. One who feels a temptation must not fall, but enter into battle. He who conquers is freed from one temptation, and advances forward and upward to find a new temptation there—and so on, until the end of his life. Oh, when will we comprehend the significance of the evil which tempts us, so that we might arrange our lives according to this understanding? The strugglers are finally crowned, and pass on to the next life, where there are neither sicknesses nor sorrows, and where they become inwardly pure like angels of God, free from the sting of tempting inclinations and thoughts. This is how the triumph of light and good is being prepared, and it will be revealed in all of its glory on the last day of the world.

FRIDAY
I Cor. 4:5–8; Matt. 13:44–54

Arriving in Nazareth, the Lord found no faith there. His visible simplicity hindered the Nazarenes from seeing His invisible glory and Divinity. Does not the same occur with a Christian? Christian dogmas are very simple in appearance; but for the mind which enters into them, they represent an all-embracing harmonious system in and of themselves, which was not—nor could ever be—generated by any creature's mind. Proud-mindedness, casting a fleeting glance at the simplicity of the Gospel, is repelled by it and begins to build his own house of knowledge, which he deems enormous and full of broad horizons. It is in fact no more than a towering house of cards, and the horizons are no more than mirages, phantom products of a heated imagination. But there is no point in telling him. He and his brothers are ready with their critical attacks to immediately cast anyone who tries to dissuade them from the mountain into the abyss, but the truth always passes unharmed through their midst and goes on to other souls capable of receiving it.

SATURDAY
Rom. 9:1–5; Matt. 9:18–26

The woman with the issue of blood said: *If I may but touch His* [the Lord's] *garment, I shall be whole* (Matt. 9:21), and she received healing according to her faith. We who are carnal need physical contact in order to receive intangible strength. The Lord arranged things this way. His Holy Church has a visible structure. Its various parts embrace us, and we touch them. The power of God, found within the Church, is received through such contact by those who have a receptacle—faith—which says: "If I may but touch, I shall be made whole." The Church is the body and garment of the Lord. The most visible parts, which we touch, are the Divine Mysteries, particularly Baptism and Chrismation, and the Sacrament of the Lord's Body and Blood in conjunction with the Sacrament of Confession. But contact with all the other aspects can draw needed strength from the Lord, Who is everywhere. He sees each person who does this, and says to such a one's heart, "Be bold, My child!" Freethinkers, antagonistic toward the external rites of the Church, thus deprive themselves of the opportunity to enter into contact with the inner, Divine, all-animating power. This is why they remain sick and, exhausting themselves with a flow of vain thoughts and feelings, they dry up spiritually and die.

SIXTH SUNDAY AFTER PENTECOST
Rom. 12:6–14; Matt. 9:1–8

The Lord forgives the sins of the man sick of the palsy. One should rejoice; but the evil mind of the learned scribes says: *This man blasphemeth* (Matt. 9:3). After the miracle of the healing of the man sick of the palsy—a confirmation of the comforting truth that *the Son of man hath power on earth to forgive sins* (Matt. 9:6)—the people glorified God. But nothing is said about the scribes, probably because they continued to weave their deceitful questions even after such a miracle. The mind without faith is a schemer; it constantly hammers out its evil suspicions and weaves blasphemy against the whole realm of faith. As for miracles—it either does not believe in them, or it demands a tangible one. But when a miracle is given that would obligate one to submit to the Faith, this mind is not ashamed to turn away from it, distorting or slandering the miraculous works of God. It treats irrefutable evidence of God's truth in the same way. Such a mind is sufficiently and cogently presented with both experiential and intellectual proof, but it covers even this with doubt. Sort out all that it produces and you will see that in this there is only deceit, although its own language calls it cleverness, and you are unwillingly led to the conclusion that cleverness and deceit are one and the same. In the realm of faith the Apostle says, *We have the mind of Christ* (I Cor. 2:16). Whose mind is outside of the realm of faith? The evil one's. That is why deceit has become his distinguishing characteristic.

MONDAY
I Cor. 5:9–6:11; Matt. 13:54–58

The Nazarenes did not believe the word of the Lord, because when He lived among them, He had no attractive luster or outward dignity that might have commanded involuntary respect. "We know Who He is," they said; "there can't be anything extraordinary about Him." Their reaction, however, did not induce the Lord to assume an imposing appearance. He remained extremely simple in appearance. Later, the Apostles bore themselves the same way, as did all those who truly followed and emulated them. Why is this so? Because there is no man-made luster that could fully correspond to the light of life in Jesus Christ. Moreover, we recognize that it is better to relegate external appearance to the lowest value, so that it does not obstruct what is within. Let him who has eyes to see look directly at the latter, without arresting his attention upon the former. The Holy Apostle Paul expressed it like this: *We have this treasure in earthen vessels* (II Cor. 4:7). If we could see the outward appearance of those persons whom we now revere and call upon in prayer, we would not believe our eyes—they were so simple. But to this day, those who have come to know the life in Jesus Christ abandon what is outward and turn fully within. That is why the former falls away on its own, but the latter is raised up and grows. It often happens that no one even notices this inner brightness, not even the one who possesses it. The human eye is evil; it is not shown what is truly good, as long as it is capable of harming it.

TUESDAY
I Cor. 6:20–7:12; Matt. 14:1–13

A rumor of the Lord's works reached Herod, and he immediately concluded that John had resurrected. He could have thought anything, yet he thought of no one but John. Who led his thoughts in that direction? His conscience. From it you cannot hide unconscionable deeds; you cannot correct its judgment with anything. Herod assumed the right to behead John, and no one denied that he had the right, but his conscience spoke, and he could not muffle its words with anything. That is why he immediately saw John. How many similar instances do we know of where the conscience pursues a sinner and paints the subject and deed of a sin, so that he sees them even outside himself! There is a voice within us that we must acknowledge is not our voice. Whose is it? God's. He Who gives us our nature, gives us this voice. If it is God's voice, we must obey it, for creatures dare not contradict their Creator. This voice says that God exists, that we completely depend upon Him, and therefore we cannot but have a reverent fear of God. Having this fear, we must fulfill God's will, indicated by the conscience. All of this comprises the word of God, written in our nature, read and offered to us. And we see that people of all times and all countries hear this word and heed it. Everywhere people believe in God, everywhere they listen to their conscience and await the future life. Only now has it somehow become fashionable to not acknowledge these truths. This is how the naturalists[23] behave, which means that the teaching which the naturalists preach is unnatural.

WEDNESDAY
I Cor 7:12–24; Matt. 14:35–15:11

Not that which goeth into the mouth defileth a man; but that which cometh out of the mouth, this defileth a man (Matt. 15:11). The Lord said this not because He did not favor fasting, or because He considered it unnecessary for us. No, He Himself

---

[23] Naturalism is a philosophy which holds that "nature is all there is," and that all phenomena are thus explainable in terms of natural causes, without reference to the Divine and the supernatural.—ED.

fasted, and taught the Apostles to do so, and He established fasts in His Holy Church. Rather, He said this so that not only we would fast by eating little or only uncooked food, but we might also keep the fast in our soul, not indulging it with desires and passionate inclinations. This is the important thing. Fasting serves as a powerful means for this. The foundation of the passions is the flesh; when the flesh is emaciated, then it is as if the passions are undermined and their fortress is destroyed. Without fasting, overcoming the passions would be a miracle, similar to being in a fire and not being burned. How can he who profusely satisfies his flesh with food, sleep, and rest keep anything spiritual in his mind and in his intentions? It would be as easy for him to renounce the earth, to contemplate and strive for the invisible world, as it is for an old decrepit bird to rise up from the earth.

THURSDAY
I Cor. 7:24–35; Matt. 15:12–21

Out of the heart proceed evil thoughts (Matt. 15:19). From where in the heart? Their root lies in the sin which lives within us; and their branching out, multiplying, and particular appearance in each person come from that person's own will. What should one do? First, cut off all that comes from your will. This would be like someone tearing leaves from a tree, cutting off branches and twigs, and chopping the trunk almost to its roots. Then, do not allow new sprouts to come up, and the root itself will dry up. That is, do not allow evil thoughts to proceed from your heart, and repel and drive off those that do; and the sin which lives in us, not receiving sustenance, will slacken and grow completely weak. In this lies the essence of the commandment: *Be sober, be vigilant* (I Peter 5:8). *Take heed unto thyself* (I Tim. 4:16). *Gird up the loins of thy mind* (I Peter 1:13). Along with attentiveness, one must have discernment. Not only bad things proceed from the heart, but also good things; yet, one should not fulfill every good thing suggested by the heart. What one should truly fulfill is determined by discernment. Discernment is a gardener's knife; some branches it cuts off, while others it grafts in.

FRIDAY
I Cor. 7:35–8:7; Matt. 15:29–31

In everyday affairs you cannot do anything properly without attentiveness; and, in spiritual matters, attentiveness takes the first place. It notices what is bad and brings it before the inner judge. It is the guard of the inner chamber, where the best course of action is discussed, and then it protects the one who carries out the decisions. This is not surprising, because the spiritual life in its fullness is called a sober life, and in patristic writings we encounter mostly words about soberness or attentiveness, for they are one and the same thing. Therefore, how important it is to make a habit of attentiveness! The initial labor of those who have begun to be concerned about their souls is usually directed toward this. And their work only begins to resemble work from the point where attentiveness begins to be gathered within themselves. Ordinarily, attentiveness is all outward, and not inward. From this moment the inner life is conceived, and with this attentiveness it matures and strengthens. What does this mean? It means standing with the mind in the heart before the Lord and consciously discussing and undertaking everything before His face. This job, obviously, is complicated. It is practiced with prayer, and it strengthens prayer as much as it is strengthened by it.

SATURDAY
Rom. 12:1–3; Matt. 10:37–11:1

He that receiveth a prophet in the name of a prophet shall receive a prophet's reward; and he that receiveth a righteous man in the name of a righteous man shall receive a righteous man's reward (Matt.

10:41). With this statement all misunderstandings connected with almsgiving are resolved. The questions "Who is begging?" and "Where are the alms going?" almost always, if not suppress then significantly diminish good intentions for the poor. The Lord says to those who ask these questions: Your reward is determined according to how you receive the beggar and help him. Do not look at the one who is asking, but at your thoughts. The value of your deed will be commensurate with your thoughts. The right thoughts to have about a poor person can be defined in this way: He who has mercy on the poor is lending to God; or, *Inasmuch as ye have done it unto one of the least of these My brethren, ye have done it unto Me* (Matt. 25:40). Thus, receive everyone in need as you would the Lord, and do what you can for him with the thought that you are doing it for God, and you will receive a reward from the Lord, not only as if you had received a prophet and a righteous man, but as if you had received the Lord Himself.

SEVENTH SUNDAY AFTER PENTECOST
Rom. 15:1–7; Matt. 9:27–35

According to your faith be it unto you (Matt. 9:29), said the Lord to the two blind men, and immediately their eyes were opened. The greater the faith is, the greater is the influx of Divine power. Faith is the receiver, the mouth, and the receptacle of grace. Just as one person's lungs are large while another person's are small, and the large take in more air, while the small take in less, so one person has a large degree of faith, and another a small degree, and one person's faith receives more gifts from the Lord, and another person's, fewer. God is everywhere, encompasses everything and contains all, and loves to dwell in human souls. However, He does not forcibly enter them, even though He is Almighty, but enters as if by invitation; for He does not want to infringe upon the power which man has over himself, or infringe upon man's right to rule his own house—a right which He has granted. Whoever opens himself through faith, God fills; but whoever closes himself through unbelief, God does not enter, though He is near. Lord! Increase our faith, for faith, too, is Thy gift. Each of us should confess: *I am poor and needy* (Ps. 69:6).

MONDAY
I Cor. 9:13–18; Matt. 16:1–6

The Pharisees and Sadducees wanted the Lord to show them a sign, but they did not see the sign before their very eyes. The Lord Himself was the sign. His teaching and works clearly showed Who He was, and no additional evidence was needed. *The works that I do ... they bear witness of Me* (John 10:25), He said to the Jews. The Lord denounced them, saying: *Ye can discern the face of the sky; but can ye not discern the signs of the times?* (Matt. 16:3). Why did this happen with them? Because they lived an outward life and did not enter within themselves. Without collectedness, attentiveness, and self-searching it is impossible to notice or comprehend the works of God. This has continued until this day. Christianity is before everyone's eyes as the true sign of God, but those who look at it do not see this, are shaken in faith, and step away. Their eyes lose the ability to see the stamp of divinity in it, and they are ready like the Jews to ask for special signs from heaven. But a sign is not given and shall not be given, because those who seek this do so only to tempt, and not in order to walk the path of Christ. Just enter onto this path, and from the first step you will see that it is Divine, that it leads to God and brings God nearer to you. The Lord said to the Jews: *There shall no sign be given ... but the sign of the prophet Jonah* (Matt. 12:39). The Lord foresaw today's unbelievers as well, and prepared for them an answer: *Then shall appear the sign of the Son of man in heaven: and then shall all the tribes of the earth mourn.* (Matt. 24:30).

TUESDAY
I Cor. 10:5–12; Matt. 16:6–12

Beware of the leaven of the Pharisees and of the Sadducees (Matt. 16:6), said the Lord. The Sadducees are a model of carelessness; the Pharisees represent people who are outwardly zealous. The former do nothing; as for the latter, although they look very busy, nothing comes of them. Similar to these are members of our modern society who are enticed by the ideas of humanism. You hear them talk only about the good of the people, but no good ever comes to the people, for it is all talk and no action. Their humanism is feigned; they only take on the appearance of humaneness, but in reality they are egoists. Speech does not require sacrifice. They speak lavishly, but when the matter touches sacrifices, they retreat. Nowadays almost everyone is an actor. Some show off in front of others as being zealous for good, and particularly for enlightenment, and they are all quite satisfied when their own verbal testimony portrays them as really being this way. Therefore, as soon as some charitable undertaking comes up among us, talk is everywhere, but deeds do not come to fruition. Do not expect sacrifices from them; they have no need to help others as long as their own affairs are going well. But it also happens that, without going to any great pains to think of ways to help their neighbors, they give alms in order to be left alone. The Lord has condemned both categories, and has commanded us to be filled with sincere love for one another, which does not like to show off.

WEDNESDAY
I Cor. 10:12–22; Matt. 16:20–24

When the Holy Apostles confessed the Savior to be the Son of God, He said that He *must ... suffer ... and be killed* (Matt. 16:21). The work had ripened, and it remained only to complete it through His death on the Cross. The same thing occurs in the course of a Christian's moral progress. While he is struggling against his passions, the enemy still hopes somehow to tempt him. But when the passions have calmed down and the enemy no longer has enough power to awaken them, he presents external temptations of all sorts, such as slanders, and, moreover, of the most sensitive kind. He aims to give rise to the thought, "So what did you work and struggle for? No good will come of it for you." But when the enemy thus prepares a war from without, the Lord sends down the spirit of patience to His struggler, thereby preparing a lively readiness in his heart for all sorts of suffering and hostility, before the enemy has time to stir up trouble. Just as the Lord said about Himself that He *must suffer,* so spiritual strugglers also feel a sort of thirst for sorrows. And when suffering and hostility come, they meet them with joy, and drink them in like a thirsty man drinks cooling water.

THURSDAY
I Cor. 10:28–11:7; Matt. 16:24–28

The Lord demands resolute self-denial of those who want to follow Him: *Let him deny himself* (Matt. 16:24). It could be expressed like this: Cast aside your interests and pursue only the interests of the Lord. You will be fulfilling this when you always do what is pleasing to Him. How can one do this? Mind carefully what is in you, and what is around you on the outside, and discern strictly in one or another situation, be it internal or external, how to act in the way that is most pleasing to God. Then, not pitying yourself and not inserting your own calculations, act accordingly, with complete self-denial. You say, "It's complicated to determine this." No, it's not complicated. We have been given clear and definite commandments. They express what we can do to be pleasing to the Lord. All that remains is to apply them to the given situation, and this does not present any great problem. Having common sense is enough. If you cannot figure something out, ask your spiritual father or someone else whose words you respect, and act according to his directions. But it is better to refine your discernment through reading the word of God and the writings of the Fathers, so that you will always have an arbiter with you.

FRIDAY
I Cor. 11:8–22; Matt. 17:10–18

Concerning John the Baptist, the Lord said: *Elias is come already, and they knew him not* (Matt. 17:12). Why was this? Because they did not heed the ways of God and were not interested in them. They had a different mentality, different tastes, different views on things. Outside the sphere of Divine things, their shrewdness was in play, but within this sphere they did not understand anything, due to their estrangement from it. One's inner mentality forms a feeling for things, which immediately notices and determines what is familiar to it, no matter how concealed it may be. An artist, a scientist, and an economist look at one thing with equal attention, but each one makes a judgment in his own way—one according to its beauty, the second according to causal relations, the third according to gains from it. So it was with the Jews: as was their disposition, so did they judge concerning John, and then also about the Savior, and since they did not have a godly disposition, they did not understand those who carried out the work of God. Similarly, people these days understand neither the Forerunner nor the Lord—and they do with them what they like. A hidden persecution of Christianity has arisen, and it has begun to break out openly, such as recently occurred in Paris.[24] What

---

[24] St. Theophan is probably referring here to the uprising that took place in Paris in the spring of 1871, which resulted in the short-lived Paris Commune. This government forced a separation of the church from the state, made all church property public property, and excluded the practice of religion from schools.—ED.

was done there on a small scale is what we must expect with time in great proportions. Save us, O Lord!

SATURDAY
Rom. 13:1–10; Matt. 12:30–37

A good man out of the good treasure of the heart bringeth forth good things: and an evil man out of the evil treasure bringeth forth evil things (Matt. 12:35). What you put in the treasury is what you receive: if you put in gold, you will take out gold; if you put in copper, you will take out copper. Of course, copper can be passed off as gold; but an expert will immediately recognize the forgery. How can we arrange it that our treasury contains only gold, that is, so that our heart holds only good? The heart by its nature is a treasury of good things; evil came later. Take the surgical knife of attentiveness and self pitilessness, separate what is unnatural, and cut it out. One after the other, the evil things will leave, while the good will grow in strength and spread. What will remain, at last, will be only good. The question is how to determine what is natural and unnatural. Do not listen to today's naturalists. They explain everything inside out: what is natural is unnatural for them; while what is unnatural is natural for them. They call evil good, and good evil. Look at what the Lord says in the Gospels and the Holy Apostles say in their writings, and determine what is natural in accordance with their instructions. In such a manner, at last, you will gather much good and will bring it forth out of your heart. Pray to the Holy Spirit: "O Treasury of good things, place a treasure of good in my heart!"

EIGHTH SUNDAY AFTER PENTECOST
I Cor. 1:10–18; Matt. 14:14–22

Before the miraculous feeding of the five thousand, the Lord's disciples wanted the people to be sent away, but the Lord said to them, *They need not depart, give ye them to eat* (Matt. 14:16). Let us learn this saying, and each time the enemy suggests to us to refuse someone who asks for something, let us say on behalf of the Lord, *They need not depart, give ye them to eat,* and let us give them whatever we find at hand. The enemy destroys the desire to offer charity, and suggests that perhaps the asker is not worthy of alms. But the Lord did not investigate the worthiness of those who were sitting there. He served everyone equally, while, of course, not everyone was equally devoted to Him. Perhaps even those who later cried, *Crucify Him!* were there. Such is God's overall Providence for us: *He maketh His sun to rise on the evil and on the good, and sendeth rain on the just and on the unjust* (Matt. 5:45). If only the Lord would help us even a tiny bit to be merciful, as our Heavenly Father is merciful (cf. Luke 6:36)!

MONDAY
I Cor. 11:31–12:6; Matt. 18:1–11

Except ye be converted, and become as little children, ye shall not enter into the Kingdom of Heaven (Matt. 18:3). The structure of a child's heart is a model for all. Children, before egotistical strivings have arisen in them, are a model for imitation. What do we see in children? Complete faith which does not reason, undebating obedience, sincere love, peace and lack of worry under their parents' roof, and liveliness and freshness of life, with agility and a desire to learn and become more perfect. But the Savior particularly emphasizes one of their virtues—humility: *Whosoever shall humble himself as this little child, the same is greatest in the Kingdom of Heaven* (Matt. 18:4). For as soon as there is true humility, all of the virtues are there. It is revealed perfectly when the other virtues have already blossomed in the heart and reach maturity; it is their crown and protection. This is the mystery of spiritual life in our Lord Jesus Christ. Whoever is higher is more humble, because he more clearly and tangibly sees that it is not he who labors successfully, but the grace which is in him (cf. I Cor. 5:10); and this is *the measure of the stature of the fullness of Christ* (Eph. 4:13). For an essential aspect of Christ Jesus is that He *humbled Himself, and became obedient unto death* (Phil. 2:8).

TUESDAY
I Cor. 12:12–26; Matt. 18:18–22; 19:1–2, 13–15

Wanting to know how many times one should forgive his brother, St. Peter asked with the suggestion: *forgive … till seven times?* (Matt. 18:21). Saying this, he thought that he had chosen the greatest quantity. How short human patience is! The Lord, applying His long-suffering to our infirmities, defined it thus: *I say not unto thee, Until seven times: but, Until seventy times seven* (Matt. 18:22). This is the same as saying: always forgive, and do not think about not forgiving. All-forgivingness will be the distinctive feature of a Christian spirit, as all-forgivingness is the source and constant support of our life in the Lord, coming from God Himself. Always forgiving everyone for everything is the outer garment of Christian love, which, according to the Epistle, *suffereth long, and is kind, is not easily provoked, beareth all things* (I Cor. 13:4–7). It is the most faithful guarantee of forgiveness at the Last Judgment—for if we forgive, our Heavenly Father will also forgive us (cf. Matt. 6:14). In such a manner—if you want to go to heaven—forgive everyone sincerely, from the bottom of your heart, so that not even a shadow of hostility remains.

WEDNESDAY
I Cor. 13:4–14:5; Matt. 20:1–16

In the parable about the hirelings, even he who worked only one hour was rewarded by the master of the house the same as the others. The hours of the day in this parable are an image of the course of our life. The eleventh hour is the final period of this life. The Lord shows that even those who lived without serving Him up to that moment can begin to work and can please Him no less than the others. Therefore, old age is no excuse. Let no one despair, supposing that there is no point in beginning to work. Begin, and do not be afraid. The Lord is merciful—He will give you all that He gives others: here, according to the order of grace, and there, according to the law of justice. Just have more fervor, and grieve more contritely about the carelessness in which almost all of your life was spent. You will say, "The master of the house summoned those in the parable—so, let the Lord call me." But isn't He calling? Could it really be that you do not hear the voice of the Lord in the Church, saying, *Come unto Me all ye,* and the Apostle's call, *As though God did beseech you by us: we pray you in Christ's stead, be ye reconciled to God* (II Cor. 5:20)?

THURSDAY
I Cor. 14:6–19; Matt. 20:17–28

Christianity fully satisfies our striving for precedence—but how? Through a method totally opposed to the one used in the world. Do you want to be first? Be a servant to everyone, that is, be the last among them. This is just as essential as it is to attune your life and your disposition to the example of Christ the Lord. The Lord says: *The Son of man came not to be ministered unto, but to minister, and to give His life a ransom for many* (Matt. 20:28). The Lord ministers, and even washes the feet of His disciples. There is no need, therefore, to be ashamed of ministering to someone. Minister in any way possible, and with whatever means you can. There are opportunities every step of the way: feed someone who is hungry, clothe someone who is naked, bring a stranger into your home, visit someone who is sick and even take care of him, and do not refuse all other help to those who ask it. Serve not only the body, but also the soul: give understanding and advice, point out a good book, console, and support. A word is a powerful means to help; through such a word one's soul extends itself and, joining another soul, gives him strength.

FRIDAY
I Cor. 14:26–40; Matt. 21:12–14, 17–20

My House shall be called the house of prayer; but ye have made it a den of thieves (Matt. 21:13). Everyone knows that being in church calls for reverence, the collecting of one's thoughts, profound Divine contemplation, and standing in the presence of God—but who fulfills this? People go to church with a desire to pray, to stand there for a while with warm fervor; but then thoughts begin to wander, and bargaining begins in one's head that is even louder than that which the Lord found in the temple in Jerusalem. Why is this so? Because the way one stands in church is a reflection of one's entire life. As people live, so do they behave in church. A church influences and somewhat supports movements of the spirit, but then the usual course of one's spiritual constitution takes over. Therefore, if you want your time in church to consist in worthily standing before the face of the Lord, prepare for this in your ordinary life. Go about as much as you can in a prayerful frame of mind. This labor will bring you to the point that in church too you will stand reverently all the time. This reverence will inspire you to be reverent in your ordinary life as well. Thus you will go ever higher and higher. Say, "O Lord, help"—and begin!

SATURDAY
I Rom. 14:6–9; Matt. 15:32–39

Yet again the Lord miraculously fed the people accompanying Him, to show that He is always ready to provide generously for

THOUGHTS FOR EACH DAY OF THE YEAR

believers. He could have done this at every opportunity, but He did not, in order not to break them from their usual way of life—likewise established, maintained, and supported by Him. Such is God's general Providence. The main, all-embracing actions of Providence were accomplished in the beginning, at the ordering of all things. But, having arranged everything and set it into motion, God did not bind Himself in any way, but reserved for Himself the freedom to usher in extraordinary help when necessary. He acts like the master of a house who establishes rules but, while maintaining them, does not bind himself to them. Rather, he regards them with the authority and good intentions usual to the master of a house. Those who oppose the Faith do not understand the meaning of God's Providence and, broadening it in their minds beyond its proper boundaries, and not seeing the realization of their ideas, they deny this very Providence. The providence which they demand does not exist, but that Providence which the Lord God is well pleased to establish and preserve unquestionably does exist.

Ninth Sunday after Pentecost
I Cor. 3:9–17; Matt. 14:22–34

The Holy Apostle Peter, with the Lord's permission, gets out of the ship and walks on the water; then he yields to the movement of fear and begins to drown. The fact that he decided upon such a singular act, hoping in the Lord, deserves no reprimand—otherwise the Lord would not have allowed him to do this. The reprimand came because he did not sustain the original state of his soul. He was filled with inspired hope in the Lord's ability to do anything, and this gave him the boldness to entrust himself to the waves. Several steps were already made along this new path—it was necessary only to stand more firmly in hope, gazing at the Lord, Who is near, and at the experience of walking in His strength. Instead, he gave himself over to human thoughts: "The wind is strong, the waves are great, and water is not solid"—and this shook loose and weakened the strength of his faith and hope. Because of this he broke away from the Lord's hands and, left to the operation of nature's laws, began to drown. The Lord rebuked him: *O thou of little faith, wherefore didst thou doubt?* (Matt. 14:31), showing that in this lay the entire reason for his danger. Behold a lesson for all who undertake something, great or small, with the aim of pleasing the Lord! Keep your first state of faith and hope, from which a great virtue is born—patience in doing good, which serves as the basis for a God-pleasing life. As long as these dispositions are maintained, inspiration for laboring on the path begun does not go away, and obstacles, no matter how great they may be, are not noticed. When these dispositions weaken, the soul is filled with human reasoning about human methods of preserving one's life and conducting the affairs one has begun. But since these human methods always turns out to be powerless, fear enters the soul—how should one act? From this comes waverings about whether or not to continue, and in the end one completely turns back. Here is what you must do: if you begin, persevere—chase away troubling thoughts, and be bold in the Lord, Who is close.

Monday
I Cor. 15:12–19; Matt. 21:18–22

The Lord condemned the fig tree to fruitlessness because in appearance it was so covered with leaves that there ought to have been fruit on it, but none could be found. In applying this to the Christian life, the leaves represent outward works of piety and outward spiritual asceticism, while the fruits represent inner dispositions. According to the law, the former should proceed from the latter. However, out of condescension to our infirmity, the latter should at least develop together with the former. When the former are strong but the latter are not even budding, a false life results, which expresses itself like this: to seem, but not to be. At first, perhaps, this unfortunate state is not in one's thoughts, but then it appears unnoticeably and establishes itself as a way of life. When one applies himself excessively to externals and becomes passionately attached to them, his attention toward his heart is suppressed, his spiritual feelings die away, and coldness settles in. At this stage spiritual life freezes, and there remains only an appearance of piety, but no piety. One's behavior is proper on the outside, but inwardly everything is wrong. The consequence of this is spiritual fruitlessness–works are done, but they are all dead.

Tuesday
I Cor. 15:29–38; Matt. 21:23–27

When the Lord asked the question about John the Baptist, the chief priests and the elders thought, "If we answer this way or that, either way is detrimental for us," and that is why they decided it would be better to use ignorance as a cover. Their self-interest tied their tongue and did not allow them to witness to the truth. If they had loved truth more than themselves, the words would have been different, as would their works. Their interests buried the truth and would not let it reach their hearts. Their interests kept them from forming a sincere conviction, and made their hearts indifferent to the truth. This is how it always is—egotistical strivings are the primordial enemies of truth. All other enemies follow them and act by means of them. If one investigates how all delusions and heresies have arisen, it turns out that this is precisely the source of them all: In words, truth is truth; but in reality, the truth hinders us in one regard or another and must be eliminated, and a lie must be set in its place which is more favorable to us. Why, for example, are there materialists and nihilists? Because the idea of God the Creator, Provider, and Judge, together with the idea of the spirituality of the soul, hinders those people from living in grand style according to their inclinations, and so they push the idea aside. It is clear from the worthlessness of their premises that the nihilists are not guided by the truth. They want everything to be just as they think it is, and every phantom that reflects their thoughts is exhibited by them as a witness to the truth. If they would sober up even a little, they would immediately see their lie. But they feel sorry for themselves, and therefore remain as they are.

WEDNESDAY
I Cor. 16:4–12; Matt. 21:28–32

In the parable about the two sons, the second promptly said, "I go," but went not. This is an image of all hasty good intentions that lack the constancy, will, and patience to fulfill them. A light heart is immediately ready for every good thing presented to it, but a will that is neither firm nor loves labor refuses to do something from the very beginning. This infirmity is found in nearly everyone. How can one avoid such unreliability toward oneself and others? This is how: do not begin anything without thinking it over and calculating whether there will be enough strength for the undertaking. This is what the Lord asked us to do in the parables about the man who set off to war and the other who set about building a house. What is this calculation? These parables are related by the Lord in order to instruct us to arm ourselves in advance with self-denial and patience. Look to see whether you have these buttresses that all laborers for goodness have. If you have them, begin the undertaking; but if not, then first store them up. If you stock yourself up with them, then no matter what you meet on the path to your goal, you will endure and overcome it all, and you will bring your undertaking to a conclusion. Calculating does not mean that as soon as the deed becomes a bit difficult you drop it, but rather that you should inspire yourself for every labor. From this there will come firmness of will and constancy in deeds. And it will never be the case with you that you say "I go," and then go not.

THURSDAY
II Cor. 1:1–7; Matt. 21:43–46

The chief priests and Pharisees perceived that the Lord was telling parables on their account, that He was opening their eyes so that they would see the truth. But what did they do with this? They thought about how to kill the Lord. If their common sense had not been distorted by their prejudice, then even if they could not believe, as the clarity of the instruction required, they would at least have carefully considered the truth of the Savior's words. Their prejudice pushed them onto a crooked path, and they then proved to be God-killers. It has always been this way, and it is this way now. The Germans, and our people who have followed after them and become Germanized in their mentality, immediately cry out whenever they come across a miracle in the Gospels, "Not true, not true; this didn't happen and couldn't happen, this needs to be crossed out."[25] Is not this the same as killing? Look through all the books of these clever men—in none of them will you find any indication as to why they think this way. Not one of them can say anything against what the Gospel truth proves, and not one cares to comprehend the arguments which sober-minded people use to convict their falseness; they only continue insisting that [what is written] could not be, and that is why they do not believe the Gospels. And you cannot do anything with them—they are ready to defy God Himself.

---

[25] St. Theophan is referring here to "higher Biblical criticism," which was popular in eighteenth- and nineteenth-century Germany, and continues to be popular today. This system of investigation purports to make determinations about the authorship of Biblical writings, and whether or not events described in Scripture actually occurred.—ED.

Friday
II Cor. 1:12–20; Matt. 22:23–33

Concerning the manner of the future life, the Lord said that people there will not marry and will not be given in marriage, that is, our everyday earthly relationships will have no place there. It would follow that none of the norms of earthly life will either. Neither science, nor art, nor governments, nor anything else will exist. What will there be? God will be all in all. And since God is spirit, He unites with the spirit and acts on what is spiritual. All life there will be a continuous flow of spiritual movements. There can be only one conclusion drawn from this: since our goal is the future life, and what is here is only a preparation for it, then to spend all the time of one's life only on what is appropriate to this life alone and has no relevance to the future life means to go against our purpose, and to prepare ourselves for a bitter, most bitter lot. We are not absolutely required to drop everything; but while working as much as is necessary for this life, we must turn our main concern toward preparation for the future life, trying wherever possible to turn even earthly, menial labor into a means for achieving this goal.

Saturday
Rom. 15:30–33; Matt. 17:24–18:4

The Lord paid the required temple tribute and kept all other practices, both temple-related and civic. He fulfilled this and taught the Apostles to do the same, and the Apostles in turn passed this same law on to all Christians. Only the spirit of life was made new; externally all remained as it had been, except what was clearly against the will of God—for instance, participating in sacrifices to idols, etc. Then Christianity gained the upper hand, displaced all the former practices, and established its own. One would expect that it would thus have become easier for the spirit of Christianity to develop and strengthen. So it was, but not for everyone. A large percentage mastered external Christian practices but stopped there, not concerning themselves with the spirit of life. It is the same today. Out of the entire sum of Christians, who proves to be a Christian in spirit? What are the others? They bear the name as if they were alive, but, behold—they are dead. When the Apostles preached the Gospel, their word drew God's portion out from the midst of the pagan world. Now, through the same word, the Lord chooses His portion from amidst the Christian world. *Whoso readeth, let him understand* (Matt. 24:15), and let him take care to find out for certain whether he is in the Lord's portion. If he cannot be certain of this, let him take care to belong to the Lord, for in this alone lies salvation.

Tenth Sunday after Pentecost
I Cor. 4:9–16; Matt. 17:14–23

This kind goeth not out but by prayer and fasting (Matt. 17:21). If this kind goes out by the prayer and fasting of another person, then it is even less able to enter one who fasts and prays. What protection! Although there are a huge number of demons and all the air is packed with them, they cannot do anything to one who is protected by prayer and fasting. Fasting is comprehensive temperance, and prayer is comprehensive communication with God. The former defends from the outside, whereas the latter directs a fiery weapon against the enemies from within. The demons can sense a man of abstinence and prayer from a distance, and they run far away from him so as to avoid a painful blow. Is it possible to think that where there is no fasting and prayer, there is already a demon? Yes, it is. The demons lodging in a person do not always reveal their presence, but lurk there, stealthily teaching their host every evil and turning him away from every good. This person is certain that he is doing everything on his own, but meanwhile he is only fulfilling the will of his enemy. Just commence prayer and fasting, and the enemy will immediately depart, waiting on the side for an opportunity to somehow return again. And he really will return, as soon as prayer and fasting are abandoned.

MONDAY
II Cor. 2:4–15; Matt. 23:13–22

Woe unto you ... for ye shut up the Kingdom of Heaven against men (Matt. 23:13). This can be said to hierarchs who neither teach the people the saving path themselves nor compel the priests to teach them. This can also be said to priests who leave the people in neglect, not taking care to explain to them what is necessary for the salvation of the soul. Due to this, the people remain in blindness. Some remain in the certainty that they are proceeding properly; others, although they notice that things are not going the right way, do not go where they should, because they do not know how and where to go. This causes various silly ideas to spread among the people; this is why schismatics, Molokans, and Khlysts[26] find acceptance among them, and this is how every evil teaching finds convenient access to them. A priest usually thinks that everything is fine in his parish, and rushes into action only when this evil has already spread and exposed itself. But then nothing can be done about it. A priest must consider it the first priority of his conscience to continually instruct the adults in the knowledge of the Christian Faith, and to prepare the young generation from their first conscious years, explaining to them what they can and must know. There is no need to wait for school. This must be done orally, gathering the children in

[26] The term schismatics refers to those Old Ritualists who were not in communion with the Russian Church. Molokans and Khlysts were Russian sects.—TRANS.

the church and at home on Sunday evenings, or whenever and however it is convenient.

TUESDAY
II Cor. 2:14–3:3; Matt. 23:23–28

Cleanse the inner so the outer will be clean. Our outward behavior in society is almost always proper—we fear the judgment of people and restrain ourselves. If we give ourselves over to vices outwardly, this is the end—it means that all shame is lost. But when one's visible behavior is proper, the inner tenor of thoughts and feelings is not always proper. Here complete freedom is given to pleasing oneself, which is satisfied outwardly to the degree that the eyes of men can bear it and as far as it can hide its works from human sight. This is precisely what a whited sepulcher is. Furthermore, inner uncleanness makes what is on the outside unclean. Cleanse yourself inwardly, and then the exterior will become clean, and you will be entirely clean. You will be made into a vessel that is fit for all the good uses of a householder. One must marvel at how the inside remains neglected; after all, no one wants perdition. Truly, the enemy keeps such a soul in blindness—[he says] that there is no problem as long as there are no obvious sins, or he teaches the soul to put off what is important until tomorrow. "Tomorrow we'll work seriously on ourselves, as we ought; but now let my soul take some pleasure in passionate thoughts and dreams, if not deeds." Let us be on our guard that we do not grow old in such a frame of mind, lest correction become impossible for us, like teaching an old man new things.

WEDNESDAY
II Cor. 3:4–11; Matt. 23:29–39

How many mercies the Lord revealed to Jerusalem (that is, to the Jews)! And, in the end, He was still forced to say: *Behold, your house is left unto you desolate* (Matt. 23:38). It is well known to all what the consequences of this were: the Jews are homeless to this day.[27] Does not a similar thing occur with the soul? The Lord cares for the soul and teaches it in every way. An obedient soul traverses the path indicated, but a disobedient soul remains in opposition to God's calling. However, the Lord does not abandon even this soul, and uses every means to bring it to reason. If stubbornness increases, God's influence increases. But there is a limit to everything. A soul becomes hardened, and the Lord, seeing that there is nothing more that can be done with this soul, abandons it to its fall, and it perishes like Pharaoh. Let anyone who is beset by passions learn from this the lesson that he cannot continue indulging himself indefinitely without punishment. Is it not time to abandon those passions—not just to deny oneself occasionally, but to decisively turn away? Indeed, no one can say when he will overstep the limit. Perhaps God's long-suffering is just about to end.

THURSDAY

II Cor. 4:1–6; Matt. 24:13–28

He that shall endure unto the end, the same shall be saved (Matt. 24:13). However, not everyone who endures will be saved, but only he who endures on the Lord's path. This life is given to us for that reason—to endure. Everyone endures something, even through to the very end. But enduring does not lead to benefit if it is not for the sake of the Lord and His Holy Gospel. Step onto the path of faith and the Gospel commandments; occasions to endure will multiply, but from that moment endurance will begin to bring forth crowns. That endurance which before was empty, will be made fruitful. The enemy brings such blindness

---

[27] This text was written long before the establishment of the State of Israel.—ED.

upon us that the endurance which is encountered on the path of good seems heavy and unbearable, while what he inflicts on those who serve the passions seems light and free, although it is actually heavier and more dismal than what people bear in struggling against the passions and opposing the enemy! But we are blind, and do not see this. We labor, endure, and strain ourselves to the breaking point for the sake of the enemy, unto our own perdition.

Friday
II Cor. 4:13–18; Matt. 24:27–33, 42–51

Watch; for ye know not what hour your Lord doth come (Matt. 24:42). If only this were remembered, there would be no sinners. But it is not remembered, although everyone knows that it is unquestionably true. Even the strictest ascetics were not strong enough to easily keep this in mind, but they made efforts to fix it in their consciousness so that it would not leave. One would keep a coffin in his cell, another would beg his fellow ascetics to ask him about his coffin and grave, another would keep pictures of death and the Judgment, and others would do other things. If death does not touch a soul, the soul does not remember it. But in no way can what immediately follows death not touch a soul; a soul cannot but be concerned about this, since it is the judgment of its fate for eternal ages. Why does a soul not remember this? It deceives itself that death will not come soon, and that perhaps somehow things will not go badly for it. How bitter! It goes without saying that a soul which abides in such thoughts is careless and self-indulgent. So, how can it think that judgment will go favorably for it? No, one must behave like a student who is facing an exam: no matter what he does, the exam does not leave his head. Such remembrance does not allow him to waste even a minute in vain, and he uses all his time to prepare for the exam. When will we acquire a mind-set like this?

SATURDAY
I Cor. 1:3–9; Matt. 19:3–12

The Lord says that God Himself originally blessed the marriage union, and put this law into our nature. About those who do not want to get married [for the sake of the Kingdom of Heaven], He said: *He that is able to receive it, let him receive it* (Matt. 19:12). It is clear that although He admitted that marriage is a natural law, it is not so indispensable and inevitable that there is no room for celibacy. He allows celibacy, but guards it with a condition that brings it nearer to the law of nature. A eunuch from birth is celibate according to natural law. However, he who by his own will puts himself in the same state as that of a natural eunuch, who is such by birth without the participation of will, places himself on the same level with him as regards physical needs. Consequently, in this sense, both the former and the latter are natural celibates. Why is the state of a spiritual eunuch—self-imposed celibacy— considered unnatural? Because people do not understand nature. For them "natural" means what is natural for the body; but what is natural for the spirit, and what becomes natural for the body as a consequence of the spirit's influence, people do not want to consider natural. It would be a different matter if these were all materialists, but this is not the case. Discuss some other subject with them, and they will speak reasonably.

ELEVENTH SUNDAY AFTER PENTECOST
I Cor. 9:2–12; Matt. 18:23–35

The Lord concluded the parable about the two debtors with the following words: *So likewise shall My Heavenly Father do also unto you, if ye from your hearts forgive not every one his brother their trespasses* (Matt. 18:35). It would seem that such a small thing is required: forgive and you will be forgiven. When you are forgiven, you are received into mercy; and when you are brought into mercy, you have become a participant in all the treasures of mercy—salvation, and Paradise, and eternal bliss. What a great acquisition for such a small thing as forgiving! Yes, it is a small thing, but for our self-love there is nothing more difficult than forgiving. We might still forgive some unintentional annoyance dealt us in private that no one sees. But if the offense is just a bit more sensitive, and takes place in front of people, don't even ask—there is no forgiveness. There are circumstances when, whether you want to or not, you are not allowed to express your displeasure—and so you remain silent. However, only your tongue is silent. Meanwhile, your heart speaks and builds evil plans. Raise the annoyance yet another degree, and there is no restraint. Neither shame, nor fear, nor loss, nor any other thing will restrain you. Egoism which has reached the boiling point makes a person as though insane, and he who gives in to it begins to talk foolishly. The people most subject to this unfortunate state are usually not just anyone. The more civilized one is, the more sensitive he is to insults, and the less forgiving. Relations will often remain smooth on the surface, but inwardly there is clearly discord. Meanwhile, the Lord requires that we forgive with our whole heart.

Monday
II Cor. 5:10–15; Mark 1:9–15

The Lord began His sermon thus: *The time is fulfilled, and the Kingdom of God is at hand: repent ye, and believe the Gospel* (Mark 1:15). At the end of the ages it will also be said: the time is fulfilled, the Kingdom is at hand. But this statement will not be followed by *repent ye, and believe* but by "come out to the Judgment." The time for repentance and labors of self-improvement will have ended. Let everyone give an account of what good or evil things he did in his body. And so, while there is time, hurry to use this time unto your salvation. The Father's embrace is open to receive all who come with a sincere feeling of contrition about the past and with a desire to serve God henceforth by the zealous fulfillment of His holy commandments. For each of us death is the end of this age; it is the door to the other life. Look into this more often and determine for yourself more truly: what will happen then? And having determined this without pitying yourself, begin laboring to prepare that which in you is not ready, that you might enter the place where joy is unending. Labor to push aside all that could give the servants of outer darkness the right to prevail over us and carry us away to their realm, whence there will no longer be a way out.

TUESDAY

II Cor. 5:15–21; Mark 1:16–22

The Lord taught in the Capernaum synagogue, and everyone marveled at His teaching: *for He taught them as one that had authority, and not as the scribes* (Mark 1:22). This authority is not a commanding tone, but the power of influence on souls and hearts. His word entered within, and bound itself to human consciences, showing that all was as He said. This is how a word which is imbued with Divine power, a word from the Spirit, or an anointed word, always is. This is how it was with the Holy Apostles, and after them with all influential teachers, who spoke not from learnedness, but as the Spirit gave them the gift of prophecy. It is a gift of God—which can only be acquired through labors—to master it in one's heart and life, and not just by learning. Wherever this occurs the word is imbued with cogency, because it moves from heart to heart. In this is the power of the word over souls. The scribes, speaking and writing from their learnedness, were not given such power, because they spoke from their head and mixed into their head their own philosophizing. Life is not found in the head, only the tip of life. Life is in the heart, and only what comes forth from the heart can influence the currents of life.

WEDNESDAY
II Cor. 6:11–16; Mark 1:23–28

The demon praised the Savior, but the Savior said to him, *Hold thy peace, and come out of him* (Mark 1:25). Demons never say or do anything with a good purpose—they always have something evil in mind. So it was here. The Lord, not exposing their snares, resolved it with a word: *Hold thy peace, and come out.* He did not want to converse long with an evil spirit. Here is a lesson for us. A person manages to do very little of something good before a demon sits nearby and begins to trumpet in his ears: "You are this and that." Do not listen and do not enter into conversation with this flatterer, but immediately say point-blank, "Hold thy peace and come out," and erase his tracks with sighs and self-reproach, then cense the place where he was with contrite prayer. He wants to give rise to self-opinion and self-esteem, and then to inflate self-praise and vainglory from them. In the spiritual life, all those thoughts and feelings are the same as thieves in everyday life. Like thieves that enter a house to rob its goods, so these demons, taking root in a soul, destroy all that is good in that soul and cast it away, so that nothing remains that the Lord might praise later.

THURSDAY
II Cor. 7:1–10; Mark 1:29–35

In the morning, rising up a great while before day, He went out, and departed into a solitary place, and there prayed (Mark 1:35). Here is a lesson to get up early and devote the first hours of the day to prayer in solitude. The soul, renewed with sleep, is fresh, light, and capable of being permeated, like fresh morning air. Therefore, it asks on its own to be allowed to go where all of its joy is found, to go before the face of the Heavenly Father, to the company of the angels and saints. It is more convenient for the soul to pray at this time instead of later, when the cares of the day are already piled upon the soul. The Lord orders everything. You must receive a blessing from Him for your deeds, for the teachings you need, and for your necessary strengthening. Hasten as early as possible, before anything interferes, to lift yourself up to the Lord in mind and heart in solitude, to confess your needs and intentions to Him, and to beg for His help. Having attuned yourself by prayer and thoughts of God from the first moments of the day, you will then spend the whole day in reverence and fear of God, with collected thoughts. From this come discretion, steadiness, and harmony in deeds and mutual relations. This is a reward for the labor which you compel yourself to undertake in your morning solitude. Thus, even for worldly people this makes good sense and is not something alien to their goals.

FRIDAY
II Cor. 7:10–16; Mark 2:18–22

At the Transfiguration a voice from heaven uttered, *Hear ye Him* (Matt. 17:5). Why is this so? Because the fruit of obedience was being shown to them. It was as if the Heavenly Father were saying: Do you want to attain this? Hear what He will suggest and command you to do. If you go on His path, you will undoubtedly enter into the realm of light, which will not embrace you from without, but will come forth from within, and always keep you in a state in which all of your bones will utter: it is good for us to be this way. You will be filled with the light of joy, the light of goodwill, the light of knowledge; all sorrows will pass away, the dissonance of the passions will disappear, and falsehood and delusion will disperse. On the earth you will become heavenly; from among the earthborn you will become Divinely born; from among transitory things you will become eternally blessed. Then all will be yours, because you yourselves will become Christ's. He who loves Christ the Lord is beloved of the Heavenly Father, and both will come to him and make Their abode with him. This is the light of the Transfiguration!

SATURDAY
I Cor. 1:26–29; Matt. 20:29–34

The two blind men of Jericho cry out, and the Lord returns their sight to them. But could these blind men have been the only ones in those places? Of course not. Why did these receive vision, but not the others? Because those did not cry out; and they did not cry out because they did not have hope; they did not have hope because they did not please God; they did not please God because they had little faith. When real faith comes to a man, he begins to please God from that very moment; with pleasing God comes hope, and from all of this comes prayer, compelling all kinds of help from above. Such people meet no refusal. They know how to ask, and they truly know that they must ask. They understand the limits to their asking, and they have patient persistence in prayer. All of this is indispensably necessary for success, for prayer by itself has feeble wings.

TWELFTH SUNDAY AFTER PENTECOST
I Cor. 15:1–11; Matt. 19:16–26

A rich man shall hardly enter into the Kingdom of Heaven (Matt. 19:23). Here is meant a rich man who sees within himself the many means and powers that lead to his prosperity. But as soon as one who has many possessions cuts off all attachment to them, extinguishes within himself all reliance on them, and ceases to see them as his substantial support, then in his heart he is the same as one who possesses nothing. To such a one is the road to the Kingdom opened. Riches then not only do not hinder him, but they help him, for they provide the means for charitable works.

Riches are not the danger, but rather reliance upon them and attachment to them. This thought can be generalized in this way: whoever relies on something and is attached to it is rich in that thing. Whoever relies on God alone and cleaves to Him with all his heart is rich in God. Whoever relies on something else turns his heart to it instead of to God. Such a person is rich in this other thing, but not in God. Here are meant such things as family, connections, intelligence, rank, spheres of activities, and so forth. From this it follows that he who is not rich in God has no entrance into the Kingdom of God.

Monday

II Cor. 8:7–15; Mark 3:6–12

The Lord forbade both people and demons to praise Him when He was on the earth, but required that people believe in Him and fulfill God's commandments. The Lord has the same law now, and it will be the same at the Judgment: *Not every one that saith unto Me, Lord, Lord, shall enter into the Kingdom of Heaven; but he that doeth the will of My Father which is in heaven* (Matt. 7:21). This is why in church [the great doxology] begins with "Glory to God in the highest," and toward the end it says, "Heal my soul.... Teach me to do Thy will." Without this, praise of God has no worth. For then it does not proceed from the soul, but is only sent up from the tongue in someone else's words, and that is why the Lord pays no attention to it. One must arrange things so that others praise the Lord when they see our works, so that our life will be praise to God, for He does all things in all people, as long as you do not get in the way. It is to Him that praise for one's deeds ascends. Each person must become the fragrance of Christ; then even without praise there will be unceasing glorification of the Lord. A rose does not speak, but its fragrance spreads far in silence. This is how all Christians ought to live.

TUESDAY
II Cor. 8:16–9:5; Mark 3:13–19

The Lord chose the Apostles, *that they should be with Him, and that He might send them forth to preach, and to have power to heal sicknesses, and to cast out devils* (Mark 3:14–15). Every Christian is chosen—and is chosen for similar deeds, namely: to be with the Lord through unceasing remembrance of Him and awareness of His omnipresence, through the preaching and fulfillment of His commandments, and through a readiness to confess one's faith in Him. Where such a confession is made, it is a loud sermon for those who hear it. Every Christian has the power to heal infirmities—not of others, but his own, and not of the body, but of the soul, that is, sins and sinful habits—and to cast out devils, rejecting the evil thoughts sown by them and extinguishing the excitement of the passions inflamed by them. Do this and you will be an apostle, a fulfiller of what the Lord chose you for, an achiever of your calling as an evangelizer. When you first succeed in all this, then perhaps the Lord will appoint you as a special ambassador—to save others after you have saved yourself, and to help those who are tempted, after you yourself pass through all temptations, all experiences of good and evil. But your job is to work upon yourself: for this you are chosen. The rest is in God's hands. He who humbles himself shall be exalted.

WEDNESDAY
II Cor. 9:12–10:7; Mark 3:20–27

If a kingdom be divided against itself, that kingdom cannot stand (Mark 3:24). As long as single-mindedness for sinful evil is the quality within us, the kingdom of darkness and sin is strong in us; but when God's grace attracts to itself the part of the spirit held captive by sin, freeing it from captivity, then there occurs a division within: sin on one side, good on the other. As soon as a person, as a result of this awakening, unites his consciousness and freedom with the good, sin loses all support and starts to decay. Constancy in the good intention that has been undertaken and patience in labors for its sake completely thwart sin and destroy it. Then begins the kingdom of good within, and it remains until some evil thought steals in and, attracting the will to itself, once again brings about divisions. Merely give entrance to the sinful stirring which has arisen, unite with it and set it in action, and again the good will begin to weaken, and evil will grow, until it destroys the good entirely. This is the nearly continuous history of the inner life of those who are weak-hearted and do not have a strong disposition.

THURSDAY

II Cor. 10:7–18; Mark 3:28–35

He that shall blaspheme against the Holy Spirit hath never forgiveness (Mark 3:29). Does it take long to fall into this terrible sin? Not long at all, for behold the sins of this nature: "Great or excessive hope in God's grace; despair or lack of hope in God's compassion; contradicting manifest and confirmed truth, and rejection of the Orthodox Christian Faith. Some add to this jealousy over spiritual gifts which a close one receives from God; obstinacy in sin and chronic wickedness; carelessness about repentance before departure from this life" (*Orthodox Confession,* part 3, question 38). See how many paths there are! Begin to walk any of these, and it will be difficult to return. It will carry you to a devouring abyss. Opposition to the truth begins with small doubts arising through evil words or writings. If you leave them unattended or untreated, they will lead to unbelief and obstinacy therein. People also reach despair unnoticeably: "I will repent," they say, and then they sin. Thus it goes on several times; then, seeing that repentance does not come, they say to themselves, "Let it be, you can't control yourself," and then they give themselves over to the full power of sin. A huge number of sins gather; and at the same time one permits oneself a great deal of opposition to the obvious attraction of God's grace. When in such a condition a person comes to the thought of improving himself, the multitude of his sins restrain him, while his opposition to grace takes away his boldness to approach the Lord. He then decides, "My guilt is too great for it to be remitted." This is despair! Beware of the rudiments of unbelief and love of sin, and you will not fall into this chasm.

FRIDAY
II Cor. 11:5–21; Mark 4:1–9

Behold, there went out a sower to sow (Mark 4:3). Since the time that this Sower went out to sow, He has not ceased to sow. In the beginning He sowed personally, then through the Apostles, and at last through Divine Scripture and Divinely wise teachers. To this day the word of God's truth is being sown everywhere. Just be prepared to manifest yourself as good ground, and you will be sown without fail. God will raise up what has been sown. How do you make yourself into good ground? With attention and study of the word of God, sympathy and love toward it, and readiness to immediately carry out what you learn. With such a mind-set, not a single word will lie on the surface of your soul, but all will enter within. Uniting with the elements of the spirit which are dear to it, it will take root and sprout. Then, being nourished—from above through spiritual inspirations, and from below through good desires and labors—it will grow into a tree and will flower and give fruit. God Himself arranged everything around us this way, and this is why we cannot but be amazed at our fruitlessness. But all of this is due to our inattentiveness and carelessness.

Saturday
I Cor. 2:6–9; Matt. 22:15–22

Render therefore unto Caesar the things which are Caesar's; and unto God the things that are God's (Matt. 22:21)—render unto each what is his. Hence there is a law: do not please God in one way alone, but in whatever way you can and ought to please Him; direct all of your strength and every means toward serving God. Having said, *Render unto Caesar the things which are Caesar's,* the Lord showed that such work is pleasing to Him. If by the things which are Caesar's you understand all the necessary and important practices of earthly life in general, and by the things that are God's, all observances of the Church established by God, then it turns out that all the paths of our life are filled with means for salvation. Just take heed and use everything, and act everywhere in accordance with God's will, as God wants from you—and your salvation is at hand. You can set yourself so that not a single step is taken without its being a deed pleasing to God and, consequently, a step toward salvation—for the path of salvation proceeds along the path of God's will. Walk in God's presence, take heed, discern, and set about immediately without self-pity to do that deed which your conscience shows you at each given moment.

Dormition of the Most Holy Theotokos
Thirteenth Sunday after Pentecost
For Dormition: Phil. 2:5–11; Luke 10:38–42, 11:27–28

Mary hath chosen that good part (Luke 10:42). The Dormition of the Mother of God represents a good end to such a choice. At her Dormition the Savior Himself received her soul into His arms. Many saints were made worthy of the same. In various ways and to varying degrees, all those who choose that good part encounter this. At the time this choice is made, the saints foresee this end through hope, and even feel it to a certain degree. But then labors, struggles, and forcing of oneself come, one after another, and obscure the chosen path. The good end of that good part remains as a guiding star. It is as a faraway shining light for a traveler who is overtaken by darkness. Hope is the stimulator of energy and the maintainer of patience and constancy in what was begun, while hope itself is strong through faith. People make their choice according to faith, and through hope they are firm in their choice, while through patience they attain that good end.

MONDAY
II Cor. 12:10–19; Mark 4:10–23

The Lord breathed the breath of life, and man became in the image of God. It is the same with one's own rebirth: the beginnings of a new life are established and one's image is renewed by the breath of the Spirit of God; and whence and how it comes is not known. This is the point of departure; from here the work of raising up the image to a perfect likeness begins. When we are reborn according to the image of the Creator by the Lord's Spirit, we are transfigured from glory to glory—but not without us, our work and effort. However, it is God Who creates and restores us by the grace of the Most Holy Spirit, according to faith in the Lord. Behold the ideal and method of fulfilling in oneself the image and likeness of God! People so often write about and discuss education. Meanwhile, in the word of God it is all defined in a few words. Undertake only to fulfill what is prescribed, and education will proceed successfully to its goal. This is God's path, but it does not exclude human paths—on the contrary, it gives them direction and crowns their success. When only the human remains, education is usually insufficient, even detrimental, and often totally perverts those being educated; then the rest of life goes awry. Where those educated in a distorted manner multiply, all of society becomes more and more distorted, both in life and in its attitudes. The end is universal distortion; one bends in one direction, another bends in another.

TUESDAY
II Cor. 12:20–13:2; Mark 4:24–34

The parable about the gradual growth of wheat from seed portrays, with respect to each man, the gradual growth of what is hidden in a man's heart, sown and watched over by God's grace, while with respect to mankind, it is the gradual increase in the body of the Church, or the community of those saved in the Lord Jesus Christ, according to the order established by Him. Through this parable the question is settled: why to this day is Christianity not universally embraced? Just as a man who has cast seed into the ground sleeps and rises, and the seed sprouts and grows up on its own without his knowing how, so the Lord, placing the seed of Divine life in the ground, has given it freedom to spread on its own, subordinating it to the natural flow of events, and not forcing these events. He only watches over the seed, assists it in individual circumstances, and gives the general direction. The reason for this lies in man's freedom. The Lord wants man to submit to Him on his own, and awaits the inclination of his freedom; this matter takes time. If all depended only on God's will, everyone would have been a Christian long ago. Another thought: the body of the Church is being created in heaven; from the earth come only materials, formed also by heavenly agents. The word from heaven traverses the earth and attracts those who desire this. Those who take heed and follow, enter like raw material into God's laboratory—the Church—and here are remade according to patterns given from heaven. Those who are remade, upon their departure from this life pass into heaven and there enter into the house of God, each where he is fit. This goes on unceasingly, and consequently the work of God does not stand still. A universal triumph of Christianity is not required for this. The house of God is created invisibly.

WEDNESDAY
II Cor. 13:3–13; Mark 4:35–41

The disciples are sailing across the sea; a storm arises and places them in a dangerous situation, while the Lord sleeps. They call out to Him, *Lord, save us!* and He calms the storm with one word. This is another real presentation of the order of Divine Providence. All people and nations, as well as the Church, are sailing across the sea of life on their own by means of the natural and supernatural powers placed in them, according to the order established by God. The Lord rests, although He also abides amidst moving events; He Himself begins to act when an unavoidable misfortune threatens which could turn the direction of events to oppose His Divine plans. He is everywhere, preserves everything, and warms everything with the breath of His love; but He leaves His creatures to act on their own, by means of the powers given by Him, according to the laws and order everywhere established and upheld by Him. He is not personally intervening in all things, even though everything proceeds from Him and without Him nothing occurs. He Himself is always prepared to act when it is necessary, according to His boundless wisdom and truth. Prayer is the receptor of God's actions. But the best prayer is: "Lord! Thou knowest all things. Do with me as Thou willest!"

THURSDAY
Gal. 1:1–10, 20–2:5; Mark 5:1–20

My name is Legion: for we are many (Mark 5:9). Spirits are bodiless, and therefore they do not fill or take up space like bodies. This explains why it is physically possible for many spirits to reside in one person. That it is possible morally for spirits to do this is understandable from their amorality or their absence of all moral principles. That it is possible for people is understandable from their many-sided contact with the dark realm of the unclean powers, due to the way people's souls are ordered. But this only explains what is possible; the reality of demonic possession is subject to conditions which we do not have the ability to determine. We can only say that spirits do not always enter in a visible way, and possession is not always demonstrated through the possessed person's actions. There is an unseen, hidden demonic possession. There is also a power of spirits over minds, apart from the body, when the demons lead them wherever they wish, through the passions working in them. People think that they are acting themselves, but they are actually the laughingstocks of unclean powers. What can we do? Be a true Christian and no enemy power shall overcome you.

FRIDAY
Gal. 2:6–10; Mark 5:22–24, 35–6:1

Having resurrected the daughter of Jairus, the Lord commanded her parents strictly, *that no man should know it* (Mark 5:43). Thus are we commanded: do not seek glory, and do not train your ear for human praise, even if your deeds are of such a nature that it is impossible to hide them. Do what the fear of God and your conscience urge you to do, and as to what people say, act as though it had never been said. Look after your soul—as soon as it inclines the slightest degree in the direction of seeking glory, return it to its place. A desire for people to know what you have done is provoked by a desire for praise. When there is praise the goal is achieved; but this undermines one's energy and suppresses the praiseworthy activity, and consequently suppresses the continuation of praise. Thus, one who wants people to know of his good works is his own betrayer. It is a good thing for people to praise what is good—for why would someone not praise what is good? But do not keep this in your thoughts; do not expect it and do not seek it. Indulge yourself in this and you will be totally spoiled. One indulgence leads to another. Increase the frequency of the same deeds and they will become a habit, and you will become a lover of praise. When you come to that point, then not all of your deeds will be praiseworthy, and praise will cease. Because you lack praise from others, you will begin to praise yourself, and this is what the Lord called sounding a trumpet before oneself. This is even worse. The soul then becomes petty, and chases solely after tinsel. Do not expect true good to come from such a soul.

SATURDAY

I Cor. 4:1–5; Matt. 23:1–12

He that is greatest among you shall be your servant (Matt. 23:11). As the Lord tells us, greatness is measured not by birth, not by power, not by the measure of abilities and resources, but by the ability to provide good for others. He who is more tireless and acts more extensively in this is the greatest. Just as the head of a family, once he becomes the head, is sincerely concerned for the whole family, and considers it an honor and advantage to set them all at ease, to arrange that things will be good for everyone—so in a Christian society, he who wants to be the greatest must take on complete care for the Christian comforting of all those in his sphere of existence and in the area of activity which he has chosen for himself. But it is even better to abandon every thought about greatness and take heartfelt care to serve as much as possible for the good of those around you, and then you will be the greatest in the eyes of God, and people will perhaps recognize you as such also. If only all those in high positions would make this law of Christ the law of their conscience, what prosperity and ease would arise immediately among us! But the misfortune is that the majority of them begin quickly to serve themselves and their own interests, and almost always combine this with demands to be served rather than serving others. They soothe their conscience with the fact that official affairs are running well. This is why there are many superiors, but good does not prosper in our midst, and not all good institutions bring forth the good that is expected of them.

FOURTEENTH SUNDAY AFTER PENTECOST
II Cor. 1:21–2:4; Matt. 22:1–14

A king arranged a wedding for his son. He sent once for those who were bidden and sent for them a second time, but because of earthly cares they did not come—one was occupied at home, another with business. A new invitation was made to others, and the wedding chamber was furnished with guests. Among them was found one not dressed for the wedding, and he was therefore cast out. The meaning of this parable is clear: the wedding is the Kingdom of Heaven, the invitation is the preaching of the Gospel, those who refused are those who did not believe at all, and the one who was not dressed for the wedding believed, but did not live according to his faith. Each of us must discern for himself to which category he belongs. That we are bidden is clear, but are we believers? Indeed it is even possible to be among believers, to be called by that name, and completely lack faith. One person does not think at all about faith, as though it did not exist; another knows a little about it and is satisfied; another interprets the Faith in a distorted way; another relates to it with complete animosity. All are considered to be Christians, although they have absolutely nothing which is Christian. If you believe, determine whether your feelings and deeds conform to your faith—these are the garment of the soul, by which God sees you as dressed for the wedding or not. It is possible to know the Faith well and be zealous for it, but in actual life to serve the passions—to dress, that is, in the shameful clothes of a sin-loving soul. Such people are one way in word, but another way in the heart. On their tongue is, "Lord, Lord!" but within they are saying, "Have me excused." Examine yourself, whether you are in the Faith (cf. II Cor. 13:5) and wearing the wedding clothes of the virtues, or wearing the shameful tatters of sins and passions.

MONDAY
Gal. 2:11–16; Mark 5:24–34

The woman with the issue of blood had only to touch the Lord with faith, and power went out of the Lord into her: *Straightway the fountain of her blood was dried up* (Mark 5:29). The issue of blood is an image of the passionate thoughts and intentions that incessantly spring forth from the heart, if it has not yet been cleansed from all sympathy to sin—this is our sinful disease. It is sensed by those who have repented and zealously strive to keep themselves pure not only outwardly, but inwardly as well. Such people see that evil thoughts incessantly proceed from the heart, and they grieve over this and seek healing. But it is not possible to find such healing in oneself or others. It comes from the Lord or, more precisely, it comes when the soul touches the Lord and power goes out of the Lord into the soul. In other words, it comes when tangible contact with the Lord occurs, to which a special warmth and inner burning testifies. When it happens, the soul immediately feels that it *was healed of that plague* (Mark 5:29). This is a great good; but how can it be attained? The woman with the issue of blood pressed toward the Lord and received healing—we too must press toward the Lord, proceeding without laziness by the narrow way of inner and outer spiritual struggles. Everything is narrow for those who go by this way, and the Lord is not in sight. But then suddenly, there is the Lord. And what joy! *The Kingdom of God cometh not with observation* (Luke 17:20).

TUESDAY
Gal. 2:21–3:7; Mark 6:1–7

From whence hath this Man these things? And what wisdom is this which is given unto Him? (Mark 6:2). Thus spoke the people of Nazareth about the Lord, having known His former life of low estate. The same happens with everyone who truly follows the Lord. He who strictly holds to the path of the Lord changes completely once he has labored to overcome all that is not right within himself. His gaze, walk, speech, and behavior—His whole constitution—all bear the mark of a special harmony and dignity, even though he may have come from a lowly background and have no education. Then there is heard: *From whence hath this man these things?* If things bodily and visible are so transformed, what can be said of the inner things of the soul, which are more directly and closely subject to the action of transforming grace, and to which the externals serve only as an expression and consequence? How bright, exact, and definite are his thoughts about everything! How true is his judgment about what exists and happens! His viewpoint on everything is higher than that of philosophers! And his intentions, actions, and undertakings? All is pure and holy, reflecting heavenly brightness. In truth, this is a new person! He did not receive an education, did not attend university lectures, and did not have a good upbringing at all, yet he is most well mannered and wise. Attentiveness toward himself, labor over himself, prayer, and drawing near to God have refashioned everything through God's grace; and no one saw how it happened. That is why the question arises: *From whence hath this man these things?*

WEDNESDAY
Gal. 3:15–22; Mark 6:7–13

When the Lord sent the Holy Apostles to preach, He commanded that they not take anything with them but the clothes on their back, the sandals on their feet, and a staff in their hand. They were to have no cares about anything, and to enter into this work as if everything were fully provided. Indeed, the Apostles were completely provided for, without any external provisions. How was this arranged? Through their complete devotion to the will of God. That is why the Lord arranged for them not to have any need for anything. Their preaching moved the hearts of their listeners, who fed and sheltered them. But the Apostles did not think of this and did not expect anything, committing all to the Lord. That is why they patiently bore any unpleasantness they might have encountered. Their only care was to preach, and their only sorrow was if people would not listen to their preaching. From this came the purity, independence, and great fruitfulness of their preaching. The same is needed today as well, but our infirmity demands external provision, without which we will not take a step. This, however, is not a reproach against our apostles of today. In the beginning they definitely find comfort in being provided for, but then the thought of it disappears from their mind, and through their very labor they are raised up to the state of committing themselves to God. Very likely it is from that moment that their preaching begins to be truly fruitful. Dedication to God is a high level of moral perfection, and people do not reach it immediately, at the moment they understand its value. It comes on its own after one labors on oneself.

THURSDAY
Gal. 3:23–4:5; Mark 6:30–45

And people *ran afoot thither out of all cities ... and came together unto Him* (Mark 6:33), that is, to the Bethsaida desert, where the marvelous satisfying of five thousand with five loaves of bread and two fishes was performed. What drew the people to the Lord? A feeling for the Divine. The Divinity of the Lord, hidden under the cover of human nature, revealed itself in word, deed, gaze, and in all that was visible in the Lord. The manifestations of the Godhead awakened a feeling for the Divine hidden in the heart of the people, and through it drew them to the Lord. No one has power to hold back such a movement toward the Lord, not even the one who feels it, because it is deeper and stronger than all other movements. When the Savior manifested the same Divinity later, it drew people of every tongue under the heavens to Him. It has been the same throughout the entire history of the Church, even to this day. A small sign of the Divine draws people to itself. What can one conclude from this universal experience of our spirit's aspiration for the Divine, which takes place at all times? One can conclude that the source of this experience is the Divine, the supernatural, the Godhead. This aspiration lies at the foundation of our spirit and constitutes its nature, as anyone can see from our intellectual, aesthetic, and practical concerns. But there cannot be lies and deception in nature. Consequently, they do not exist in this aspiration for the Godhead. From this it follows that God and the Divine exist, and that the naturalists, in rejecting what is supernatural, are going against the nature of the human spirit.

FRIDAY
Gal. 4:8–21; Mark 6:45–53

Be of good cheer: it is I; be not afraid (Mark 6:50). Here is the pillar of our hope! Whatever misfortune or sorrow there might be, remember that the Lord is near, and be inspired through courageous patience. As He then suddenly appeared before the Apostles who were in danger on the sea, so will He show His help and protection suddenly to you when you are in danger. He is everywhere and is always ready with His protection. Only stand with Him or before Him in faith, prayer, hope, and devotion to His holy will. Your spirit will be joined to the Lord, and from this comes every good thing. However, this does not mean that there will immediately be dignity, glory, and honor, and other such things. External things might remain as they are, but there will arise a courageous and placid abiding in the order of events which it pleases the Lord to arrange for a person. And this is the main thing that everyone in danger should seek: happiness on the inside, not on the outside. Inner blessedness always exists among those who are in a living union with the Lord.

SATURDAY
I Cor. 4:17–5:5; Matt. 24:1–13

Because iniquity shall abound, the love of many shall wax cold (Matt. 24:12). Love is destroyed by transgressions; the more sins there are, the less love there is. Where all is sin, do not look for love. Therefore, he who seeks the spread of love and the diminishing of the lack of love ought to be concerned with decreasing sin and curtailing the love of sin. This is the true foundation for humanism! Having taken up this work, one must use all means to oppose sin. Outward sins are the fruit of inner sinfulness. Inner sinfulness is rooted in egoism and its offspring. Consequently, humanists need to make it a rule for themselves to suppress egoism by all means. Egoism is suppressed most forcefully by not allowing one's own will. Do not allow yourself to have your own will, and soon you will overcome egoism. On the other hand, no matter what means you want to use against egoism, you will not be able to do anything if you give freedom to your will. Hence it follows that wherever people seek their own little will in all things, they are seeking an expansion of egoism and the drying up of love, and they are seeking greater evil. Yet such is the spirit of the current time—and evil is growing.

FIFTEENTH SUNDAY AFTER PENTECOST
II Cor. 4:6–15; Matt. 22:35–46

The Lord offered the commandment concerning love for God and one's neighbor, and immediately supplemented it with the teaching about His Sonship to God and His Divinity. Why was this? Because true love for God and for people is possible in no other way than by the operation of faith in the Divinity of Christ the Savior—that He is the Incarnate Son of God. Such faith arouses love for God; for how can one not love God, Who has loved us so much, Who did not even spare His Only Begotten Son, but gave Him up for us? Faith brings this love to complete fulfillment, or to what it seeks—and love seeks a living union. To attain this union, one must overcome one's sense of God's justice, which punishes sin. Otherwise it is terrifying to approach God. This feeling is overcome through the conviction that God's righteousness has been propitiated by the death on the Cross of the Son of God [cf. I John 2:2, 4:10; Heb. 2:17]. Such a conviction comes from faith. Consequently, faith opens the path of love for God. This is the first thing. The second thing, faith in the Divinity of the Son of God—Who took flesh, suffered, and was buried for our sake—gives us a model of love for one's neighbor; for it is love when one lays down his life for his beloved. Faith also gives strength for the manifestation of such love. To have such love, one must become a new person instead of an egotistical person—one must become a self-sacrificing person. Only in Christ does a person become a new creature, but we can only be in Christ if we unite with Christ by faith and by a grace-filled rebirth through the Holy Mysteries received with faith. Hence it follows that people without faith who expect at least to maintain good moral conduct do so in vain. Everything must be taken together; it is impossible to divide a man. All of his aspects must be taken care of.

Monday
Gal. 4:28–5:10; Mark 6:54–7:8

The Lord rebukes the Pharisees not for their outward observances and rules of conduct, but for their passionate attachment to them—for limiting themselves to the external worship of God with no concern for what was in their heart. It is impossible to be without externals. The highest internal things require the external as their expression and garment. In reality, internal things are never alone, but are always united with the outer; only in false theories are they separated. But again, it is obvious that externals alone are nothing; their worth comes from the presence of the internal things contained within them. Thus, once the inward ceases to be, the outward might as well not be there. Meanwhile, we have a weakness for outward and visible things, in which the internal is depicted and takes a definite form. And we do so to such an extent that, having fulfilled that which is external, we remain at peace, without even thinking that there might be internal things. And since the inward is harder to attain than the outward, it is quite natural to get stuck on the latter, without striving for the former. What can we do? We must govern ourselves and keep the internal things in mind, always pushing ourselves toward them through the externals, only considering a work to be real when the internal and external are united in it. There is no other way. Attentiveness toward oneself, sobriety, and vigilance are the only levers for raising up our nature, which is corpulent and has a penchant for lowly things. Notice that those who possess the internal never abandon the external, although they attach no special value to it.

Tuesday
Gal. 5:11–21; Mark 7:5–16

There is nothing from without a man, that entering into him can defile him: but the things which come out of him, those are they that defile the man (Mark 7:15). This and similar passages—for example, *But meat commendeth us not to God* (I Cor. 8:8)—are usually cited by those who do not like to fast, supposing that they thereby sufficiently justify the fact that they do not fast according to the rule and custom of the Church. Everyone who is faithful to the Church knows how invalid this excuse is. Fasting decrees that we abstain from some foods not because they are defiled, but because we can more conveniently refine our flesh by this abstinence—something crucial for inner progress. This meaning of the law of fasting is so essential that those who consider some foods to be defiled are numbered among the heretics. For those who are not well-disposed to fasting it is better not to insist on this point, but on the point that fasting is not obligatory, although it is definitely the means for overcoming sinful urges and the strivings of the flesh. There is no way that they can resist on this point. If inner progress is obligatory, then the means by which it is obtained is also obligatory, namely, fasting. Each person's conscience says this to him. In order to soothe their conscience, they assert: I'll compensate for my omission of fasting in another way; or, fasting is harmful for me; or, I'll fast when I want to, but not during the established fasts. However, the first excuse is inappropriate because no one has yet managed to cope with his flesh or to order his inner life properly without fasting. The last excuse is also inappropriate, because the Church is one body, and to separate oneself from others within it means opposing its good order. One can remove oneself from the general customs of the Church only by leaving it; but, while someone is a member of it, he cannot say this or demand that. The second excuse has a shade of validity. Indeed, among the limitations of fasting, the obligation is lifted from those upon whom fasting acts destructively, because the fast was established not to kill the body, but to mortify the passions. But if one were to conscientiously count the true number of such people, it would be seen that they are so few that they do not even count. Only one real reason remains—lack of desire. There is no point in arguing with this. You will not be brought to Paradise against your will. But when you are condemned to hell you will go whether you want to or not—you will be grabbed and thrown there.

WEDNESDAY
Gal. 6:2–10; Mark 7:14–24

From within, out of the heart of men, proceed evil thoughts, adulteries, fornications, murders, thefts, covetousness, wickedness, deceit, lasciviousness, an evil eye, blasphemy, pride, foolishness (Mark 7:21–22). Here common sins are listed; but all the rest also, both large and small, proceed from the heart, and the form in which they proceed are evil thoughts. The first seed of evil falls as a thought to do this or that. Why and how does this occur? Some of these instances can be explained by known laws of the joining and linking of ideas and images, but only some of them. Another, more significant portion comes from the self-propelled irritation of the passions. When a passion lives in the heart, it cannot help but demand satisfaction. This demand is revealed in an urge for something or other; with the urge is united some object or another. From this comes the thought: "Here is what I need to do." Here the same thing happens as, for example, when one is hungry: feeling hunger, one feels an urge for food; with the urge comes the thought of the food itself; from this follows finding something and eating it. The third and, perhaps, largest portion proceeds from the unclean powers. The air is filled with them; they dart around people in packs. Each, according to what kind of demon it is, spreads its influence around itself to people with whom it comes into contact. Evil flies from them like sparks from a red hot iron. Where it is readily accepted, a spark is instilled, and with it the thought of an evil deed. Only by this can one explain why evil thoughts arise, for unknown reasons, in the midst of activities which decisively are not related to them. But this variety of reasons does not require a variety of ways to react to evil thoughts. There is one law: an evil thought has come—cast it out and the matter is finished. If you do not cast it out the first minute, it will be harder the second minute, and yet harder the third minute; and then you will not even notice how sympathy, desire, and the decision will be born; then the means will appear ... and a sinful act is at hand. The first opposition to evil thoughts is sobriety and prayerful vigilance.

THURSDAY
Eph. 1:1–9; Mark 7:24–30

What moved the Syro-Phoenician woman to come to the Lord and be so persistent in her petition? The convictions that had been formed within her. She was convinced that the Savior had the power to heal her daughter, and she came to Him. She was convinced that He would not leave her petition without fulfillment, and she would not stop asking. Convictions are the sum of one's whole life, upbringing, current thinking, impressions from one's surroundings and the teachings one has received, and various incidents and activities in life. One's mind works under the influence of all this, and arrives at certain convictions. Meanwhile, one must keep in mind that God's truth is everywhere, and it presses into the soul of man from everywhere. Truth lies in the heart of man. God's truth is imprinted in all creatures. God's truth is in the customs and dispositions of man and it is also in his teachings to a greater or lesser degree. But falsehood is everywhere as well. He who is of the truth gathers the truth, and is full of true, saving convictions, whereas he who is not of the truth gathers lies and is full of false convictions and fatal delusions. Whether a person is of the truth or not of the truth—let each one examine for himself; meanwhile, God's judgment awaits everyone....

FRIDAY
Eph. 1:7–17; Mark 8:1–10

Having filled four thousand with seven loaves of bread, the Lord *straightway ... entered into a ship, and came into the parts of*

THOUGHTS FOR EACH DAY OF THE YEAR

Dalmanutha (Mark 8:10), as if nothing special had been done. Such is the true doing of good—to do it continually, not paying attention to what has been done and, always forgetting what is past, to stretch forward to what is ahead. This comes naturally for those who are filled with goodness. Just as a strong man lifts heavy weights without noticing, while a weak man who has lifted a small weight cannot seem to forget it, so one who is strong in goodness does every good without strain, whenever the occasion arises, while one who is weak in goodness cannot manage without straining. The good is memorable to him, and he keeps glancing at it and looking back. A good heart craves to do good, and is not satisfied until it has done good in abundance, as a man is not satisfied until he has eaten his fill. While hunger is felt, dinner is remembered, but when the hunger has been satisfied, all is forgotten. So it is with a truly good person: a good deed is remembered before it is completed, but once it is done, it is forgotten.

SATURDAY
I Cor. 10:23–28; Matt. 24:34–44

Watch therefore; for ye know not what hour your Lord doth come (Matt. 24:42). To be vigilant does not mean to sit with your arms folded, but rather to keep in mind that the Lord will come suddenly, and so to behave and conduct your affairs so as to be ready to meet Him at any instant, not fearing reproach and condemnation. How is one to do this? Very simply. Walk in the commandments without breaking a single one. And if it happens that you break one, immediately cleanse yourself through repentance and by fulfilling what needs to be done. Then everything in you will be clean. Do not leave sin on your soul for even a minute; immediately repent, weep in your heart, and run to your spiritual father to confess and receive absolution, and then get down to business again, in accordance with God's commandments. If you set out zealously to have your life in good order, it soon will be; just do not remain in a fall for long. In such a case falls will become ever rarer and will eventually cease completely, with the help of the all-healing grace of God. Then the joyful assurance will dwell in you that you will not meet the Lord unprepared.

Sixteenth Sunday after Pentecost
(II Cor. 6:1–10; Matt. 25:14–30)

The parable about the talents offers the thought that life is a time for trading. That means that it is necessary to hasten to use this time as a person would hurry to a market to bargain for what he can. Even if one has only brought bast shoes, or only bast,[28] he does not sit with his arms folded, but contrives to call over buyers to sell what he has and then buy what he needs for himself. No one who has received life from the Lord can say that he does not have a single talent—everyone has something, and not just one thing. Everyone, therefore, has something with which to trade and make a profit. Do not look around and calculate what others have received, but take a good look at yourself and determine more precisely what lies within you and what you can gain for what you have, and then act according to this plan without laziness. At the Judgment you will not be asked why you did not gain ten talents if you had only one, and you will not even be asked why you gained only one talent on your one, but you will be told that you gained a talent, half a talent, or a tenth of its worth. And there will be a reward—not because you received the talents, but because you gained. There will be nothing with which to justify yourself—not with being a member of the nobility, or with poverty, or with a lack of education.

---

[28] Bast is tree-bark, from which shoes and other items are woven. Thus St. Theophan means here very inexpensive, unsophisticated items.—Trans.

What has not been given to you will not be demanded of you. But you had hands and feet. You will be asked, what did you gain with them? You had a tongue—what did you gain with it? In this way the inequalities of earthly states will be leveled out at God's Judgment.

MONDAY
Eph. 1:22–2:3; Mark 10:46–52

The blind man of Jericho raised his voice when he learned that the Lord was walking by. His cry reached the Lord. Nothing surrounding the Lord could interfere with His hearing it, and the Lord called the blind man over and restored his sight. At every time and in every place the Lord does not just walk by, but is there; He governs the whole world. As human thinking would have it, this means that He has many cares; furthermore, multitudes of angels surround Him with their doxologies. But if you are able to raise your voice like the blind man of Jericho, nothing will stop your cry from reaching the Lord; He will hear and fulfill your petition. It does not depend on the Lord; He Himself is near, and everything you need is already prepared with Him—it is you who are holding things up. Succeed in raising your voice to the measure of the Lord's hearing, and you will immediately receive everything. What then is this measure? Faith, hope, and devotion to God's will. But even these have their own measures. What then should these measures be? Ask someone who has prayed and received what he requested. He will say to you, "I prayed about this and that, and I received according to my request. Now I need this and that and I've been praying and haven't received it, and I know why: because I cannot in any way ascend to the measure of prayer that I had earlier." It turns out that it is impossible to determine this measure with literal precision. Only one thing is definitely true: that the matter depends on us, and not on the Lord. As soon as you reach the point where you are capable of receiving, you will unquestionably receive.

TUESDAY
Eph. 2:19–3:7; Mark 11:11–23

The fig tree covered with leaves was splendid in appearance, but was not honored with approval by the Lord because there was no fruit on it, and there was no fruit because there was no inner fruit-bearing power. How many such fig trees there are in the moral sense! In appearance all is proper, but on the inside there is nothing. They are steady, honorable, and fulfill all that is Christian, but they do not have the spirit of life in Christ Jesus. That is why they do not have living fruit. What is in them only seems to be fruit, but it is not. In what lies the spirit of life in Christ Jesus? To this we say: one part is from the Lord, and the other is from us. What is from the Lord is essentially a fruit-bearing spiritual power, but from us there is only a receiver for this power. Concern yourself more with the latter. The root of this is the feeling that you are perishing, and that if it were not for the Lord, you would perish. From this you will have a heart that is broken and humbled, in everything you do throughout your life. Furthermore, since the future is unknown, since there are many enemies and you can stumble every moment, then salvation is effectuated in fear and trembling, along with the unceasing cry: "By the judgments which Thou knowest, save me!" Woe unto him who rests on something other than the Lord; woe unto him who has worked for something other than the Lord! Ask yourself, you who labor in works which are considered God-pleasing: "For whom are you working?" If your conscience boldly answers, "Only for the Lord"—it is good; but if not, you are building a house upon sand. These are several indications of a fertile inner spirit. You can understand other things according to this.

WEDNESDAY
Eph. 3:8–21; Mark 11:23–26

The Lord said that, if you do not forgive others' trespasses against you, then your Heavenly Father will not forgive you your trespasses. Who does not forgive others? A righteous person, or rather one who considers himself righteous. To such a person nothing remains other than to judge, pronounce sentences, and demand the punishment of the guilty. Does a man who feels sinful have any time for [considering the sins of] others? Would his tongue dare to judge another and demand satisfaction from him, when his own conscience unceasingly convicts him and unceasingly threatens him with God's righteous judgment? So, is it better to sin than to be self-righteous? No—be zealous for righteousness in every way; but with all of your righteousness, recognize that you are an unprofitable servant, and recognize this with undivided thought, that is, not with the thought of your unworthiness in the foreground, while the feeling of righteousness hides in the background. Rather, preserve a full awareness and sense of yourself as unprofitable. When you attain this, (and it takes a while to get there, for it is not acquired suddenly), then no matter how your brother trespasses against you, you will not call him to account, because your conscience will keep repeating, "You deserve more than this; this is not enough for you." Then you will forgive him; and having forgiven, you yourself will be made worthy of forgiveness. So, for your whole life, let there be forgiveness after forgiveness, and at the Judgment all shall be forgiven you.

THURSDAY
Eph. 4:14–19; Mark 11:27–33

The Savior proved that He was sent from heaven using the testimony of John the Forerunner. But [the leaders of the Jews] were silent, for there was nothing to say to the contrary, yet they did not believe. Another time He proved the same thing through His deeds, and they thought up a new trick: [*He casteth out devils*] *by the prince of the devils* (Matt. 9:34; Mark 3:22). When this trick was exposed as completely inapplicable, they were again silent, but nevertheless did not believe. Thus unbelievers never believe, no matter what you tell them and how convincingly you prove the truth. They cannot say anything to the contrary, while they nevertheless do not believe. One might say that their mind is paralyzed; after all, they reason sensibly about other things. Only when the issue touches upon faith do they become confused in their concepts and words. They also become confused when they present their opinions as a substitute for the tenets of the Faith given by God. Here their doubt raises such a buttress that it is like a mighty cliff. If you hear their entire theory through, you will see that a child could figure out that this is a spider's web; but they do not see it. What unfathomable blindness! One can explain the obstinacy of unbelievers as their not wanting to believe, but where does this lack of desire come from? Why in this case does it get such power that it makes a sensible man consciously cling to an illogical way of thinking? This is darkness. Is it not from the father of darkness?

FRIDAY

Eph. 4:17–25; Mark 12:1–12

The Old Testament Church and God's care for it is depicted in the parable about the vineyard. The New Testament Church succeeded the Old, and so this parable can be applied to it as well. Since each Christian is also a living church of God, it can refer to him as well. The latter is more needful for us. What is the vineyard? It is the soul that has received remission of sins, the grace of rebirth, the gift of the Holy Spirit as a promise of the inheritance of the eternal Kingdom, the word of God, the

THOUGHTS FOR EACH DAY OF THE YEAR

Holy Mysteries, and a guardian angel. Who are the husbandmen? Consciousness and freedom. They receive the gifts and give a commitment to cultivate them and bear fruit to the Lord. Who are the careless husbandmen? Those who want to use the advantages of being a Christian as befits the outward order of their lives, but do not bring forth worthy spiritual fruits for the Lord. Who are those sent by the Lord? The conscience and the fear of God, the word of God, and teachers and pastors, by whom the Lord wants to grant understanding to the careless. Those who do not want to change themselves do not heed them. Some drive them away and try to muffle their voice. Others even start to be at enmity against the Lord Himself, when they reject faith in Him in various forms. In the end, they will be miserably destroyed (cf. Matt. 21:41).

SATURDAY

I Cor. 14:20–25; Matt. 25:1–13

The parable of the ten virgins has been read. St. Macarius the Great portrays the meaning of it thus: "The five prudent and vigilant virgins ... had taken in the vessel of their heart the oil of the supernatural grace of the Spirit—a thing not conformable to their nature. For this reason they were able to enter together with the Bridegroom into the heavenly bridal chamber. The other, foolish ones, however, content with their own nature, did not watch nor did they betake themselves to receive the oil of gladness in their vessels. But still in the flesh they fell into a deep sleep through negligence, inattentiveness, laziness, and ignorance, or even through considering themselves justified. Because of this they were excluded from the bridal chamber of the Kingdom because they were unable to please the Heavenly Bridegroom. Bound by ties of the world and earthly love, they did not offer all their love and devotion to the Heavenly Spouse, nor did they carry with them the oil. But the souls who seek the sanctification of the Spirit, which is a thing that lies beyond natural power, are completely bound with their whole love to the Lord. There they walk; there they pray; there they focus their thoughts, ignoring all other things. For this reason they are considered worthy to receive the oil of Divine grace.... But other souls, who remain on the level of their own nature, crawl along the ground with their earthly thoughts. They think only in a human way. Their mind lives only on the earthly level. And still they are convinced in their own thought that they look to the Bridegroom and that they are adorned with the perfections of a carnal justification. But in reality they have not been born of the Spirit from above and have not accepted the oil of gladness."[29]

SUNDAY BEFORE THE EXALTATION OF THE CROSS
Gal. 6:11–18; John 3:13–17

As Moses lifted up the serpent in the wilderness, even so must the Son of man be lifted up: That whosoever believeth in Him should not perish, but have eternal life (John 3:14–15). Faith in the Son of God, crucified in the flesh for our sake, is *the power of God unto salvation* (Rom. 1:16). It is the living source of vivifying moral aspirations and dispositions—the receptacle of the abundant grace of the Holy Spirit, which always abides in the heart, and of timely secret inspirations sent from above at the hour of need. Faith combines one's convictions, which attract God's goodwill, with power from above. Both of these are what make up the possession of eternal life. While this life is kept intact, a Christian is unyielding, because by cleaving to the Lord, he is one in spirit with the Lord, and nothing can overcome the Lord. Why do people fall? From weakening of faith. If Christian convictions weaken, moral energy weakens as well. To the degree of this

[29] St. Macarius the Great, *The Fifty Spiritual Homilies and the Great Letter,* trans. George A. Maloney (New York: Paulist Press, 1992), Homily 4.6, pp. 52–53.—ED.

weakening, grace is crowded out of the heart, and evil urges raise their head. An inclination toward these urges comes at a convenient hour, and there is a fall. Be a watchful guardian of the Faith in everything it encompasses, and you will not fall. In this sense St. John says that *whosoever is born of God doth not commit sin* (I John 3:9).

MONDAY
Eph. 4:25–32; Luke 3:19–22

Herod is an image of self-love, irritated by his troubled conscience, and reproached by the truth. And self-love seeks to escape this unpleasantness through violence. John the Forerunner is an image of the truth persecuted by self-love, when this self-love possesses the means to do this. No matter how one softens the truth with all the condescension and turns of speech that tender love can invent, not desiring to injure or wound another's heart, the face of truth will nevertheless appear before the eyes of the conscience, and stir up a tempest of denunciation within. Selfishness is nearsighted and cannot see that the denunciation is not coming from without but from within, and it rises up with all of its strength against the external accuser. By blocking his lips, this selfishness hopes to silence the inner voice as well. It does not succeed, however, because it does not direct its concern in the right direction. One must appease the conscience. Then, no matter how many external accusers there are, they will not disturb inner peace, but will, on the contrary, only deepen it, compelling one to gather calming convictions within: faith in the crucified Lord, sincerity of repentance and confession, and firmness in the resolution to do nothing against one's conscience. One must look in this direction, and not keep putting all Johns into prison; for the word of God's truth walks everywhere upon the earth, and each one is an accusing John to you.

TUESDAY
Eph. 5:20–26; Luke 3:23–4:1

The honorable Cross is brought out for veneration in the middle of Great Lent in order to inspire those who toil in fasting to patiently bear to the end the yoke they have taken. Why is this also done in September? Is it accidental? But there are no accidents for the Providential Wisdom that arranges all things. This is why: The harvest is taken from the field in September—at least, here [in Russia]. And so, in order that some Christians might not feel too satisfied and say, *Soul, thou hast much goods laid up for many years; take thine ease, eat, drink, and be merry!* (Luke 12:19), and so that others might not become fainthearted because of scarcity, the elevated Cross is brought before all. It reminds the former that the support of well-being is not in possessions, but in their bearing of the cross in a Christian, inner way, if God's goodness should bring external plenitude; and it inspires the latter to possess their souls in patience, through the certainty that they will go from the cross directly to heaven. Therefore, may some endure, knowing that they are traveling a smooth path to the Heavenly Kingdom; and may the others enjoy outward comforts with fear, not sealing the entrance to heaven against themselves.

WEDNESDAY
Eph. 5:25–33; Luke 4:1–15

The devil approaches the God-man with temptations. Who among men is free of them? He who goes according to the will of the evil one does not experience attacks, but is simply turned more and more toward evil. As soon as one begins to come to himself and intends to begin a new life according to God's will, the entire satanic realm immediately enters into action. They hasten to scatter the good thoughts and intentions of the penitent in any way they can. If they do not manage to turn him aside, they attempt to hinder his good repentance and confession. If they do not manage to do that, they contrive to sow tares amidst the fruits of repentance and disrupt his labors of cleansing the heart. If they do not succeed in suggesting evil, they attempt to distort the truth. If they are repulsed inwardly they attack outwardly, and so on, until the end of one's life. They do not even let one die in peace, and even after death they pursue the soul, until it escapes the aerial expanse where they hover and have their haunts. You ask, "What should we do? It's dismal and terrifying!" For a believer there is nothing frightening here, because demons only bustle around a God-fearing man, but do not have any power at all. A sober man of prayer shoots arrows against them, and they stay far away from him, not daring to approach, and fearing the defeat that they have already experienced. If they succeed in something, it is due to our blundering. We slacken our attention or allow ourselves to be distracted by their phantoms, and they are right there and disturb us more boldly. If you do not come to your senses in time, they will whirl you about; but if a soul does come to its senses, they again recoil and spy from afar to see whether it is possible to approach again somehow. So be sober, watch, and pray—and the enemies will do nothing to you.

THURSDAY
Eph. 5:33–6:9; Luke 4:16–22

The Lord not only came *to preach the acceptable year* (Luke 4:19), but He brought it as well. Where is it? In the souls of believers. The earth will never become Paradise under the current state of affairs; but it is and will be an arena of preparation for the heavenly life. The rudiments of heavenly life are placed in the soul and the possibility for this lies in God's grace, while grace was brought by our Lord Jesus Christ—Who brought, consequently, the acceptable year for souls. He who listens to the Lord and fulfills all that is commanded by Him receives grace, and with its power enjoys the acceptable year within himself. This truly occurs in all who sincerely believe and act according to faith. You will not fill your soul with this "acceptableness" by thinking; you must act, and it will enter in on its own. There might not be any outer peace whatever, just inner peace, yet it cannot be separated from Christ. But it always happens that as soon as inner peace is established, outer disturbances are neither bitter nor heavy. Consequently, the acceptable year is there even in this respect—it only seems like a cold winter on the outside.

FRIDAY

Eph. 6:18–24; Luke 4:22–30

The people of Nazareth marveled at the word of the Lord, but nevertheless they did not believe: envy prevented them, as the Lord Himself revealed. Every passion opposes truth and goodness, but envy does so most of all, because falsehood and spite make up its essence. This passion is the most unjust and poisonous, both for the one who bears it and for the one against whom it is directed. It occurs on a small scale with everyone when someone equal or inferior gets the upper hand. Egoism becomes irritated, and envy begins to gnaw away at the heart. This is not so tormenting if the road is still open to you; but when it is blocked off, especially by the one you already envy, then envy's aggression is unstoppable, and peace is impossible. Envy demands the overthrow of one's enemy from his place at the summit, and will not rest content until it somehow attains this, or until it destroys the envier. Good natured, well-wishing people, whose kindly sentiments prevail over egotistical ones, do not suffer from envy. This is also the way for any person tormented by envy to extinguish it. You must hasten to inspire goodwill, especially toward the one whom you envy, and manifest it in deed. Then envy will immediately abate. If you repeat this several times, with God's help it will entirely subside. But if you leave it the way it is, if you do not overcome yourself and force yourself to do good to the one you envy, it will torment you, dry you up, and send you to your grave.

<h2 style="text-align:center">SATURDAY</h2>
I Cor. 15:39–45; Luke 4:31–36

If ye believe not that I am He, ye shall die in your sins (John 8:24). *There is none other name under heaven, given among men, whereby we must be saved* (Acts 4:12). We must receive remission of sins, and we can receive it in no other way than by faith in the Son of God, Who was crucified in the flesh for our sake—but on the condition that we do not desire to indulge in sinful habits and deeds. For when we sin, we have only Him as an intercessor before the Father. He who has given his word to abstain from sins must accept the helping grace of the Most Holy Spirit. However, this grace descended to the earth after the Lord ascended to sit at the right hand of God the Father, and is only given to those who believe in this marvelous economy of our salvation, and who with this faith approach the Divine Mysteries—the Mysteries which were established in the Holy Church of the Lord through the Apostles. Thus, he who does not believe in the Lord as He is, cannot be pure of sins. Because he has not been cleansed of sins he shall die in them, and shall be judged of them according to their weightiness. If someone wants to do a good deed for someone that is of eternal value, guide him in faith in the Lord, in true faith, not allowing philosophizing or wavering. Those who directly or indirectly impair faith in the Lord must be considered everlasting evildoers, for they wreak an evil that nothing can correct, and its power stretches to all eternity. Their ignorance does not justify them, for how can they not know the truth that is known to the whole world? Their opposing beliefs do not justify them, for if you should only start strictly testing them you would immediately shake their strength; a person cannot rely on anything other than faith in the Lord. Those who do not properly examine the foundations, faith, and teachings to which they adhere, go astray in faith. An exact investigation of the conditions for salvation will lead to the conviction that they can only be met through God Incarnate, Who died on the Cross and sent the Holy Spirit down to the earth. In this lies the essence of the Christian Faith. He who sincerely believes this way will not die in his sins, for he bears within himself the power which brings forgiveness. The unbeliever is already condemned, for he bears this condemnation within himself.

EIGHTEENTH SUNDAY AFTER PENTECOST
II Cor. 9:6–11; Luke 5:1–11

The fishermen toiled for an entire night and caught nothing. But when the Lord entered their ship and, after preaching, commanded them to cast their net, they caught so many that they could not pull them out, and the net broke. This is an image of all work done without God's help, and of work done with God's help. When someone works, wanting to achieve something through his strength alone, everything falls apart. But when the Lord draws near to him, one good thing after another flows in. In the spiritual-moral sense, the impossibility of success without the Lord is tangibly evident: *Without Me ye can do nothing* (John 15:5), said the Lord. And this law acts in all things. Just as a branch that is not grafted onto a tree not only does not bear fruit, but dries up and loses its life as well, neither can people bring forth fruits of truth valuable for eternal life if they are not in living communion with the Lord. They might sometimes have some good, but it is good in appearance. In reality it is of poor quality, like a wild apple that appears red but is sour to the taste. It is also tangibly clear in an external, worldly sense: someone struggles and struggles, but it all comes to no good. When God's blessing descends, you do not even know where everything comes from. Those who are attentive toward themselves and the paths of life know these truths from experience.

MONDAY
Phil. 1:1–7; Luke 4:37–44

I must preach the Kingdom of God to other cities also: for therefore am I sent (Luke 4:43). Our priesthood needs to take "for therefore am I sent" as an immutable law. The Apostle commanded them, in the person of St. Timothy, to *be instant in season, out of season; reprove, rebuke, exhort* (II Tim. 4:2). The Lord and the Holy Spirit, Who filled the Apostles on the day of Pentecost, brought the truth to the earth, and the truth walks the earth. Its transmitters are the mouths of God's priests. If any priest closes his mouth, he blocks off the path to the truth, which demands to enter the souls of believers. That is why the souls of believers grow weary, when they do not receive the truth. The priests themselves must feel weariness, since the truth, not receiving an exit, burdens them. Relieve yourself of this weight, priest of God. Pour forth streams of Divine words unto your own joy and to the enlivening of the souls entrusted to you. If you see that you yourself do not have the truth, get it: it is in the Holy Scriptures. Then, filling yourself with it, pass it on to your spiritual children. Just do not be silent. Preach, for it is unto this that you have been called.

TUESDAY
Phil. 1:8–14; Luke 5:12–16

The leper fell down before the Lord and besought Him: *Lord, if Thou wilt, Thou canst make me clean. The Lord said: I will: be thou clean. And immediately the leprosy departed from him* (Luke 5:12). So also does every moral leprosy immediately depart as soon as one falls down before the Lord with faith, repentance, and Confession—it truly departs and loses all power over him. Why does the leprosy sometimes return again? For the same reason that bodily diseases return. One who has recovered is told, "Do not eat that, do not drink this, do not go there." If he does not obey, the disease again flares up. So it is in the spiritual life. One must be sober and vigilant, and must pray—then the disease of sin will not return. If you are not attentive toward yourself, if you allow yourself to see, hear, say, and do everything indiscriminately, how can sin not flare up and take power once again? The Lord charged the leper to fulfill all according to the law. This means that after Confession one must receive a penance and faithfully fulfill it; within it is concealed great preventive strength. But why do some say: "This sinful habit has overcome me, I cannot manage myself"? Either because repentance and Confession were not complete, or because after making precautionary changes they adhere only weakly to them, or indulge themselves. They want to do everything without toil and self-coercion, and are laughed at by the enemy. Resolve to stand unto death and show this resolve in deed, and you will see what power there is in this. It is true that in every insurmountable passion that appears, the enemy is mastering one's soul, but this is no justification; for he immediately flees as soon as you produce an inner change with God's help.

WEDNESDAY
Phil. 1:12–20; Luke 5:33–39

It is unbecoming for the children of the bridechamber to fast while the bridegroom is with them, said the Lord, and thus He pronounced the law that even with virtues and spiritual endeavors everything has its place and time. And this is so crucial that an untimely and inappropriate deed loses its value, either entirely, or in part. The Lord arranged everything in visible nature with measure, weight, and number. He also wants everything in the moral realm to be decent and in order (cf. I Cor. 14:40). Inner decency consists in a joining of each virtue with all the virtues in conjunction, or a harmony of virtues, so that none stand out needlessly, but all are in accord, like voices in a choir. Outward decency gives each deed its place, time, and other connections. When all of this is properly arranged, it is like a beautiful lady dressed in beautiful clothes. Virtue which is decent both inwardly and outwardly is desirable. It is Christian good sense that makes it this way. With elders it is discernment, acquired through experience and the sensible examination of the Lives of saints in the light of the word of God.

THURSDAY
Phil 1:20–27; Luke 6:12–19

And He continued all night in prayer to God (Luke 6:12). Here is the foundation and beginning of Christian All-night Vigils. Prayerful ardor chases away sleep, and exhilaration of the spirit does not allow one to notice the passing of time. True men of prayer do not notice this; it seems to them that they had just begun to pray, and meanwhile day has already appeared. But until one reaches such perfection, one must take on the labor of vigils. Solitaries have borne this and continue to bear it. Cenobites too have borne this and continue to bear it. Reverent and God-fearing lay people have borne this and continue to bear it. But although vigil comes with difficulty, its fruit remains in the soul, directly and constantly present—tranquility of soul and contrition, along with the weakening and exhaustion of the body. It is a state very valuable for those who are zealous about prospering in the spirit! That is why in places where vigils are established (on Athos), they do not want to give them up. Everyone acknowledges how difficult it is, but no one has a desire to rescind this order of things, for the sake of the profit which the soul receives from vigils. Sleep, more than anything, relaxes and feeds the flesh; vigils, more than anything, humble it. One who has enough sleep is burdened by spiritual deeds and is cold toward them. He who is vigilant is quick in movement like a gazelle, and burns in spirit. If the flesh, like a slave, must be taught to be good, there is no better way to succeed in this than through frequent vigils. Here the flesh fully feels the power of the spirit over it and learns to submit to it, while the spirit acquires the habit of reigning over the flesh.

FRIDAY
Phil. 1:27–2:4; Luke 6:17–23

The Lord blesses the poor, those who hunger and weep, and the persecuted, under the condition that it is all for the sake of the Son of man. This means that He blesses a life which is surrounded by every kind of need and deprivation. According to this saying, pleasures, ease, and esteem are not something good—and indeed, this is the way it is. But while a person finds rest in these things, he does not realize this. Only when he frees himself from their spell does he see that they are not good things of themselves, but only phantoms. A soul cannot do without consolations, but these should not be of the senses. It cannot do without treasures, but these should not of gold and silver, not in luxurious houses and clothes, and not in outward plenitude. It cannot get by without honor, but this lies not in people's servile bows. There are other consolations, other kinds of pleasure, and other kinds of honor, but these are spiritual, akin to the soul. He who finds them does not want the outward ones. Not only does he not want them, but he scorns and hates them, because they obstruct the spiritual and do not allow one to see it. They keep a soul in darkness, drunkenness, and phantoms. This is why such people with all their soul prefer poverty, sorrow, and obscurity, and they feel good amidst them, as though behind some safe enclosure against the spell of the deceptions of the world. What about those people who have all these [treasures of the world] without trying? They should relate to all of these things, according to the word of the Holy Apostle, as one who possesses not (cf. I Cor. 7:30).

SATURDAY
I Cor. 15:58–16:3; Luke 5:17–26

But that ye may know that the Son of man hath power on earth to forgive sins (He said unto the sick of the palsy) I say unto thee, Arise, and take up thy couch, and go into thine house (Luke 5:24). Remission of sins is an inner, spiritual miracle. Healing from paralysis is an outward miracle—a natural action of God upon the world, something physical. Through this event the influx of God's power is proven and confirmed, both in the spiritual realm and in the physical world. The purpose of the physical miracle was to bring about the spiritual one, for in the spiritual lies the goal of everything. The Lord does not coerce one's freedom, but gives understanding, inspires, and amazes. One of the best means for this is an outward miracle. The miracle began at the time that man was created as a rational creature, directed by freedom. This connection is so essential, that those who reject the supernatural action of God in the world also reject the freedom of man, along with the recognition that the latter must necessarily call forth the former. On the other hand, those who confess the truth of God's influence in the world beyond the natural flow of phenomena can say boldly: we feel free. The recognition of freedom is as strong and irresistible as the recognition of one's existence. Freedom urgently demands the direct providential actions of God; consequently, the acknowledgment of these actions stands as firmly as the recognition of freedom.

NINETEENTH SUNDAY AFTER PENTECOST
II Cor. 11:31–12:9; Luke 6:31–36

The fundamental, original commandment is: Love! It is a small word, but it expresses an all-encompassing thing. It is easy to say that you must love, but it is not easy to attain love to the necessary degree. It is also not exactly clear how to attain it. This is why the Savior surrounds this commandment with other explanatory rules: *Love thy neighbor as thyself* (Matt. 19:19, 22:39; Mark 12:31), and, *As ye would that men should do to you, do ye also to them likewise* (Luke 6:31). Here is shown a degree of love that one can call boundless; for is there any limit to one's love for oneself? And is there any good which one would not want for himself from others? However, this injunction is not impossible to fulfill. The matter depends upon having perfect compassion toward others, in order to fully transfer their feelings to yourself, to feel the way they feel. When this occurs, there will be no need to point out what you must do for others in a given situation: your heart will show you. Just take care to maintain compassion. Otherwise egoism will immediately approach and return you to yourself and confine you within yourself. Then you will not lift a finger for the sake of someone else, and will not look at him, though he might be dying. When the Lord says, *Love thy neighbor as thyself,* He means that our neighbor instead of our own selves should be within us, that is, in our heart. If our "I" remains there as before, we cannot expect anything good to come of it.

MONDAY
Phil. 2:12–16; Luke 6:24–30

Woe to those who are rich, who are full, who laugh, and who are praised. But good shall come to those who endure every wrongful accusation, beating, robbery, or imposed hardship. This is completely opposite to what people usually think and feel! The thoughts of God are as far from human thoughts as heaven is from the earth. How else could it be? We are in exile, and it is not remarkable for those in exile to be offended and insulted. We are under a penance, and the penance consists of deprivations and labors. We are sick, and bitter medicines are most useful for the sick. The Savior Himself did not have a place to lay His head for His whole life, and He finished His life on the Cross. Why should his followers have a better lot? The spirit of Christ is the spirit of preparedness to suffer and good-naturedly bear all that is sorrowful. Comfort, conceit, splendor, and ease are all foreign to its strivings and tastes. Its path lies in the fruitless, cheerless desert. Its model is the forty-year wandering of the Israelites in the desert. Who follows this path? Anyone who sees Canaan beyond the desert, overflowing with milk and honey. During his wandering he too receives manna—however, not from the earth, but from heaven; not bodily, but spiritually. All glory is within.

TUESDAY
Phil. 2:17–23; Luke 6:37–45

Judge not, forgive, give…. It seems like nothing but expenses, without any profit. But behold what is promised: if you do not condemn, you will not be condemned; if you forgive, you will be forgiven; if you give, you will be given to. Right now the profit is not visible, but it will undoubtedly come for one who makes these expenditures from the heart. It will come precisely at that time when he needs exoneration and forgiveness the most. How he will rejoice when he is suddenly made worthy to receive such good gifts as if for nothing! And, on the other hand, how another will sorrow and grieve because he did not know how to manage his property profitably! He would now forgive everything and give away everything, but it is too late: everything has its time. Not everyone pursues only the kind of profit that comes directly into his hands almost immediately after the expenditure.[30] A Russian proverb says, "Throw bread and salt behind you, and you will find it in front of you." The actions in the above-mentioned cases really are like throwing something, but in these cases they

---

[30] That is, some people hold out for the greater gain of a long-term investment.—ED.

are not thrown underfoot to be trampled, but into the hands of God. These hands are true, and sure to return what they receive. Just add faith and hope.

WEDNESDAY
Phil. 2:24–30; Luke 6:46–7:1

Why call ye Me, Lord, Lord, and do not the things which I say? (Luke 6:46). Why do they call Him Lord, but do not do the Lord's will—that is, why do they not acknowledge His lordship in their works? Because they only call with their tongue, and not with their heart. If their heart were to utter: "Lord, Thou art my Lord," then complete readiness would abide therein to submit to the One Whom they confess as their Lord. But since this is not the case, their deeds do not match their tongues; whereas, deeds always match the heart. Well, what then—is there no use in calling: "Lord, Lord"? No, that's not it. But it is necessary to make the external word match the inner word, which is the feeling and disposition of the heart. Sit and reflect upon the Lord and upon yourself: what is the Lord and what are you? Think about what the Lord has done and still does for you, why you live, and how it will end. You will immediately come to the conviction that there is no other way than to steadfastly fulfill the Lord's entire will. There is no other path for us. This conviction gives birth to a readiness to fulfill in deed what is expressed by the word "Lord." With such readiness a need for help from above will be awakened, and from it the prayer: "Lord, Lord! Help me and give me strength to walk in Thy will." And this call will be pleasing to the Lord.

THURSDAY
Phil. 3:1–8; Luke 7:17–30

St. John the Forerunner sends his disciples to ask the Lord if He is the One Who should come or whether they should they look for another. He does not ask this for himself but for his disciples, for he knew precisely Who Jesus Christ was, being informed of this from heaven. The disciples sought an answer to this question not out of empty inquisitiveness, but out of a sincere desire to know the truth. To such as these there is no need to say much; the Lord did not speak, but only indicated what had been accomplished by Him at that time. Divine works witnessed to His Divinity. It was so obvious, that the questioners no longer questioned. This is the way it always is. The power of God lives in the Church; a sincere seeker of the truth immediately feels it and is sure of this truth. This sureness through experience puts an end to all questions and sets one completely at ease. For someone who does not want to believe and, having lost his faith, begins to seek in the Church and in Christianity not the foundations of the Faith, but grounds to justify his unbelief, no signs are satisfactory. He considers his unbelief well grounded, although its foundations are petty and insignificant. This is what his heart wants, and therefore it is tolerable.

Friday
Phil. 3:8–19; Luke 7:31–35

Whereunto then shall I liken the men of this generation (Luke 7:31), that is, unbelievers? If the Lord poses this question as if in perplexity, is it not even more appropriate for us to be perplexed by acts of unbelief? One might ask: how can people go against something that is obvious in every respect? And yet they do. The fact that Satan resists is not surprising—such is his name: "the opponent of truth and goodness. He clearly sees that God exists, that God will judge him and condemn him, and that death is already prepared for him, but he is nevertheless defiant—and not for the sake of anything except evil, and consequently, for greater ruin to himself. Are not unbelievers being controlled by this spirit of fighting against God? At least according to the understanding we have of the soul and its operations, unbelief—given the obviousness of the foundations of faith—is as inexplicable as a sinner's slavery to sin after he has clearly seen that sin is destroying him. And here is another contradiction! Only unbelievers and lovers of the passions deny the existence of Satan and the unclean spirits. Those who should stand up for them most of all, totally deny them. Is it not from them [the demons] that this teaching comes? The demons, who are of the darkness, love the darkness, and teach people to say that they do not exist, and that in moral life things takes shape by themselves, without the demons' snares and deceit.

SATURDAY
II Cor. 1:8–11; Luke 5:27–32

I came not to call the righteous, but sinners to repentance (Luke 5:32). What a consolation for sinners! But it is necessary to leave sins and do only good and, when doing good, to continue to call oneself a sinner not only with the tongue, but in the heart. Do not sin, but as a true sinner repent and call out to the Lord for forgiveness. When you are disposed in such a way, it means that you stand in the truth. As soon as you give way to self-righteousness and start considering yourself sinless, know that you are turning aside from the right path and have gone over to those for whom there is no salvation. How we can combine a proper life with feelings of sinfulness is something only asked by scribes, who write but do not do. For one who follows the path of action, this is so clear that he cannot understand how it could be any other way.

TWENTIETH SUNDAY AFTER PENTECOST
Gal. 1:11–19; Luke 7:11–16

The Lord saw a mother weeping over the death of her son and had compassion on her. Another time He was called to a marriage, and rejoiced together with the family. By this He showed that to share ordinary, everyday joys and sorrows is not contrary to His spirit. This is what true, reverent Christians do, who live their lives in fear [of God]. However, they distinguish some of life's everyday customs from others, for much has entered into these customs upon which God cannot look favorably. There are customs that come from the passions, which are devised for their indulgence. Others are nourished by vanity and cares. He who has the spirit of Christ will be able to distinguish the good from the bad. He adheres to the one and rejects the other. He who does this with the fear of God is not alienated by others, though he does not act like them, because he always acts in the spirit of love and compassion toward the infirmities of his brothers. Only a spirit of zeal beyond measure rubs people the wrong way and produces disharmony and division. Such a spirit cannot refrain from teaching and criticizing. But the one [with the spirit of Christ] is only concerned with ordering his and his family's life in a Christian way. He does not permit himself to interfere in the affairs of others, saying to himself, "Who set me as a judge?" He quietly makes everyone well-disposed to himself, and inspires respect for those customs to which he holds. He who gives orders to everyone makes himself unloved, and evokes disapproval for the good customs to which he holds. Humility is needed in such cases—Christian humility. It is the source of Christian good sense, which knows how to act well in given situations.

MONDAY
Phil. 4:10–23; Luke 7:36–50

How could it be that although Simon the Pharisee reveres the Lord and invites Him to his home, he is scandalized when he sees that He shows favor toward a sinful woman and permits her to approach Him? Why does he think to himself, *If He were a prophet* (Luke 7:39), and so forth? Because he has busied himself with entertaining, and has therefore ignored a sensible understanding of how God does things. These two realms, worldly and spiritual, have completely different characteristics and laws. Meanwhile, our mind, when it is preoccupied with something, begins to judge according to that thing. According to worldly customs, one must not have contact with an obviously sinful woman. This is how Simon judges, forgetting that repentance makes everyone pure and puts sinners on par with the righteous. He thinks that the sinful woman should not be there, and that if the Savior does not chase her away, it is probably because He does not know who she is. Another thought immediately follows this one: If He does not know, then what kind of prophet is He? He did not say this in words, but only thought it, although there was no outward change in his appearance or in how he was treating his guests. But the Lord saw his heart and corrected him accordingly. He suggested to him that sinners also have a place beside Him, and that the sinful woman, who had prostrated before Him in her heart, revered Him more than did Simon, who honored Him with nothing but food. Externals lead a person to a feeling of self-righteousness which is disagreeable to the Lord, while inner qualities always keep him in a feeling of his worthlessness before the face of the omniscient Lord.

TUESDAY
Col. 1:1–2, 7–11; Luke 8:1–3

The Lord preaches, while the women minister unto him of their substance (cf. Luke 8:3) and, as it were, are thus participants in his very preaching. It is not given to everyone to preach the Gospel, but everyone can help spread it and be participants in this, the most important matter on earth. There have been many such participants, both men and women, at the time the Holy Apostles preached, and then at the time of their successors, and finally, throughout the entire history of the Church. Such participants exist to this day.

Our apostles in the Caucasus and in various areas of Siberia labor zealously, suffering every need and deprivation. They continue the work of the Lord and the Holy Apostles. Those women and men who send aid to them join the ranks of the women who served the Lord, and become worthy of equal recompense. The Lord said, *He that receiveth whomsoever I send receiveth Me* (John 13:20). This means that He equates Himself with the one who is sent to preach, consequently, that He equates the service rendered to His messengers with service rendered to Him. According to the law of His goodness and justice, the way a person receives someone determines the reward he will receive (cf. Matt. 10:41). This would seem to be sufficient incentive to not hold back one's hand from donating to assist the great work of preaching the Gospel.

WEDNESDAY
Col. 1:18–23; Luke 8:22–25

When they boarded the ship to sail to the other side of the lake, did the Apostles think that they would meet with a tempest and expose their lives to danger? Meanwhile, a tempest suddenly arose and they did not expect to remain alive. Such is the path of our life! You do not know how or from where danger will sweep in, capable of destroying us. Air, water, fire, beasts, man, a bird, a house—in a word, everything around us—could suddenly be transformed into a weapon for our death. From this comes a law: live in such a way that every minute you are ready to meet death, and fearlessly enter into its realm. This minute you are alive, but who knows whether you will be alive the next? Keep yourself according to this thought. Do everything you have to, according to the routines of your life, but in no way forget that you could immediately move to a land from which there is no return. Not remembering this will not postpone the appointed hour, and deliberately banishing this crucial change from your thoughts will not lessen the eternal meaning of what will happen after it.

Commit your life and everything into God's hands. Spend hour after hour with the thought that each hour is the last. From this the number of empty pleasures will decrease, while at death this deprivation will be immeasurably recompensed with a joy that has no equal among the joys of life.

THURSDAY
Col. 1:24–29; Luke 9:7–11

Hearing about the works of Christ the Savior, Herod said, *John have I beheaded; but Who is this?* (Luke 9:9). And he desired to see Him. He desired to see Him and sought an opportunity for this, but was not made worthy, because he sought not unto faith and salvation, but out of empty curiosity. Inquisitiveness is the tickling of the mind. Truth is not dear to inquisitiveness, but news is, especially sensational news. That is why it is not satisfied with the truth itself, but seeks something extraordinary in it. When it has contrived something extraordinary, it stops there and attracts other people to it. In our days, it is the German mind that does this.[31] The Germans are obsessed with contriving things. They have covered the whole realm of the truth of God with their contrivances as with a fog. Take dogma, ethics, history, the word of God—all are so overloaded with contrivances that you cannot get to the truth of God. Meanwhile, these things interest them and those with the same mind-set. The truth of God is simple; can a proud mind study it? Such a mind would rather think up its own things: sensational things, although empty and as weak as a spider's web. To see that this is so, look at the current theories of the creation of the world: they are like a somnambulistic or drunken delirium.[32] And yet how good they

[31] See pp. 110 and 166 above.—ED.

[32] St. Theophan is referring here to modern naturalistic theories of the origin of the world and of living things. See p. 272 below.—ED.

seem to those who invented them! How much energy and time are wasted on this—and all in vain! The deed was accomplished simply: *He spake, and they came to be. He commanded, and they were created* (Ps. 148:5). No one can think up anything better than this solution.

FRIDAY
Col. 2:1–7; Luke 9:12–18

The miraculous feeding of the multitude in the desert is an image of the feeding of the faithful with the Holy Communion of the Most Pure Body and Blood of the Lord. The Lord is sitting apart; the multitude is made to sit in groups; the Apostles are intermediaries—they receive the bread and give it out. So it is now: believers are all divided into groups—small individual churches in which the Lord, invisibly present, gives out His Body and Blood through the apostolic successors. As He said to the Apostles then, so now to their successors does He say, *Give ye them to eat* (Luke 9:13). As then, so now do the believing multitudes stand steadfastly before the Lord in fasting, in hearing the word, and in a prayerful desire to be healed from sins when they prepare to approach the Divine Mysteries. Thus the mystery begun by the Lord's appearance has continued until now and will continue until the end of the world. And in the world to come there will be a communion of a different sort, for the Lord has promised to give us to eat of the hidden manna and of the tree of life (cf. Apoc. 2:7, 17). Our first parents' own mystical communion was also arranged in the earthly Paradise—eating from the tree of life. In the Old Testament Church its image is the eating of the paschal lamb. Thus, mystical communion began with the human race and will be with it unto eternal ages—in various forms, but in the one meaning of true communion with the Lord, for *in Him was life; and the life was the light of men* (John 1:4). It is fitting for those who are created according to the image of God to be in such communion with Him, Who is the brightness of the Father's glory, and the express image of His person (cf. Heb. 1:3).

SATURDAY
II Cor. 3:12–18; Luke 6:1–10

The Lord's disciples plucked the ears of grain, rubbed them in their hands and ate them on the Sabbath—a deed very unimportant both in appearance and in essence. Meanwhile, the Pharisees could not restrain themselves and rebuked them. What made them raise this issue? In appearance, unreasonable zeal; but in essence, the spirit of judging. This spirit picks on everything and presents it in a dismal state of lawlessness and prejudice. This infirmity, to a greater or lesser degree, is common to almost all people who do not pay heed to themselves. Not everyone will express judgmental thoughts in word, but it is rare for a person to refrain from such thoughts. Someone [a demon] crouches by the heart and stirs up the spirit of judging, and the heart pours it forth. But at the same time the critic himself is prepared to do bad deeds as long as no one sees, and is constantly in a bad state about something. It is as if he judges and condemns in order to recompense his inwardly insulted and pent-up feeling of righteousness with attacks on others, groundless as they may be. He who loves righteousness and stands for it, knowing how difficult it is to attain correctness in deeds and even more so in feelings, will never judge. He is rather ready to cover with leniency not only the small, but even the great transgressions of others. The Lord does not judge the judging Pharisees, but indulgently explains to them that the disciples did something that anyone would excuse if they thought about it rightly. And it is almost always this way: if you think reasonably about your neighbor's action you will find that it does not at all have the serious, terrible character that it seemed to have at first.

TWENTY-FIRST SUNDAY AFTER PENTECOST
Gal. 2:16–20; Luke 8:5–15

The thorns and thistles which choke the word of Divine truth, in addition to being riches, pleasures, and cares of this life, must also be understood at the current time to be various false teachings, spread by scholars who have lost the truth and lost the way to it. Among us such teachings differ much: some publicly and openly go against the truth; others do so by oblique hints that are nevertheless understood by those toward whom they are directed. In essence they act like carbon monoxide poisoning: they enter unnoticeably and cloud the head, leading to a loss of clear consciousness of everything around. He who is affected by this kind of "carbon monoxide poisoning" begins to rave like one who is asleep, for everything already appears to him not at all as it is, not as it appears to one who is in his right mind. When you meet such a person you see that not only is all truth suppressed in him, but any feeling for the truth is also stifled, and a lie has penetrated all the components of his mind. What should one do? Do not listen to these ravings or read them; and when they are unintentionally heard or read, throw them out of your head. When they are not thrown out—submit them to reason, and they all will scatter like smoke.

MONDAY
Col. 2:13–20; Luke 9:18–22

Whom say the people that I am? the Lord asked (Luke 9:18). In answer to this the Apostles related the current opinions among the people concerning Him, formed according to the nature of people's views at that time. Some said that He was John the Baptist, others that He was Elijah, others that He was one of the ancient prophets resurrected. How do people answer today? Also in various ways, each according to his own way of thinking. What sort of answers could be given by materialists, atheists, and the soulless, who are descended from apes, when they believe in neither God nor the soul? Spiritists get away with the same response as the Arians, which was denounced at the First Ecumenical Council. Deists see God as being very far from the world, and since they cannot contain in their system the mystery of the Incarnation, they answer like the Ebionites[33] and Socinians.[34] You will encounter similar responses in Russian society, for the aforesaid three types of personalities exist and are multiplying among us. But thanks be to the Lord, we still have an extremely predominant number of sincere believers and those who strictly maintain the apostolic confession that the Lord Jesus Christ is the Incarnate, Only Begotten Son of God, the Savior and Redeemer of the human race, Who even in Paradise was promised to our progenitors. Which party will prevail is known only to God. Let us pray that we preserve within us the light of Christ, and that the darkness of false teachings be driven away. We have a weakness for bad things, and therefore it would not be surprising if a lie took the upper hand. Even now it is walking the streets of town openly, while in the past it cautiously hid from the gaze of Christian believers.

TUESDAY
Col. 2:20–3:3; Luke 9:23–27

Do not be ashamed to confess the Lord Jesus Christ as the Incarnate Son of God, Who redeemed us through His death

---

[33] An early, heretical sect of Jewish Christians, originating in Palestine. They did not believe in Christ's Divinity and insisted on following the Jewish law.—ED.

[34] A Protestant sect begun by Lelio Sozzini (1525–62) and his nephew Fausto Sozzini (1539–1604), having roots in the Anabaptist movement. They rejected belief in the Holy Trinity and in the Divinity of Christ.—ED.

on the Cross, Who through His Resurrection and Ascension opened for us the entrance into the Kingdom of Heaven. If you are ashamed, then He will be ashamed of you *when He shall come in His own glory, and in His Father's, and of the holy angels* (Luke 9:26). Now it has become fashionable in society to not talk at all about the Lord and about salvation, whereas in the beginning these precious subjects were all that people talked about. One's talk more readily flows from the place where the heart abides. Can it really be that people's hearts abide less with the Lord? Judging from the talk, this must be the case. Some do not know Him at all, and others are cold toward Him. Fearing encounters with such people, even those who are warm toward the Lord do not direct conversation toward Him, and the priesthood is silent. These days, discussion about the Lord and Savior and about our main concern—salvation—is excluded from the range of conversation acceptable in society. "What?" you say, "Is that really all we're supposed to talk about? Why only about that?" It is possible to talk about anything, but it must be done in a way that is underscored by the spirit of Christ. Then it would be possible to guess whether the speaker is Christian or pagan. Now, however, it is impossible to guess what they are, either by their talk or by their writings. Look through all the periodicals—what don't they write about? But no one wants to make Christian conversation. Strange times!

WEDNESDAY
Col. 3:17–4:1; Luke 9:44–50

Whosoever shall receive Me, receiveth Him that sent Me (Luke 9:48), says the Lord, and He that sent Him is God. Consequently, whosoever confesses the Lord, confesses God; whereas whosoever does not confess Him, does not confess God. You will say: I confess Christ to be a great, most wise, universal teacher. No— confess Him as He Himself speaks of Himself: that He and the

Father are One, Persons of one Divine nature, separate, but one in honor and co-reigning. If someone does not confess Him in this way, no matter how much he honors the Lord, it is the same as if he did not confess Him. Not confessing Him, he does not confess the Father either; he does not confess God. That is why, no matter what displays you make of honoring God, you do not honor Him if you do not confess the Lord Jesus Christ as the Only Begotten Son of God, Who was Incarnate for our sake, and Who saved us through His death on the Cross. It is not all the same which god one confesses, as long as one confesses one: those who worship the sun and the stars or invented beings are not called honorers of God, because they do not consider God to be God. Thus, whosoever does not confess the Lord is not an honorer of God, because he does not confess the God Who is the true God. The true God does not exist without the Son, Who is co-eternal and co-unoriginate. Therefore, once you cease to confess the Son, you no longer confess the true God. Only God will discern what your confession is worth; but since God is revealed to us as the true God, apart from this revelation one cannot have the true God.

Thursday
Col. 4:2–9; Luke 9:49–56

How should one relate to unbelievers who do not confess the Lord? The same way as the Lord related to the village that did not receive Him. Youthful zeal, full of ardor, wanted to send down fire from heaven upon them, but the Lord Himself restrained it: *Ye know not what manner of spirit ye are of* (Luke 9:55). The Lord and Savior did not do anything to those who did not receive Him, though receiving Him is what salvation itself consists in; but passing them by, He went to another village, leaving them to themselves. The same applies now: let unbelievers go their own way, while believers go theirs. God exists, and He will sort everyone out in good time. One must pity them and pray for them; one must desire that they come to know the truth and try to find opportunities to hint to them about it. But when they openly start attacking the truth, give them a rebuff that is loving, yet brings them to their senses—and that is enough.

FRIDAY
Col. 4:10–18; Luke 10:1–15

In the next world, will there be such condescension toward those who do not accept the Lord as He showed toward those living on the earth? No, there will not be. Sending the "Seventy" to preach, the Lord commanded them that when they were not received, they should say in the streets: *Even the very dust of your city, which cleaveth on us, we do wipe off against you: notwithstanding, be ye sure of this, that the Kingdom of God is come nigh unto you* (Luke 10:11). That is, we do not need anything of yours. It is not with self-interest that we walk and preach, but to proclaim peace and the Kingdom of God unto you. If you do not want to receive this blessing, then let it be as you wish—we will go on. Thus it was commanded for the present time; but how will it be in the future? *It shall be more tolerable in that day for Sodom, than for that city* (Luke 10:12). Therefore, unbelievers have nothing to give them hope of the Lord's lenience. While on the earth they take their liberties, but as soon as death comes, the entire storm of God's wrath will come down upon them. It would be a great misfortune to be as the unbelievers! They do not even have joy on the earth, because without God and the Lord Jesus Christ, the Savior and Redeemer, even here everything is dismal and dreary. As to what will happen there, it is impossible to describe it in words or to imagine it. It would be more tolerable to be destroyed, but even that will not be given to them.

SATURDAY
II Cor. 5:1–10; Luke 7:2–10

What a radiant figure the centurion is! How did he reach such faith that he surpassed all the Israelites, who had been raised on revelation, prophecies, and miracles? The Gospel does not indicate how, but only paints a vivid picture of his faith and tells how the Lord praised him. The path of faith is a secret, concealed path. Who can even explain to himself how the convictions of faith are formed in the heart? The Holy Apostle resolved this in the best way by calling faith God's gift. Faith truly is God's gift, but unbelievers are not without responsibility, and, consequently, they themselves are at fault for the fact that this gift is not given to them. If there is no recipient for this gift, it is not given, for there is nothing to receive it with. In such a case to give it would be the same as to waste it. How a soul is made a worthy recipient of the gift of faith is difficult to determine. Extreme humility could be seen in the centurion, despite the fact that he was a powerful, virtuous, and sensible man. In general, is it not through humility that this great mercy, which gives faith, is attracted? This is not at all surprising. At the very least it is known to everyone that unbelievers are always of a proud spirit, and that faith most of all requires the mind's submission beneath its yoke.

TWENTY-SECOND SUNDAY AFTER PENTECOST
Gal. 6:11–18; Luke 16:19–31

The parable about the rich man and Lazarus shows that those who do not live as they should will suddenly wake up to reality, but that they will no longer have the opportunity to correct their state. Their eyes will open and they will clearly see where the truth lies. Remembering that on the earth there are many who are blind as they were, they will want someone to be sent from the dead to assure them that one must live and understand things only according to the Lord's revelation and in no other way. But they will be denied even this, because for those who desire to know the truth, revelation alone is a witness. On the other hand, for those who do not desire it and do not love the truth, even the very resurrection of one of the dead would not be convincing. The feelings of the rich man in this parable are probably felt by everyone who departs this life. Consequently, according to the belief of that world, which will be the belief of all of us, the only guidance for us on the path of life is the Lord's revelation. But there, for many, this belief will have come too late—it would have been more useful here, but not everyone had it. Let us, at least, believe the testimony of those there, putting ourselves into their state. Those who are in torments do not lie. Pitying us, they want our eyes to be opened, so that we will not come to the place of their torment. We cannot say about this subject, as we often do about ordinary affairs, "Maybe somehow things will pass." No, it will not somehow pass. We must be thoroughly certain that we will not find ourselves in the place of the rich man.

MONDAY
I Thess. 1:1–5; Luke 10:22–24

No man knoweth ... Who the Father is, but the Son, and he to whom the Son will reveal Him (Luke 10:22). The Son was on earth and revealed everything necessary for us Himself and through the Holy Spirit, Who acted in the Apostles. Consequently, what you find in the Gospels and the apostolic writings is all you will and can know about the Father and Divine things. Do not seek more than this, and do not think to find the truth about God and God's plans anywhere else aside from this. What a great treasure we possess! Everything has already been said. Do not rack your brains, just accept with faith what has been revealed. It has been revealed that God is One in Essence and Triune in Persons: the

Father, Son, and Holy Spirit. Accept this with faith and uphold it. It has been revealed that the Tri-hypostatic God created all through the Word and preserves all in His right hand, in His Providence is over all things. Accept this with faith and uphold it. It has been revealed that we were in a blessed state and fell, and that for our restoration and redemption the Son of God, the Second Person of the Most Holy Trinity, was incarnate, suffered, died on the Cross, resurrected and ascended into heaven. Accept this with faith and uphold it. It has been revealed that he who desires to be saved must believe in the Lord and, receiving Divine grace in the Holy Mysteries, must live, with its help, according to the Lord's commandments, struggling against the passions and lusts by means of spiritual endeavors that correspond to them. Accept this with faith and do it. It has been revealed that whoever lives according to God's direction will enter after his death into radiant dwelling places, the foretaste of eternal bliss. But whoever does not live this way will, upon death, begin to experience the torments of hell. Accept this with faith and thus teach yourself and inspire yourself to do good and to perform spiritual endeavors. Accept all this with faith and keep it faithfully. There is no need to rack your brains over your own invented things. Do not listen to those who show off their intelligence, for they do not know where they are going.

TUESDAY
I Thess. 1:6–10; Luke 11:1–10

The Lord gave a common prayer for everyone, combining in it all of our needs, spiritual and bodily, inner and outer, eternal and temporal. But since it is impossible to include everything one needs to pray to God about in life in only one prayer, a rule is given after the common prayer for individual requests: *Ask, and it shall be given you; seek, and ye shall find; knock, and it shall be opened unto you* (Luke 11:9). So is it done in the Church of

God: Christians pray in common about common needs, but each privately sets his own needs and requirements before the Lord. We pray in common in churches according to established rites, which are nothing other than the Lord's Prayer, explained and presented in various ways. Privately, at home, everyone asks the Lord about his own needs in whatever way he can. In church one can also pray about one's own concerns, and at home one can also pray with a common prayer. We must concern ourselves about only one thing: that when we stand at prayer, at home or in church, we have true prayer in our soul: a true turning and lifting up of our mind and heart to God. Let everyone do this as he is able. Do not stand like a statue, and do not mutter the prayers like a wound-up machine that plays songs. No matter how long you stand like that, and mumble the prayers, you have no prayer, when your mind is wandering and your heart is full of empty feelings. But if you stand at prayer and are accustomed to it, what does it cost you to draw your mind and heart there as well? Draw them there, even if they have become stubborn. Then true prayer will form and will attract God's mercy, and God's promise: *Ask, and it shall be given you,* will be fulfilled. Often it is not given because there is no petition, only a posture of petitioning.

WEDNESDAY
I Thess. 2:1–8; Luke 11:9–13

The Lord prevails upon us to pray with the promise that we will be heard, explaining this promise as the compassion of a natural father who is favorably disposed to the petitions of his children. But here He hints at the reason why our prayers and petitions are sometimes not heard or are not fulfilled. A father will not give His children a stone instead of bread, or a serpent instead of a fish. If a natural father does not do this, how much more will the Heavenly Father not do it? And yet our petitions are not infrequently similar to petitions for a serpent and a stone. It seems to us that we are asking for bread and fish; while the Heavenly Father sees that what is requested will be for us a serpent and a stone, and He does not give us what we ask for. A father and mother pour out heartfelt prayers for their son before God, that He arrange what is best for him, but in addition they express what they consider to be better for their son, that is, that he be alive, healthy, and happy. The Lord hears their prayer and arranges for their son what is best, not according to the understanding of those asking, but as it is in reality for their son: He sends a disease from which their son dies. Those who think that everything ends with the present life will feel that the Lord has not heard them, but rather did the opposite of what they asked, or left the person about whom they prayed to his own fate. But those who believe that the present life is only a preparation for the next life have no doubt that the son for whom they prayed fell sick and died precisely because their prayer was heard and because it was better for him to leave here than to remain here. You will say, "Why pray, then?" No, you must not refrain from prayer, but when praying for specific things you must always keep in mind the condition: "If Thou Thyself, O Lord, deemest this to be salvific." St. Isaac the Syrian advises us to shorten all prayer to this: "Thou knowest, O Lord, what is needful for me: do unto me according to Thy will."

THURSDAY
I Thess. 2:9–14; Luke 11:14–23

When a strong man armed keepeth his palace, his goods are in peace: But when a stronger than he shall come upon him, and overcome him, he taketh from him all his armor wherein he trusted, and divideth his spoils (Luke 11:21–22). This allegory explains how demonic power over souls is destroyed by the Lord. While a soul is in sin, its evil spirit possesses it, although it may not always be clearly demonstrated. The evil spirit is stronger than the soul, and this is why it does not fear an uprising on the soul's part.

It rules and tyrannizes over it without resistance. But when the Lord comes to a soul, attracted by faith and repentance, He tears apart all of Satan's bonds, casts out the demon and deprives it of all power over this person's soul. While this soul serves the Lord, the demons cannot prevail over it, for the soul is strong through the Lord, Who is stronger than they are. When the soul takes a false step and roams away from the Lord, the demon again attacks and overcomes it, and for the soul, the poor thing, the last state is worse than before. This is the general, unseen order of phenomena in the spiritual world. If only the eyes of our mind were opened, we would see the worldwide battle of spirits against souls: first one side, then the other overcomes, depending upon whether the soul communes with the Lord through faith, repentance, and zeal for good works, or falls back from Him through carelessness, lack of concern, and coolness toward doing good.

Friday
I Thess. 2:14–19; Luke 11:23–26

He that is not with Me is against Me; and he that gathereth not with Me scattereth (Luke 11:23). It turns out that one can labor for a whole century and think that all sorts of good has been gathered, but it was all for nothing if it was not gathered with the Lord. What does it mean to gather with the Lord? To labor and act according to faith in the Lord, according to His commandments, with the help of His grace, being inspired by His promises—to live so that the spirit of one's life is the spirit of Christ. There are two domains in the world: good and evil, truth and falsehood. Only good and truth make up a true possession which is lasting and valuable; but good and truth come only from the Lord, and are acquired only with His help. It is clear that he who does not gather with the Lord will not gather truth and goodness. He will not gather what could be called a true possession, which is lasting and valuable. No matter what such a person gathers, it is all of no use; it is all vain labor, a vain waste of energy and time.

SATURDAY
II Cor. 8:1–5; Luke 8:16–21

Nothing is secret, that shall not be made manifest; neither any thing hid, that shall not be known and come abroad (Luke 8:17). Therefore, no matter how much we hide with our bad deeds, a record of them is made independently of us, which will be presented in its time. What is the parchment on which this record is written? Our conscience. We sometimes force it to be silent—and it is silent. But although it is silent, it does its work, keeping a most precise chronicle of our deeds. What is one to do if many bad things are written there? One must wipe out what is written there. With what? With tears of repentance. These tears will wash away everything, and not a single trace will remain of these bad things that have been written. If we do not wash them away, then at the judgment we ourselves will have to read everything that was written. But since the truth will then reign in our consciousness, we ourselves will pronounce our judgment, and the Lord will confirm it. Then there will be a decision which cannot be appealed, because each person will condemn himself, and this will have nothing to do with anyone else. All of this will occur in the twinkling of an eye: you will look and see what you are. You will immediately hear from the Lord, Who is omnipresent, a confirmation of the judgment; and then it will be the end of everything....

TWENTY-THIRD SUNDAY AFTER PENTECOST
Eph. 2:4–10; Luke 8: 26–39

After the Gadarene who was possessed with devils was healed, he cleaved to the Lord and desired to be with Him always. Then, upon hearing His will, he went and preached throughout the whole city about the good things he had received. The Benefactor attracted him; His will became law for the one who received the benefaction, and the man's tongue could not resist proclaiming what had been received from Him. If only we were to keep in mind all the good things which we have received and are receiving from the Lord, there would be no ungrateful people among us; there would be no transgressors of His holy will, nor would there be people who do not love Him more than all else. Through Baptism we are saved from our ancestral sin and all of its misfortune. In repentance we are constantly washed from the sins that unremittingly cling to us. Through God's Providence we are preserved from dangers which are often not visible to us, and we receive a direction for our life which is safer for us and more favorable to our goals. Besides, all that we possess is from the Lord. That is why we must belong to the Lord with our whole soul, fulfill His will in all things, and glorify His most holy name—especially in our life and deeds, so that we might not fall behind the Gadarene who had been possessed by devils, who immediately proved himself to be so wise that he became an example worthy of everyone's imitation.

MONDAY
I Thess. 2:20–3:8; Luke 11:29–33

The queen of the south shall rise up in the judgment with the men of this generation, and condemn them (Luke 11:31). For what? For indifference to the work accomplished by the Lord before their eyes. That queen, upon hearing about Solomon's wisdom, came from afar to hear him, but these men, having before their face the Lord Himself, did not heed Him, although it was obvious that He was higher than Solomon, just as the sky is higher than the earth. And the queen of the south condemns everyone who is indifferent to God's works, because among us as well, the Lord is always as obviously present in the Gospel accounts as He was [in the days of Solomon]. Reading the Gospel, we have before our eyes the Lord with all of His marvelous works, for the Gospel is as undoubtedly true as the testimony of our own eyes. Meanwhile, who heeds the Lord as One Who has imprinted Himself upon our souls? We have closed our eyes or averted them. This is why we do not see, and not seeing, we do not devote ourselves to the Lord's works. However, this is no excuse, but rather the reason behind our heedlessness, which is as criminal as the acts that proceed from it. The work of the Lord is our top priority—that is, the salvation of our souls. Furthermore, since we must heed what comes from the Lord even if it is not directly related to us, should we not all the more heed what is directed at us for the accomplishment of our essential work, the significance of which extends throughout all eternity? Judge for yourselves how criminal it is to disregard such a matter!

TUESDAY
I Thess. 3:9–13; Luke 11:34–41

The light of the body is the eye (Luke 11:34), while the light of the soul is the mind. When the eye of the body is undamaged we see everything around us in our external life, and we know how and where to go, and what to do. So also when the mind is sound, we see everything in our inner life, in our relationship to God and our neighbor, and in how we ought to behave. The mind, the higher aspect of the soul, combines a sense of the Godhead, the demands of conscience, and aspirations for what is better than anything possessed by us or known to us. When the mind is sound, fear of God reigns in the soul, as does conscientiousness and detachment from anything outward. But when it is unsound, God is forgotten, the conscience limps on both legs, and the soul wallows in what is visible and can be possessed. In the latter instance there is a dark night for that person: concepts are confused, deeds are in disharmony, and in the heart there is a cheerless heaviness. Circumstances push him around, and he is drawn after them like a wood chip in a river current. He does not know what he has been doing up to now, what he is now, and how his path will end. On the other hand, he whose mind is sound, fearing God, conducts his affairs with circumspection and listens only to the law of his conscience, which gives a uniform harmony to his entire life. He does not immerse himself in sensible things, but takes wing through hope in future bliss. From this his view on the entire flow of life with all that it touches is clear, and for him all is full of light, as when the bright shining of a candle gives someone light (cf. Luke 11:36).

WEDNESDAY
I Thess. 4:1–12; Luke 11:42–46

The Lord begins to reproach His contemporaries by saying that they *pass over judgment and the love of God* (Luke 11:42). The drying up of righteousness and love is the root of all disharmony, both in society and in every person. It comes from the predominance of self-love or egoism. When egoism inhabits the heart an entire horde of passions settles therein. [This horde] strikes out against righteousness and love, which require selflessness; while the passions generated from it chase away all other virtues. The person becomes, by his heart's disposition, unfit for anything that is truly good. He can still *tithe mint and rue and all manner of herbs* (Luke 11:42), but he does not find within himself the courage to do anything more substantial. This does not mean that his outward behavior is disgraceful. No, it is adorned in every way with decency, but on the inside he is as "a grave which appears not, and the men that walk over it are not aware of it" (cf. Luke 11:44). The beginning of self-correction is the beginning of the appearance of selflessness in the heart, after which righteousness and love are restored. Then, one after the other, all other virtues begin coming to life. Then the person becomes comely in the eyes of God because of his heart's disposition, although on the outside he may sometimes seem unattractive to other people. But the judgment of man is not the important thing; the important thing is for God's judgment not to be against us.

THURSDAY
I Thess. 5:1–8; Luke 11:47–12:1

Beware ye of the leaven of the Pharisees, which is hypocrisy (Luke 12:1). The distinguishing feature of hypocrisy is to do everything for show. To do things in public is not yet hypocrisy, because a large portion of our necessary deeds must be done for people and, consequently, amidst them and in their view. Although those who contrive to do everything secretly do better, this is not always possible. That is why one cannot immediately reproach those who act in the sight of others with having a desire for ostentation or show. They might have a sincere desire to do good, while a necessary accompaniment to deeds done outwardly is that they are seen by others. Hypocrisy begins the moment an intention appears, not to do good, but only to show oneself doing good. And this again is not always an offense, because there can be a momentary attack of evil thoughts, which are immediately noticed and chased away. But when one has it in mind to make a reputation for himself as a benefactor, this is already hypocrisy, which enters deeply into the heart. When the hidden goal of taking advantage of the benefits of such a reputation is added to this, then hypocrisy is in full force. Let everyone look at what the Lord requires when He commands to *beware ... of the leaven of the Pharisees*. Do good according to the desire for the good of others unto the glory of God, according to the recognition that this is God's will. But take no care about how people look at it—and you will avoid hypocrisy.

FRIDAY
I Thess. 5:9–13, 24–28; Luke 12:2–12

Be not afraid of them that kill the body, and after that have no more that they can do. But I will forewarn you Whom ye shall fear: Fear Him, Who after He hath killed hath power to cast into hell; yea, I say unto you, Fear Him (Luke 12:4–5). The greatest fear we have is of death. But the Lord says that the fear of God should exceed the fear of death. When circumstances come together in such a way that it is necessary either to lose one's life or to act against what is suggested by the fear of God, it is better to die rather than to go against the fear of God. For if you go against the fear of God, then after your bodily death, which is in any case inevitable, you will meet another death which is immeasurably worse than all of the most terrible bodily deaths. If we always bore this in mind, the fear of God would not weaken in us, and we would perform no deeds contrary to the fear of God. Suppose that passions rise up. At the moment they rise up, the conscience, motivated by the fear of God, requires one to defy them. A refusal of the demands of the passions seems like a parting with life, a killing of the body. Therefore, when disturbing feelings of this type come back and begin to shake the conscience, hasten to raise up the fear of God and of His judgment and its consequences. Then fear of a most terrible death will drive away the fear of the weakest death, and it will be easy for you to stand firm in the demands of duty and conscience. This is how the wise Solomon's saying is fulfilled: *Remember thine end and thou shalt not sin unto the ages* (Sirach 7:36).

SATURDAY
II Cor. 11:1–6; Luke 9:1–6

And He sent them (the Holy Apostles) *to preach the Kingdom of God* (Luke 9:2). Then, it was only throughout Palestine, but later they were sent throughout the whole world. The preaching which was begun then has not ceased to this day. Every day we hear what has been handed down by the Holy Apostles from the Lord, in the Holy Gospels and the apostolic writings. Time does not make a difference: we hear the Holy Apostles and the Lord Himself as if they were before us, and the power which acted in them acts to this day in the Church of God. The Lord has not deprived any believers of anything: those who are the most recent have everything the first ones had. The Faith has always maintained this, and still does. But false wisdom came and made a division between the present and what was originally. It seemed to this false wisdom that there was a great gulf between them; its head began to spin, its eyes grew dim. The Lord and Holy Apostles appeared to be plunged into a seemingly impenetrable darkness. And it got what it deserved: let it reap the fruits of what it has sown: nothing but the downfall of the spirit. It wallows in darkness and does not see the light, and one cannot help but acknowledge the admission of this as sincere—but who is guilty? [This false wisdom] has beclouded itself and continues to do so. To this day, it has not stated why the words of New Testament Scripture should not be considered as the true words of the Holy Apostles and of the Lord Himself. It only cries out tirelessly, "I don't see, I don't see!" We believe, we believe that you don't see! Just stop emitting your fog—the air around you will clear, and then perhaps God's light will come in and you'll see something. "But this is the same as my ceasing to be myself." Too bad! Stop; others will have more peace. "No, I can't. I'm destined to exist until the end of the ages, and even more artful ones will arise. I began in the first-created mind, even before this visible world [came into being], and as long as the world stands I will rip like a whirlwind across the paths of truth to raise up a cloud of dust against it." But you only becloud yourself, while around you there is light. "No, I'll keep throwing dust in people's eyes; and if I can't, then let them at least know me as I am. I won't be silent,

THOUGHTS FOR EACH DAY OF THE YEAR

and you with your truth will never succeed in barring my lips."
Who does not know this? Everyone knows that your first title is
"*pizma,*"[35] the obstinate insistence on your own way, regardless of
all the evidence that unmasks your falseness. You are blasphemy
against the Holy Spirit—so await the fulfillment of the sentence
pronounced against you by the Lord.

Twenty-Fourth Sunday after Pentecost
Eph. 2:14–22; Luke 8:41–56

Openly, in front of everyone, Jairus fell at the Savior's feet and
besought the Lord to heal his daughter, and he was heard. Saying
nothing, the Lord, immediately arose and went to his house. On
His way to Jairus' house the Lord healed the woman with an
issue of blood—of course, also not without prayer on her part.
Although she did not appeal in word and did not fall down
at the Lord's feet, she had a heartfelt prayer of faith. The Lord
heard her and healed her. Here everything occurred secretly.
The woman with the issue of blood turned to the Lord in her
heart, and the Lord heard this cry of her heart and granted her
petition. Both this woman and Jairus had essentially the same
prayer, although we can discern certain degrees in them. Such
prayers full of faith, hope, and devotion never go unheard. People
sometimes say, "I pray and pray, but my prayer still isn't heard."
Labor a little to ascend to a measure of prayer that cannot be
refused, and you will see why it was not heard. Whether you
are in a prayerful state like Jairus, or in a simple, ordinary one
like everyone around him (such as the woman with the issue of
blood), when true prayer arises in your heart, it will undoubtedly
reach the Lord and incline Him to mercy. The question is how
to attain such prayer. Labor, and you will attain it. All prayer
rules have as their object to lift up those who pray to such a

---

[35] From the Slavonic, meaning "hatred" or "displeasure."—Ed.

measure of prayer, and all who prudently follow this course of prayer reach their goal.

MONDAY
II Thess. 1:1–10; Luke 12:13–15, 22–31

The Lord said to the man who asked Him to divide between him and his brother, *Who made Me a judge or a divider over you?* (Luke 12:14). Later He added: *Take no thought* (Luke 12:22) about what to eat and drink, or what to wear. Earlier He taught: *Let the dead bury their dead* (Luke 9:60). Another time he suggested that it is better not to marry (cf. Matt. 19:10–11). This means that the turning aside of the attention and heart from everything worldly, as well as freedom from vanity and worldly bonds, make up one of the characteristics of a Christian spirit. The fact that the Lord blesses marriage and supports its indissolubility, which effectually renews the commandment regarding the relationship between parents and children and attaches significance to civic authorities and order, does not efface this characteristic and does not give Christians the right to avoid preserving it and cherishing it in their hearts. Compare both things and you will see that you have a duty to keep your heart unworldly amidst the worldly order of things. How can you do this? Resolve it yourself in your own life; in this is all practical wisdom. The Lord guides you toward resolving this with the following rule: *Seek ye first the Kingdom of God* (Matt. 6:33). Direct all your concern toward having God reign in you, and everything worldly will lose its binding and burdensome spell over you. Then you will conduct your affairs outwardly, but inwardly your heart will be possessed by something else. But, if on account of this, the resolution arises to cut off even this outward relationship to worldly things, it will not be a loss for you. You will come closer to the goal which faith in Christ will give you.

TUESDAY
II Thess. 1:10–2:2; Luke 12:42–48

The parable about the steward shows how a Christian should behave with relation to worldly things. A steward diligently does his work, but in his heart he is not attached to anything. He is free from all bonds; he relates to everything externally. So also must a Christian be in relation to all worldly things. But is this possible? It is possible. As there exists outward piety without inner piety, so worldly concern which is only outward and without inner bonds is also possible. But in such a case will everything around us turn into a mere lifeless form, emitting coldness like a marble statue? No—in the midst of worldly things another life will develop which is more attractive than the fullest worldliness. Worldly things, being worldly things, will truly remain as a form, while that which warms the heart will start to proceed from another source, and whoever drinks from this source will no longer experience thirst (cf. John 4:14). But in such a case is it better to drop everything? What for? Even one who outwardly drops everything can still be attached in his heart, and one who does not outwardly drop everything can be free from bonds. Of course it is easier for one who outwardly renounces everything to control his heart. Choose what is most suitable to you—just dispose yourself to be as the Lord commands.

WEDNESDAY
II Thess. 2:1–12; Luke 12:48–59

Suppose ye that I am come to give peace on earth? I tell you, Nay; but rather division: For from henceforth there shall be five in one house divided, three against two, and two against three. The father shall be divided against the son, and the son against the father; the mother against the daughter, and the daughter against the mother; the mother-in-law against her daughter-in-law, and the daughter-in-law against her mother-in-law (Luke 12:51–53). What is the reason? Those who believe in the Lord are filled with an entirely different spirit, contrary to that which reigned in people before His coming, and that is why they are incompatible. The pagan world exclusively pursued worldly and earthly interests. The Jews, though they had indications of higher good things, finally inclined toward the path of the pagans. Coming to the world, the Lord showed people other treasures—outside of the family and society—and He awakened other aspirations. Those who accepted His teaching naturally established a way of life different from before, for which they were subjected to hostility, oppression, and persecutions. This is the division. The Apostle Paul said then that all desiring to *live godly in Christ Jesus shall suffer persecution* (II Tim. 3:12). So it was, and so it is. When worldly and earthly interests begin to prevail in society, then society looks unfavorably at those who display other, unearthly strivings. It cannot even understand how it is possible to be interested in such things. People cannot endure those who serve as representatives of a way of life which is different from theirs. This is happening now before everyone's eyes. Is this not a sign of the times?

THURSDAY
II Thess. 2:13–3:5; Luke 13:1–9

Pilate mingled the blood of some Galileans with their sacrifices, and the Lord said: *Except ye repent, ye shall all likewise perish.* The tower of Siloam fell and killed eighteen people, and the Lord again said: *Except ye repent, ye shall all likewise perish* (cf. Luke 13:2–5). This gives us an understanding that when some misfortune befalls others, we must not reason about why it happened, but must rather look at ourselves and see if there are any sins in us that deserve temporal punishment in order to instruct others, and hasten to wipe them out with repentance. Repentance cleanses sin and removes the cause which attracts misfortune. While a person is in sin, an axe is laid to the root of the tree of his life, ready to cut him down. It does not do so, because it waits for repentance. Repent, and the axe will be taken away, and your life will flow to its end in its natural course. If you do not repent, expect to be cut down. Who knows whether he will live to the next year? The parable about the barren fig tree shows that the Savior prays that Divine justice spare each sinner in the hope that he will repent and bring forth good fruits. But it sometimes happens that Divine justice no longer listens to entreaties, and perhaps He might not agree to allow someone one more year among the living. How do you know, sinner, that you are not living your last year, your last month, day, or hour?

FRIDAY
II Thess. 3:6–18; Luke 13:31–35

The Lord said about Jerusalem: *Behold, your house is left unto you desolate* (Luke 13:35). This means that there is a measure to God's long-suffering. God's mercy is ready to be eternally patient, awaiting good. But what should He do when we reach such derangement that helping us is pointless? This is why we are abandoned. So it will be in eternity as well. Everyone says, "God's mercy will not allow people to be eternally cast out." God's mercy does not want this, but what can be done with those who are completely filled with evil and do not want to correct themselves? They place themselves beyond the limits of God's mercy, and are left there because they do not want to leave. Spiritists have invented numberless reincarnations as a means for cleansing sinners. But one who is defiled by sins in one incarnation could be the same in ten more, and onward without end. As there is progress in good, so there is progress in evil. On the earth we see people embittered in evil, and they can remain this way beyond the earth, and then forever. When the end of everything comes—and it will inevitably come—what is to be done with those who are embittered in evil? Of course they will be somewhere outside of the bright realm appointed for those who worked on themselves for the cleansing of their impurities. This is hell! Would those who did not improve under the best of circumstances really improve under the worst? And if not, this is eternal hell! It is not God who is responsible for hell and the eternal torments in it, but sinners themselves. If there were no unrepentant sinners, there would be no hell. The Lord very much desires for there to be no sinners, and it is for this that He came to earth. If He desires sinlessness, this means that He desires that no one end up in eternal torments. It all depends on us. Let us agree and destroy hell with sinlessness. The Lord would be glad of this; He revealed that hell exists so that everyone would be careful not to end up there.

<h2 style="text-align:center">SATURDAY</h2>
<h3 style="text-align:center">Gal. 1:3–10; Luke 9:37–43</h3>

After coming down from the mount of the Transfiguration, the Lord healed a youth possessed by a devil. The healing was preceded by a reproach for unbelief, which was the reason that the unfortunate one had not been healed by the disciples. Whoever's unbelief this was—whether of the father who brought his son, of the people who gathered together, or perhaps of the Apostles—it is evident only that unbelief closes the doors to God's merciful intercession and help, whereas faith opens it. The Lord even said to the father, "As much as you can believe, so much will you receive" (cf. Mark 9:23). When it regards a person, faith is not a matter of thought and mind alone, but embraces the entire essence of the man. It consists of the mutual obligations of the believer and the one in whom he believes, though these might not be expressed literally. He who believes counts on the one he believes in for everything, and does not expect a refusal from him in anything. That is why he turns to him with undivided thought, as to a father, and goes to him as to his treasury, assured that he will not return empty. Such an attitude, without words, inclines the one toward whom this attitude is held. This is how it is among people. But the power of such dispositions is truly manifest when they are directed toward the Lord, Who is almighty, omniscient, and desires to give us every good; and a true believer's expectations are never betrayed. If we do not have something, and do not receive it when we ask for it, it is because we do not have the proper faith. First and foremost we must seek and introduce into our heart complete faith in the Lord. We must seek and obtain it of Him through our entreaties, for it does not comes from us, but is God's gift. When faith was required of the father of the youth, he implored, *Lord, I believe; help Thou mine unbelief* (Mark 9:24). He weakly believed, wavering, and he prayed for the strengthening of his faith. But who can boast of perfect faith, and who, therefore, does not need to pray, "Help, O Lord, mine unbelief?" If only the full force of faith were in us, our thoughts would be pure, our feelings holy, and our deeds God-pleasing. Then the Lord would heed us like a father his children, and no matter what came to our heart—and what comes to a person in this state could only be pleasing to the Lord—we would receive everything without refusal or delay.

Twenty-Fifth Sunday after Pentecost
Eph. 4:1–6; Luke 10:25–37

To the man who asked how to be saved, the Lord on His part posed a question: *What is written in the law? How readest thou?* (Luke 10:26). By this He showed that to resolve all perplexity one must turn to the word of God. And for there not to be such perplexity at all, it is best to always read Divine Scripture attentively, with discernment and sympathy, applying it to your own life, and fulfilling in your own thoughts what relates to thoughts, in your own feelings and dispositions what relates to the senses, and in your deeds what relates to deeds. He who hearkens to the word of God gathers bright ideas about all that is in him, around him, and above him. He clarifies his obligations in all aspects of life; and sacred principles, like precious pearls, are strung onto the thread of his conscience, which then precisely and definitely indicates how and when to act so that he might please the Lord. He tames the passions, which the reading of the word of God always acts to assuage. No matter what passion troubles you, begin to read the word of God, and the passion will become quieter and quieter, and at last it will calm down completely. He who enriches himself through knowledge of the word of God has above him the pillar of cloud which guided the Israelites in the desert.

Monday
I Tim. 1:1–7; Luke 14:12–15

As an indication of whom to invite to lunch or dinner, take for yourself a rule: do not do anything for your neighbor with a view to receive recompense from him here. But this does not mean that you will spend everything in vain. In due course all will be returned to you. Regarding all God-pleasing works—prayer, fasting, and almsgiving—in the Sermon on the Mount, the Lord commanded us to do them secretly. Why? Because the Heavenly Father will openly reward those who act this way. Therefore, a Christian should prepare future bliss for himself through all his labors in life. He should build himself an eternal home, and send provisions there in advance for all eternity. This is not being mercenary, because one's own material interests are limited to this life, while [the future] life is to the detriment of these interests. Furthermore, it is impossible to live this way without faith, hope, and love toward the Lord. Acting according to the commandments in hope of recompense is likewise a remote kind of activity. And yet it is closer and more intelligible to the heart than something else which is too unreal—for example, to do good for the sake of good. You will not find the latter anywhere in the Scripture. There is a higher incentive here: do everything for the sake of the Lord and do not fear loss.

TUESDAY
I Tim. 1:8–14; Luke 14:25–35

Salt is good: but if the salt have lost his savor, wherewith shall it be seasoned? (Luke 14:34). Salt represents the Lord's disciples, who, passing on His instructions to people, destroyed the moral rottenness in those people. If we call such teaching education, then the word "salt" should also be applied to this. Then the entire saying will look like this: education is a good thing, but if education has lost its savor, then what is it fit for? Throw it out! Education acts like salt when it is filled with the principles and elements of the Lord's teaching, when it itself consists of discipleship to the Lord. But as soon as it departs from this, and adopts alien teachings instead of the Lord's lessons, then it has lost its savor and becomes unprofitable. It becomes infected with the rottenness of delusion and lies, and begins to be not curative, but infectious. History has confirmed and continues to confirm this with universal experience. Why does no one heed experience? The enemy brings darkness upon everyone, and they all think that it is light; while in their teachings they remain far from the Lord's teaching.

WEDNESDAY
I Tim. 1:18–20, 2:8–15; Luke 15:1–10

The parables about the stray sheep and the lost silver piece. How great is the Lord's mercy toward us sinners! He leaves all those who are well and turns to those who are not, in order to correct them. He seeks them, and when He finds them, He Himself rejoices and calls all of heaven to rejoice with Him. How is it that He seeks them? Does He not know where we who have stepped away from Him are? He knows and sees all; but if it were merely a matter of taking them and transferring them to His own, all the sinners would again reappear in their own ranks. They must first be disposed to repentance, so that their conversion and return to the Lord will be free, but this cannot be done by command or other external order. The Lord seeks a sinner by guiding him to repentance. He arranges everything around him so that the sinner comes to his senses and, seeing the abyss into which he has been rushing, returns. All the circumstances of life are directed in this way—all encounters with moments of sorrow and joy, even words and glances. And the inner actions of God through the conscience and the other righteous feelings that lie in the heart never cease. How much is done to convert sinners to the path of virtue, yet sinners still remain sinners! The enemy covers them in darkness and they think that everything is all right, and all will pass. If anxieties arise, they say, "Tomorrow I'll stop," but they remain in their current state. Thus day after day passes; indifference to their salvation grows and grows. A bit more and it will pass over into being hardened in sin. Who knows whether conversion will come?

THURSDAY
I Tim. 3:1–13; Luke 16:1–9

The parable about the unjust steward who was denounced. Do you see how he contrived to disentangle himself from his misfortune? If only we would all manage to arrange a peaceful life for ourselves upon our departure from this life! But no: *The children of this world are in their generation wiser than the children of light* (Luke

16:8). Why did the steward go to such pains? Because disaster was near. The nearness of misfortune aroused energy and quick-wittedness, and he quickly settled everything. But is misfortune not near to us as well? Death could overtake us at any moment, and then: *Give an account of thy stewardship* (Luke 16:2). Everyone knows this, but almost no one budges. What is this blindness? No one thinks he will die right now, but all suppose that they will live another day or two. They do not know the time, but are certain that death will come sometime later. This is why misfortune is seen as something in the future. Misfortune will come later, and any thought about what to do in case of misfortune is put off. No one intends to remain careless his entire life; he simply puts off changing for the present day. But since one's entire life is composed of present days and hours, he does not take the trouble to put things in order for the future.

FRIDAY

I Tim. 4:4–8, 16; Luke 16:15–18, 17:1–4

It is impossible but that offenses will come: but woe unto him, through whom they come! (Luke 17:1). Therefore, one cannot live in a careless way, uninhibitedly. One must look around carefully so as not to offend anyone. The mind is arrogant and does not look at anyone, but it arouses offenses all around in deed and, even more, in word. Offending increases and magnifies the woe of the offender, but he does not sense this and even further expands his offenses. It is good that, in the hope of correction, God's threat against those who offend is almost never fulfilled here on earth. It is put off until the future Judgment and retribution. Only then will offenders feel how great the evil of offending is. Here almost no one thinks about whether he offends or does not offend those around him by his deeds and words. Two sins which are very great in the eyes of God are not regarded as anything by people: offending and condemning. The offender, according to the word

258

of the Lord, would be better off dead; he who condemns is already condemned. But neither the one nor the other think about it, nor can they even admit that they are sinful in any such thing. Indeed, what blindness surrounds us, and how carelessly we walk in the midst of death!

SATURDAY
Gal. 3:8-12; Luke 9:57-62

No man, having put his hand to the plough, and looking back, is fit for the Kingdom of God (Luke 9:62). That is, he who thinks he can be saved while looking back at what he should abandon for the sake of his salvation is not being saved, is not heading toward the Kingdom of God. One must once and for all be done with everything that is not compatible with the work of salvation. Those who want to be saved see this themselves, but they continually put off parting with certain attachments until tomorrow. To suddenly break with everything is too great a sacrifice. They want to give things up by degrees, so as not to be conspicuous before others, but they almost always fail. They introduce salvific practices in their lives, while the dispositions of their hearts remain as before. At first the incongruity is very sharp, but their "tomorrow" and their promises of change shut the mouths of their consciences. In such a manner, with all these "tomorrows," their consciences grow tired of saying the same thing over and over, and at last fall silent. Now thoughts start to come that things can be left the way they are. These thoughts strengthen, and then are established permanently. A person who is outwardly proper but inwardly careless is formed. This is a whited sepulcher before the eyes of God. The worst thing is that the conversion of this sort of person is as difficult as the conversion of those who have become hardened in open sins, if not more difficult. Meanwhile, he thinks that everything is fine.

Twenty-sixth Sunday after Pentecost
Eph. 5:9–19; Luke 12:16–21

Having imparted the parable about the man who became rich and planned to just eat, drink, and be merry, and for this was struck with death, not remaining alive for his supposed pleasures, the Lord concluded: *So is he that layeth up treasure for himself, and is not rich toward God* (Luke 12:21). "So"—that is, such occurs to, or such a lot befalls, those who commit both the one and the other. Those who become rich and forget about God think only about the pleasures of the flesh. Let those who desire to avoid this bitter lot not lay up [treasure] for themselves, but be rich only toward God. Since riches come from God, then devote them to God when they flow, and holy riches will come of this. Share all surplus with the needy—this will be the same as returning to God what was given by God. He who gives to a poor person gives to God. Seemingly exhausting his riches, such a person becomes truly rich—rich in good works. He becomes rich for the sake of God, in pleasing Him. He becomes rich in God, attracting His goodwill. He becomes rich from God, Who makes one who is faithful over a few things ruler over many things. He becomes rich toward God, and not toward himself, for he does not consider himself to be the owner, but only a steward and an accountant, whose entire concern consists in satisfying all who come to him in need. But he fears spending anything special on himself, considering it to be an improper use of the property entrusted to him.

Monday
I Tim. 5:1–10; Luke 17:20–25

Having said that the Son of man will appear on His day like lightning, instantly illuminating everything under heaven, the Lord added: *But first must He suffer many things, and be rejected of this generation* (Luke 17:25).... He suffered in His person at one specific time [i.e., at His Passion and Crucifixion], after which sufferings continue in the person of believers. There is suffering as they are born, as they are brought up in the spirit, and as they ward off the actions of the enemy, both inward and outward.... The sorrows, temptations, and wavering of faith due to unbelief are continual arrows. Words and writings that exude unbelief are the flaming arrows of the evil one. These days, the evil one has led many blacksmiths to forge such arrows. The hearts of believers ache when they are struck by them and see others being struck.... But the day of the Lord's glory will appear—then all the secret darkness will be revealed, and those who have suffered will rejoice with the Lord. Until that time we must endure and pray.

TUESDAY
I Tim. 5:11–21; Luke 17:26–37

Whosoever shall seek to save his life shall lose it; and whosoever shall lose his life shall preserve it (Luke 17:33). One must understand this as follows: to save your life means to pity yourself, while to lose your life means not to pity yourself—that is, on the path of the Lord's commandments, or in working for the Lord. So, it is like this: he who works for the Lord, fulfilling His commandments without pitying himself, is saved, while he who pities himself perishes. If you pity yourself, you will unfailingly turn out to be a transgressor of the commandments and, consequently, an unprofitable servant. And what is the sentence for an unprofitable servant? *Cast ye the unprofitable servant into outer darkness: there shall be weeping and gnashing of teeth* (Matt. 25:30). Make an effort to observe yourself, if only for a single day, and you will see that self-pity distorts all of our works and kills the desire to do them. Without labor and effort, you will not do anything; but if you are grieved at forcing yourself—it all stops there. There are things you must do, like it or not. Such things are done without fail, difficult as they may be.

But here self-pity is overcome by self-pity. If you do not do them, there will be nothing to eat. But since the things required by the commandments are not of that nature, then in the face of self-pity they are always omitted. Likewise, out of self-pity allowances are made when it comes to bad deeds. One hates to refuse himself what he wants and so the desire is fulfilled, even though it is either outright sinful, or will lead to sin. Thus it always goes with one who pities himself—what he should do, he does not do, and what he should not do, he indulges himself in doing; and he ends up good for nothing. What salvation can there be in this?

WEDNESDAY
I Tim. 5:22–6:11; Luke 18:15–17, 26–30

Whosoever shall not receive the Kingdom of God as a little child shall in no wise enter therein (Luke 18:17). How is one to receive it as a little child? Here is how: in simplicity, with a full heart, without a moment's thought. A rational analysis is not applicable in the realm of faith. It can have a place only on its threshold. As an anatomist divides the whole body into its parts but does not see life, so also reason, no matter how much it deliberates, does not comprehend the power of faith. Faith itself provides contemplations which, on the whole, show that faith completely satisfies all the requirements of our nature, and obliges our consciousness, conscience, and heart to receive faith. They receive it, and having received it, do not want to break from it. The same thing happens here as with someone who has tasted pleasant and healthy food. Having tasted it once, he knows that it is suitable, and he accepts it among the substances that nourish him. Chemistry is no help to him in this conviction, either before or after he tastes it. His conviction is based on personal, direct experience. In the same way a believer knows the truth of the Faith directly. Faith itself instills in him the unshakable conviction that it is faith. How, then, could faith be rational faith? The rationality of faith is to directly know that faith is faith. The intellect only ruins things, cooling faith and weakening life according to faith; but the main thing is that it is arrogant, and chases away God's grace—and in Christianity this is an evil of the first degree.

THURSDAY
I Tim. 6:17–21; Luke 18:31–34

The Lord told the disciples about His suffering, but they did not comprehend anything He said; *This saying was hid from them* (Luke 18:34). Later, the faithful *determined not to know any thing, save Jesus Christ, and Him crucified* (I Cor. 2:2). Before the time came, they did not understand any of this mystery; but when the time came, they understood, and taught everyone, and explained it to everyone. This happens with everyone, not only with regard to this mystery, but to all the other mysteries as well. What is not understood in the beginning becomes understood with time; it is as if a ray of light enters the consciousness and brightens what was formerly dark. Who is it that elucidates it? The Lord Himself, the grace of the Spirit that lives in the faithful, or one's guardian angel—but in no way is it the person himself. He is the recipient, not the cause. On the other hand, something else might remain incomprehensible for one's whole life—not only for individuals, but for all of humanity. Man is surrounded by things he does not understand. Some are cleared up over the course of his life, while others are left until the next life—they will be seen then. This applies even to minds enlightened by God. Why are things not revealed here? Because some things are incomprehensible, so there is no point in talking about them. Others are not proclaimed out of considerations of health—that is, it would be harmful to know about them prematurely. Much will become clear in the next life, but other subjects and other mysteries will also be discovered then. A created mind will never escape inscrutable mysteries. The mind rebels against these bonds, but whether you rebel or not, you cannot sever the bonds of mystery. Humble yourself, proud mind, beneath the mighty hand of God—and believe!

FRIDAY
II Tim. 1:1–2, 8–18; Luke 19:12–28

The parable of the ten pounds portrays the entire history of mankind until the Second Coming of Christ. In it the Lord speaks of Himself, of His going through sufferings, death, and Resurrection to the Heavenly Father, to reign over mankind—all of which is His birthright. Those who remain on the earth are divided into two parts: servants who serve the Lord through obedience to the Faith, and those who, because of their unbelief, do not want to have Him as king and serve Him. To those who approach the Lord through faith, with a readiness to serve Him, are given the gifts of the Holy Spirit in the Holy Mysteries: this is a pound—and every believer receives it in order to serve among other believers. When everyone from the human race who is capable of submitting to the Lord submits to Him, then He will come again, as One Who has received His Kingdom. His first job will be to judge among the servants, as to who acquired what with the grace that had been given to them. Then will follow judgment over those who did not want to have Him as king, that is, who either did not believe, or who fell away from the Faith. Imprint these truths in your mind and do not take your attention from them, for then there will be a decision, and you cannot expect any changes. Flee unbelief, but do not believe idly—bring forth the fruits of faith. Finding you faithful over a few things, the Lord will make you ruler over many things (cf. Matt. 25:21).

SATURDAY
Gal. 5:22–6:2; Luke 10:19–21

I thank Thee, O Father, Lord of heaven and earth, that Thou hast hid these things from the wise and prudent, and hast revealed them unto babes: even so, Father; for so it seemed good in Thy sight (Luke 10:21). Behold the judgment on human wisdom and reason. And this is fulfilled visibly. Revelation is now before our eyes in Divine Scripture, and clever people read it, but do not understand. One must marvel: it is written simply, but to them everything there seems to be not as it is written; it is as if it had blinded them. Babes see and understand, but for the others, what is revealed is hidden. It pleased the Heavenly Father to establish it so, and therefore there is nothing to argue about. If what was vitally necessary had not been revealed at all, then the clever ones could still object. But it has been revealed—come and partake of it!—that is why it was revealed. Just become a babe. "What—me?" you say, "Not for anything!" Well, as you like. Remain wise and rational, while understanding nothing of vital importance. Remain unable to contain it in your head—which wanders amidst the phantoms and illusions which are born from your attempts to be clever, and which keep you in total blindness, according to which you think that you can see, but are blind, and cannot see afar off (cf. 2 Peter 1:9)—that is, you see something, but as if through a thick mist. This does not show you the true path and does not lead to the goal, but only keeps you in a perpetual cycle of self-delusion. Deliver us, O Lord, from such a terrible state!

Twenty-seventh Sunday after Pentecost
Eph. 6:10–17; Luke 13:10–17

On the Feast of the Entry of the Most Holy Theotokos into the Temple, "Christ is born" begins to be sung,[36] preparing believers for a worthy meeting of the Feast of Christ's Nativity. Having understood this inspiration, act according to it. Delve deeply into the mystery of the Incarnation of the Only Begotten Son of

---

[36] The *katavasia* of the Feast of the Nativity of Christ.—ED.

God; ascend to its beginning in the pre-eternal counsel of God concerning the existence of the world and man within it; see its reflection in the creation of man; joyfully meet the first tidings of it immediately after the fall; rationally trace its gradual revelation in Old Testament prophecies and prefigurations. Understand who prepared to receive God Incarnate and how they prepared, under the influence of Divine institutions and activities within Israel. Pass, if you wish, beyond the borders of God's people and gather there rays of God's light, shining in the darkness, and ponder to what degree those chosen from among all nations reached the presentiment of the extraordinary manifestation of God's Providence for man. This will be a mental preparation. But now is the time of the [Nativity] Fast—prepare yourself, go to Confession, and receive Communion of Christ's Holy Mysteries: this will be an active and living preparation. If, as a result of all this, the Lord grants you to sense the power of His coming in the flesh—then, when the Feast comes, you will celebrate it not out of a joy foreign to you, but out of an intimate joy.

MONDAY
II Tim. 2:20–26; Luke 19:37–44

The people cry out, "Hosanna!"—while the Lord weeps. Does not something similar occur at our church celebrations? At that time [of the Lord's entry into Jerusalem], the outward appearances were triumphant, but the Lord looked at what was invisible in souls, and saw it to be worthy of weeping. With us also, on feast days the outward appearance is always festive; but is everyone's inner state this way? One person has no understanding at all of the power and meaning of feast days. Another gropingly feels something darkly, but sees nothing clearly. Hardly anyone sees, feels, or is disposed in a way worthy of the feast. Many offerings are made at our feasts. But how many of them are set aside for the Lord and for one's brethren? Either none or the most insignificant bit; almost all are taken by the belly and frivolity. This cannot be concealed from the Lord, and it is not surprising if, to speak in a human way, He weeps when we utter festive exclamations. These are those who are redeemed, justified, adopted as sons! They gave a vow and took on an obligation to walk in the Spirit and not fulfill the lust of the flesh (cf. Gal. 5:16), while here what goes on among them? The sons of the Kingdom are worse than the basest slaves!

TUESDAY
II Tim. 3:16–4:4; Luke 19:45–48

My house is the house of prayer (Luke 19:46). And indeed, just enter into a church, and it calls you to prayer. Everything there is arranged and done in order to dispose to prayer and assist him in it. Therefore, if you want to enkindle prayer in your heart, go to the church of God more often. You will not pray at home the way you can in church. There are those who pray warmly at home too, but if they pray this way at home, how much higher is their prayer in church? But when you are in church, be there not only in body, but even more so in spirit. Stand where it is quieter and, beholding the Lord before you with your mind, pour out your soul before Him. Drive away daydreams, do not allow concerns, and attend to only one task—the task of prayer. Raise up your heavy soul on high and break down its corpulence through contemplation of Divine things. If you have something [on your conscience], remove it through repentance and a promise of correction. If your conscience is not satisfied, add deeds of self-denial and love. While standing in church, store up these feelings within yourself for all the time that you will not be in church. Do not step away from the Lord in thought, but always see Him before you, that your steps might not stray from the right path to the wrong one. Then, when you come to church, it will be easier for you to be as you ought to be there. Again, by standing appropriately in church, it will be easier for you to hold your attention before the Lord when you are outside of church.... Thus your [state of] abiding in the Lord will become higher and higher. What more could one desire?

WEDNESDAY
II Tim. 4:9–22; Luke 20:1–8

The priests, scribes, and elders did not believe in the Lord. In order to raise them up to faith, He offered them a question: *The baptism of John, was it from heaven, or of men?* (Luke 20:4). Consider this without bias and your reasoning will bring you to faith. What is said about John's appearing can be said about every event accompanying the Lord's advent in the flesh, and about His very advent, and all that comes into contact with it. Let each person consider all of this, and the conclusion will be the same: *Truly this was the Son of God* (Matt. 27:54). Various thoughts can come, confusion can arise, what seem like incongruities can be encountered; but at the end of all investigations one universal conviction will result: that it is impossible to think any other way than as is shown in the Gospels and apostolic writings. *Great is the mystery of godliness: God is manifest in the flesh* (I Tim. 3:16). This remains a mystery, but if the mind compels itself by a spiritual need to investigate it, then this mystery will become clear to the mind—and it will confess this way, and in no other way. Unbelievers either do not investigate it at all as they ought to, or they investigate it superficially, with a mind alien to it, or they take on a miserable state of mind that is opposed to what is required by the Faith. To justify their unbelief, they are satisfied with the most insignificant trifle to refute the Faith. The words of unbelievers shake believers, who, being satisfied with simple faith, do not seek clarification of the foundations of the Faith. Those words take them unawares, and hence they are shaken.

THURSDAY
Tit. 1:5–2:1; Luke 20:9–18

The parable about the vineyard portrays the Old Testament Church; the husbandmen are the hierarchy of those times. Because they was not fulfilling their purpose, a sentence was pronounced upon them: to take the vineyard from them and give it to others. These others were first the Holy Apostles, then their successors— the bishops with all the priesthood. God's vineyard has been the same from the beginning of the world, and the purpose of its husbandmen was, is, and will be the same until the end of the world—to bring to the Lord fruit of the vine—saved souls. This is the task of the Christian hierarchy, and thus, our task. The extent of its fulfillment we can all see. What can one say to this? About many things we can say: Glory be to God! But about many other things one cannot help but desire better. This particularly concerns the preaching of the word of God. Perhaps a sermon is heard somewhere, yet this is only one pruning knife in the hands of the husbandmen of God's vineyard. May this not be fulfilled in us: The lord of the vineyard *shall come and destroy these husbandmen, and shall give the vineyard to others* (Luke 20:16). May these "others" not break in on their own, and destroy not only the husbandmen, but the vine itself....

FRIDAY
Tit. 1:15–2:10; Luke 20:19–26

Render therefore unto Caesar the things which be Caesar's, and unto God the things which be God's (Luke 20:25). This means that each gets what is his own. In our times, instead of "the things which be Caesar's" we should substitute "the things which are worldly," and say that worldly things have their turn, while the things of God have theirs. But everyone has rushed toward earthly things alone, and they leave the godly things behind. That is why godly things not only are left out of their proper place—that is, in the first place, as they ought to be—but are completely forgotten. A consequence of this supposedly unintentional forgetfulness is that the godly is darkened in one's consciousness, and then both its content and foundation become unclear. From this come weakness of conviction and vacillation of faith. Then there is alienation from the Faith and the influence of the winds of various teachings. Everyone goes down this path when he begins to be careless about godly things; society takes this path when in its customs it begins to ignore what God requires of it. When godly things are left in the background, then emancipation from godly requirements begins to be established in society, in the intellectual, moral, and aesthetic sense. There occurs secularization (serving the spirit of the time) of politics, customs, entertainment, and then of education and all institutions. At the current time, people do not think, speak, or write about what is God's, nor do they even keep them in mind—not in any of their undertakings. Is it surprising, given such a state of mind, that teachings contrary to the Faith find access to society and that society is inclined toward mass unbelief?

SATURDAY
Eph. 1:16–23; Luke 12:32–40

Let your loins be girded about, and your lights burning (Luke 12:35). We must be ready at every hour—one does not know when the Lord will come, either for the Last Judgment or to take you from here; for you they are the same. Death decides everything. After death comes the results of your life; whatever you've acquired, you'll have to be satisfied with it for all eternity. If you have acquired what is good, your lot will be good; if you have acquired what is evil, then your lot will be evil. This is as true as the fact that you exist. All of this could be decided this moment—here at this very moment, as you read these lines—and then, the end of everything: a seal will be set to your existence, which no one can remove. This is something to think about! But one cannot be sufficiently amazed at how little people think about it. What is this mystery which is wrought upon us? We all know that death will come at any moment, that it is impossible to escape it, but meanwhile almost no one at all thinks about it—and it will come suddenly and seize us. Even then—even when a fatal disease seizes a person, he still does not think that the end has come. Let psychologists resolve this from a scientific aspect; from the moral aspect it is impossible not to see here an incomprehensible self-delusion, alien only to one who is heedful of himself.

Twenty-Eighth Sunday after Pentecost
Col. 1:12–18; Luke 14:16–24

Many are called, but few are chosen (Matt. 22:14). All Christians are called; chosen are those Christians who believe and live in a Christian manner. In the first Christian times, preaching called people to faith; [nowadays] we are called by our birth from Christians and our upbringing among Christians. And glory be to God! We travel down half the road—that is, entrance into Christianity and the taking root of its principles in our heart— from our very childhood, without any labor. It would seem that our faith should be all the stronger, and our life all the more correct throughout all the time that follows. It used to be that way; but at a certain point in time it started to be different with us. Unchristian principles, which ruin young people, are permitted in our schools, and unchristian customs, which corrupt them after they leave school, have entered into society. If, in accordance with the word of God, there have always been only a few chosen, it is no surprise that in our time there are even fewer of them; such is the spirit of the age—antichristian! What will be next? If our manner of education and social customs are not changed, true

Christianity will weaken more and more, and at last will entirely come to an end. Only the name "Christian" will remain, but the spirit of Christianity will not be there. The spirit of the world will fill everyone. What is one to do? Pray.

MONDAY
Heb. 3:5-11, 17-19; Luke 20:27-44

The Sadducees had a seemingly insoluble objection to the resurrection; but the Lord resolved it with a few words to them, and so clearly that everyone understood and acknowledged the Sadducees to have been beaten by the truth of His word. What the Sadducees were then, unbelievers of all sorts are now. They have heaped up a multitude of fanciful suppositions for themselves, elevated them to the status of irrefutable truths and plumed themselves on them, assuming that nothing can be said against them. In fact, they are so ungrounded that it is not even worthwhile speaking against them. All of their sophistry is a house of cards—blow on it and it flies apart. There is no need to refute it in its parts; it is enough to regard it as one regards dreams. When speaking against dreams, people do not prove the absurdity in their composition or in their individual parts, but only say, "It's a dream," and with that they resolve everything. It is the same with the theory of the formation of the world from a nebula and its supports,[37] with the theory of abiogenesis[38] and Darwin's origin of genera and species, and with his last dream about the descent of man.[39] It is all like delirium. When you read

[37] That is, dust particles that allegedly served as supports for the accumulation of matter from a solar nebula. This has remained to this day as the predominant naturalistic theory of the origin of the earth.—ED.

[38] A reference to the modern naturalistic theory of how life on earth arose from inanimate matter.—ED.

[39] A reference to Charles Darwin's books *The Origin of Species* (1859) and *The Descent of Man* (1871).—ED.

them you are walking in the midst of shadows. And scientists? Well, what can you do with them? Their motto is "If you don't like it, don't listen, but don't prevent me from lying."

TUESDAY

Heb. 4:1–13; Luke 21:12–19

And ye shall be hated of all men for My name's sake (Luke 21:17). He who breathes in even a little of the spirit of the world becomes cold toward Christianity and its requirements. This indifference turns into enmity when one remains in it a long time without coming to one's senses, especially after one picks up a particle of some false teaching somewhere. The spirit of the world with its false teachings is a spirit inimical to Christ: it is of the Antichrist. The spread of this spirit is the spread of hostile attitudes toward Christianity and Christian customs. It seems that something like this is happening around us. So far, only hollow roars are sounding everywhere; but it would not be surprising if that which was prophesied by the Lord began soon: *They shall lay their hands on you and persecute you* (Luke 21:12) ... *ye shall be betrayed ... and some of you shall they cause to be put to death* (Luke 21:16). The spirit of Antichrist is always the same: what there was in the beginning will be the same now—perhaps in another form, but with the same meaning. What should we do? *In your patience possess ye your souls* (Luke 21:19). Be patient, with a firm word of confession of the truth in your mouth and in your heart.

WEDNESDAY

Heb. 5:11–6:8; Luke 21:5–7, 10–11, 20–24

The disciples were indicating to the Lord the beauty of the temple building and its furnishings, but He said, *The days will come, in which there shall not be left one stone upon another, that shall not be thrown down* (Luke 21:6). This is an inscription to go under all the beauty of this world. In appearance it seems durable and everlasting; but after a day or two you look, and it is as though it were never there—beauty withers, strength is exhausted, fame fades away, minds are overcome, and clothes are worn out. Everything carries within itself a destructive power, which does not lie like an undeveloped seed, but is an unceasing activity, and everything flows to its end. *The fashion of this world passeth away* (I Cor. 7:31). *Surely man walketh about like a phantom ... He layeth up treasure, and knoweth not for whom he shall gather it* (Ps. 38:8–9). But we keep rushing around vainly. We are caught up in cares, and there is no end to our cares. We encounter constant lessons around us, but we do everything our own way, as though we were blind and saw nothing. And it is correct to say we are blind, or blinded; we do not expect an end either to ourselves or to anything surrounding us or possessed by us. And what else? Arranging our surroundings as we see fit, we are certain that we stand firmly, like on a rock, when actually it is more like we are standing in a quagmire, just about to sink. But we do not feel this, and we give ourselves over to careless delight in passing things, as though they would always remain. Let us pray that the Lord might open the eyes of our mind, that we might see everything not as it seems, but as it is.

THURSDAY
Heb. 7:1–6; Luke 21:28–33

And take heed to yourselves, lest at any time your hearts be overcharged with surfeiting, and drunkenness, and cares of this life, and so that day come upon you unawares (Luke 21:34). *That day,* that is, the last day of the world or of each of us, comes like a thief and captures like a net. That is why the Lord says, *Watch ye therefore and pray always* (Luke 21:36). Since satiety and over-solicitousness are the first enemies of vigil and prayer, we are forewarned not to permit ourselves to be weighed down by food, drink, and worldly worries. If someone has eaten, drunk, and made merry, then has a good sleep and does the same thing again, what kind of vigil can there be? If someone is occupied solely with worldly things, day and night, will he be in a state for prayer? "What should I do?" you say. "It is not possible to go without food, and we have to procure it. That's something to care about." But the Lord did not say, "Do not work, do not eat, do not drink," but rather, do not let your heart *be overcharged* with this. Work with your hands, but keep your heart free. If you must eat—eat, but do not burden yourself with food. Drink wine when necessary, but do not let it lead to disturbance of your head and heart. Divide your outer side from your inner side, and make the latter your life's work, and the former something incidental. Keep your attention and heart on the latter, and only your body, arms, legs, and eyes on the former. *Watch ye and pray always,* that you may be made worthy to stand fearlessly before the Son of man. In order to be made worthy of this, it is necessary to establish yourself before the Lord while you are still here in your life. There is one means for this—vigilant prayer performed by the mind in the heart. He who is thus attuned will not be taken unawares on *that day.*

FRIDAY
Heb. 7:18–25; Luke 21:37–22:8

Satan entered into Judas, and taught him how to betray the Lord; he agreed, and betrayed Him. Satan entered because the door had been opened for him. What is within us is always closed; the Lord Himself stands outside and knocks, that we might open it. What causes it to open? Sympathy, predisposition, and agreement. If all of this is inclined in the direction of Satan, he enters. If, on the contrary, it is inclined toward the Lord, then the Lord enters. If Satan enters, and not the Lord, the person himself is guilty. If you do not allow thoughts pleasing to Satan, if you do not sympathize with them, or dispose yourself to their suggestions and agree to do them, Satan will come near and then leave. After all, he is not given authority over anyone. If he takes possession of anyone, it is because that person gives himself over in slavery to him. The source of all evil is one's thoughts. Do not allow bad thoughts, and you will forever close the door of your soul to Satan. That bad thoughts come—what can you do? No one in the world is without them, and there is no sin here. Chase them away, and that will end everything. If they come again, chase them away again—and so on for your entire life. When you accept thoughts and become engaged in them, it is not surprising that sympathy for them appears as well; then they become even more persistent. After sympathy come bad intentions for some sort of bad deeds. Vague intentions define themselves later by an inclination toward one thing or another. Acceptance, agreement, and resoluteness set in, and now sin is within! The door of the heart is opened wide. As soon as agreement forms, Satan jumps in and begins to tyrannize. Then the poor soul, like a slave or a pack-animal, is driven and wearied into doing indecent things. If it had not allowed bad thoughts, nothing of the sort would have happened.

SATURDAY
Eph. 2:11–13; Luke 13:18–29

Strive to enter in at the strait gate (Luke 13:24). The strait gate is a life not according to your will, not according to your desires, not for pleasing yourself. The wide gate is a life according to all of the stirrings and strivings of a passion-filled heart, without the slightest refusal of oneself in anything. Thus, the gate to the Kingdom is self-restraint. Restrain yourself in all things and it will be the same as pressing or pushing against a door to open it and squeezing your way through it. How and with what should you restrain yourself? With the commandments of God, which are opposed to the passion-filled stirrings of the heart. When you begin to be angry with someone, remember the Lord's commandment not to give place to wrath, and with this restrain your heart. When lustful movements come, bring to mind the prohibition against even looking at a woman with lust, and with this restrain your lustfulness. When you want to judge someone, remember what the Lord said, that by judging you make the Judge of heavenly things implacable toward you, and with this restrain your arrogance. Do likewise in relation to every wanton movement [of the heart]. Gather sayings from Divine Scripture against each of them and keep these sayings in your memory. As soon as some bad desire comes from your heart, bind it immediately with a saying directed against it, or tie up all of your desires and thoughts in advance with Divine words, and walk in them. It will be like you are in bonds. But in these bonds lies freedom, or an open path to the Kingdom of God.

TWENTY-NINTH SUNDAY AFTER PENTECOST
Col. 3:4–11; Luke 17:12–19

Ten lepers were healed, but only one came to thank the Lord. Is there not generally a similar proportion of people who are grateful after receiving blessings from the Lord? Who has not received good things; or, rather, what do we have in us or what happens to us that is not good for us? Even so, is everyone grateful to God, and does everyone give thanks for everything? There are even those who permit themselves to ask, "Why did God give us existence? It would be better for us not to exist." God gave you existence so that you would be in eternal bliss. He gave you existence as a gift, as a gift He has furnished you with every means for attaining eternal bliss. The matter depends on you: you need only to labor a bit for this. You say, "But I have only sorrows, poverty, diseases, misfortunes." Well, these too are among the ways to attain eternal bliss. Be patient. Your entire life could not even be called an instant compared with eternity. Even if you had to suffer unceasingly your entire life, against eternity it is nothing; and you still have moments of consolation. Do not look at the present, but at what is prepared for you in the future, and be concerned with making yourself worthy of that; then you will not notice the sorrows. They will all be swallowed up by unquestioning hope in eternal consolations, and your lips will never cease to utter thanks.

MONDAY
Heb. 8:7–13; Mark 8:11–21

The Lord and the disciples sailed to the other side of the sea. The disciples had forgotten to take bread; they had with them only one loaf, and were beginning to wonder what to do. Knowing their thoughts, the Lord reminded them of the feeding of the four thousand and the five thousand, thus leading them to the firm hope that in His presence they would not die of hunger, even if they did not have a single loaf of bread. How much anxiety comes from thoughts about an unknown future! There is only one relief from this anxiety—hope in the Lord. A sensible examination of what has come to pass for us and others enlivens and strengthens us. You will not find a single person who has never in his life experienced some unexpected deliverance from misfortune or some unexpected turn of his life for the better. Revive your soul with recollections of such instances, when gloomy thoughts begin to weary it about what to do. God will arrange everything for the better now, as He has before. Rely upon Him. Even before your deliverance from misfortune, He will send you tranquility, and you will not even notice your misfortune. *Mercy shall encircle him that hopeth in the Lord* (Ps. 31:10) Examine experiences of this in Holy Scripture, in the Lives of saints, in your own life, and in the lives of your acquaintances, and you will see, as in a mirror, how *the Lord is nigh unto all them that call upon Him* (Ps. 144:19). Then fears about your fate will not trouble your soul.

TUESDAY
Heb. 9:8–10, 15–23; Mark 8:22–26

The Lord did not heal the blind man of Bethsaida immediately—He first healed him a little, and then completely, so that he began to see everything clearly. Why the Lord did this is known to Him alone. We can take from this the following thought: if it was considered necessary to heal bodily vision gradually, then even more so is such gradualness indispensable in the enlightenment of the eyes of our mind. That is how it has been. During the period of the [Old Testament] patriarchs, Divinely revealed knowledge was not complicated. During the period under the law it became more complex and detailed. In our Christian period it is even more detailed and exalted; but is this the end? Do not expect anything higher on the earth, but in the other world there will be [something higher]. Two Holy Apostles assure us of this: Sts. John and Paul. *Now we see* everything *through a glass, darkly* (I Cor. 13:12), but then we will see everything clearly. But even there, there will be degrees of enlightenment of the mind, for the realm of the knowledge of God is boundless. God's revelation on earth is already complete; there is no point in dreaming about something higher. We have everything we need; learn it and live by it. Christian revelation does not promise new revelation in the future, but only that the Gospel will be known in the whole world, and that this universality and generality of knowledge of the Gospel is the limit of the current order of things. After this, faith will weaken, love will dry up, life will become difficult—and God's goodness will put an end to the world.

WEDNESDAY
Heb. 10:1–18; Mark 8:30–34

Having invited us to follow Him with our cross, the Lord also shows us this path, eliminating the main obstacles to it, which are not outer, but inner, rooted in the human heart. It is as though He were saying, "If you want to follow Me, first of all do not pity yourself, for he who pities himself will destroy himself. Second, do not have anything to do with cupidity, for *what shall it profit a man, if he shall gain the whole world, and lose his own soul?* (Mark 8:36). Third, do not be embarrassed by what others say or how they look at you: *Whosoever therefore shall be ashamed of Me and of My words, in this adulterous and sinful generation, of him also shall the Son of man be ashamed, when He cometh in the glory of His Father with the holy angels* (Mark 8:38)." Self-pity, cupidity, and embarrassment are the main chains by which a person is held in a life displeasing to God, on the path of passions and sin. They are the main obstacles to a sinner's conversion; they are the main object of spiritual struggle in a person who repents and who has already begun to bring forth fruits of repentance. As long as these threads are not cut, the Christian life in us is unreliable, full of stumblings and falls—if not always outer, then inner. Let everyone look thoroughly at himself. If there is anything in you of what is said above, take care to give it up—otherwise do not hope to rise to perfection in Christ, although outwardly you may be quite proper.

THURSDAY
Heb. 10:35–11:7; Mark 9:10–16

History flows on and, it seems, inexorably determines individual events. How many preparations there were to receive the Savior! At last, His closest witness, John, came—but what came of it? *They have done ... whatsoever they listed* (Mark 9:13) to John, and the Son of man suffered and was humiliated. The flow of events could not be broken; it took its own course. So the flow of history always draws everything after it. People now ask, "Where is freedom? What would it be, given such an order of events? Nothing but a phantom." Thus do fatalists usually reason.

But this all-determining necessity of the flow of events is only an appearance. In reality all human events, both common and individual, are the fruit of man's free undertakings. The common [history] flows exactly the way it does because everyone, or a majority, want this. And individual events enter into agreement with common events because someone or other in particular wants this. The proof of this is obvious: in the midst of general good there occur bad elements, and in the midst of general bad there occur good elements. Also, in the midst of a firmly established commonality are born elements which, spreading and becoming stronger and stronger, overpower the former commonality and take its place. But these elements are always a matter of freedom. What did Christianity have in common with the character of the time in which it was conceived? It was sown by several individuals who were not a result of the necessary flow of history; it attracted those who desired it, spread vigorously, and became the common cause of the humanity of the time, yet all the same it was a matter of freedom. The same is true in a bad direction: how did the West become corrupted? It corrupted itself. Instead of learning from the Gospel, they began to learn from pagans and adopt their customs—and they became corrupted. The same will happen with us: we have begun to learn from the West which has fallen from Christ the Lord, and have transferred its spirit to ourselves. It will end with us, like the West, forsaking true Christianity. But in all of this there is nothing that necessarily determines the matter of freedom. If we want to, we will drive away the Western darkness. If we do not want to, of course, we will immerse ourselves in it.

FRIDAY
Heb. 11:8, 11–16; Mark 9:33–41

The Savior sets forth a child as a model of faith and life. Simplicity of faith gives birth to simplicity of life. From both of these comes an exemplary moral system. If you let philosophizing in, it will produce disorder within, and under the appearance of a better arrangement of things, it will throw one's entire life into disorder. Philosophizing always cries, "This is not right, that's not right. Let me arrange everything in a new way; the old is worthless, boring." But it has never yet, in any place, arranged anything good; it only throws things into confusion. The mind should obey what is commanded by the Lord. True, the mind is called "the king in the head"; however, this king is not given legislative power—only executive power. As soon as it starts making laws, it piles up who-knows-what. Moral, religious, worldly, and political orders are thrown into confusion, and everything turns upside down. It is a great misfortune for society when its mind is given freedom to soar, with no restraint by Divine truth! This is God's wrath. About this is said: *Hide thyself for a little season, until the anger of the Lord hath passed away* (Is. 26:20). During this apex of intellectual willfulness it is best to seek shelter in simplicity of faith. Just as during a storm it is better to sit at home and not step out in arrogance to fight with it, so during a time of stormy trust in one's own thoughts it is better not to enter into battle with it, or to seize the weapon of philosophizing in order to resist it. Simplicity of faith is stronger than philosophizing; clothe yourself in it, as in armor, and you will keep your balance.

Saturday
Heb. 5:1–8; Luke 14:1–11

When you are invited somewhere, do not sit in the highest place. In general, always and everywhere, seek the lowest place. The entire rich content of humility is briefly expressed in this simple rule. Take this rule, sit down and examine all possible cases in your life, and in advance choose the lowest place in each of them. This will be a practice of humility, which will gradually move from external deeds to inner ones, and will form a sediment of humility there as a foundation. Time will make this seed to grow amidst this practice, and humility will at last fill all of your soul and body, and all your outward affairs. What will happen? Moral greatness will shine on your brow and attract universal respect, and the words will be fulfilled in you: *Whosoever exalteth himself shall be abased; and he that humbleth himself shall be exalted* (Luke 14:11). However, while practicing humility do not have this as your intention, but rather humility itself. In and of itself it brings a blessed good disposition to the soul. Wherever humility goes, all inner disquiet ceases and outward adversities do not produce alarming impressions. Just as a wave which meets no impediment rolls across the boundless sea without noise or crashing, so outer and inner sorrows do not strike a humble soul, but rush by, as it were, on the surface, without leaving a trace. This is, so to speak, the worldly advantage of a humble person. What light from above overshadows him, what consolations are sent, what breadth of free action is revealed! Truly, humility alone contains it all....

Sunday of the Holy Forefathers
Col. 3:4-11; Luke 14:16-24

The Holy Forefathers—what truly great people![40] If one were to generalize the thought which defines their greatness, only those who fulfill God's will for the human race—a positive will— are truly great, for there is much that happens only by God's allowance. There are also powerful figures who act apart from God's will and even against it. These too can seem great—not in and of themselves, but only because of the great opposition put forth by God's Providence to efface the evil caused by them. We know God's direct will concerning eternal salvation, but God's plans concerning the temporal sojourn of people on the earth are hidden from us. That is why it is difficult for us to determine

---

[40] The Sunday of the Holy Forefathers commemorates the righteous ones of the Old Testament.—Ed.

who is acting more rightly, more precisely according to God's will. One can only acknowledge one negative criterion as true: He who acts against what God has determined for the eternal salvation of people cannot be considered great, no matter how ostentatious his deeds, for it is evident that he is going against the obvious will of God. Although this will does not concern temporal, but rather eternal things, it is doubtless that one will of God cannot contradict the other.

MONDAY
Heb. 11:17–23, 27–31; Mark 9:42–10:1

Every one shall be salted with fire, and every sacrifice shall be salted with salt (Mark 9:49). Before this the Lord said that one must be prepared for all sorts of sacrifices and deeds of self-denial, so as to stand only on the good path. Though these sacrifices are precious to us, like our own eye, or indispensable, like our right hand, we must offer them without a moment's hesitation. For if you begrudge offering such a sacrifice, and are led away because of this from the right path to the wrong, you will be forced to suffer eternally in the future life. So, offer painful and sorrowful sacrifice here to escape torments there. Without purification by fire here one cannot be saved from the eternal fire. Everyone desiring to be saved must be salted with fire, and pass through purification by fire. All of us, according to the law of creation, must offer ourselves in sacrifice to God; but every one of us is impure. This means we must purify ourselves, so that a sacrifice pleasing to God can be made from us. But if you start to purify yourself, to tear passions from your soul, it will be painful, like being burned with fire. This operation of inner self-purification is like the operation of fire purifying metal. Metal is without feeling. If you were to give it feeling, it would feel the purifying and the burning simultaneously. The same thing occurs in a person who purifies himself. Undergoing this operation, he is as if totally burned through by fire. The purifying fire passes through all his members the way salt penetrates a body which is being preserved. And only he who subjects himself to this operation is a truly God-pleasing sacrifice. That is why it is necessary for everyone to be salted with fire, as in the Old Testament, where every sacrifice was salted before being offered as a whole-burnt offering.

Tuesday
Heb. 12:25–26, 13:22–25; Mark 10:2–12

What God hath joined together, let not man put asunder (Mark 10:9). With these words the Lord affirms the indissolubility of marriage. Only one lawful ground for divorce is indicated—a spouse's unfaithfulness. But what should one do if one discovers something like this? Be patient. We have a universal commandment—to bear one another's burdens. Even more willingly should close ones, such as spouses, mutually fulfill this with respect to one another. Unwillingness to be patient inflates unpleasant situations, which pile up into a dividing wall. What is the mind given us for? To smooth out the path of life. Prudence will work out any unpleasantness which is encountered. People divorce not because of a lack of worldly wisdom, but more out of an unwillingness to think over the state of things well, and even more from not having any goal in life other than pleasure. Pleasures cease, and satisfaction with one another ceases; on and on it goes, until divorce. The more life's goals are debased, the more frequently divorces occur on the one hand, and on the other—unlawful temporary cohabitation. The source of this evil lies in a materialistic view of the world and life.

Wednesday
James 1:1–18; Mark 10:11–16

With what love the Lord regarded children! Who does not

regard them with love? The longer one lives, the more one loves children. One sees in them freshness of life, purity, and a chaste disposition, which are impossible not to love. Looking at the innocence of childhood, some suppose that there is no ancestral sin, that each person falls himself when he comes of age and encounters immoral urges, which, it seems to him, he does not have the strength to overcome. Everyone falls himself, yet the ancestral sin is nevertheless present. The Apostle Paul sees in us the law of sin, warring against the law of the mind. This law, like a seed, is at first apparently invisible, but later comes to light and entices one. Those who are born of lepers do not manifest leprosy until a certain age, but then it is revealed, and begins to consume them just as it did their parents. Where was the leprosy before this time? It was concealed within. So ancestral sin hides until its time comes, and then it emerges and does its work. Environment means a great deal, both for suppressing this sin and revealing it. If there were no sinful elements all around, there would be nothing with which to feed this hidden sin, and perhaps it would dry up on its own. But herein is our sorrow: all around us there is a great deal of favorable food for it. There is much sin in every person as well as in society, but all of this does not necessarily determine that we will sin. Sin is always a matter of freedom—struggle and you will not fall. Only he who does not want to struggle falls. Why do we not want to struggle? There are no regulations concerning desire and lack of desire to struggle: I want to, because I want to; and I don't want to, because I don't want to. Self-rule is the original principle—one cannot go beyond it.

Thursday
James 1:19–27; Mark 10:17–27

Someone turned to the Lord with a question: *Good Master, what shall I do that I may inherit eternal life?* (Mark 10:17). What necessitated this question? Was there no Scripture? Was the law not read every Saturday for everyone? There was everything—both the Scripture and its interpreters—but differences of opinion went around in society and muddled everyone. The Pharisees said one thing, the Sadducees another, the Essenes had their own opinion, and the Samaritans theirs. In Galilee, perhaps even pagan teachings were heard, and each side put forth its own teachings with a tone of conviction. Anyone who was zealous for salvation naturally came to the question: What should I do? What should I follow, so as not to lose my soul? Our situation now is very similar to that of those times. How many teachings are circulating in our schools, in society, and in literature! For the indifferent it is nothing, but those concerned over which teaching to follow cannot help but seek a resolution: "What should I do?" And so what is the solution? The one which the Savior gave: Believe and live as God commanded, and do not listen to people's talk; let them talk. The talk of scholars too is like rumors and fashion: today one thing, tomorrow another. But you should heed only God's word, which abides unto the ages. What the Lord commanded, no philosophizing can revoke. Everything must be done, and cannot be put off. The Judgment indeed will be according to the word of the Lord, and not according to our philosophizing.

FRIDAY
James 2:1–13; Mark 10:23–32

Hearing the word of the Lord about the difficulty the rich have in entering the Kingdom of God, the disciples thought: *Who then can be saved?* In reply, the Lord said: *With men it is impossible, but not with God: for with God all things are possible* (Mark 10:26–27). It is impossible to renounce avarice without the influence of grace on the heart. It is impossible to cope with all the other predilections, with all the sin living in us, and all of its fruits, without God's grace. God's grace is given, according to faith in the Lord, in the

Mysteries of the Holy Church. Hold tightly to the Holy Church of God and to all of its institutions, and the power of God, which helps to bring about every good, will always abide with you. But at the same time, always remember that these illuminating and life-giving institutions are a means, but not the goal. That is why you should serve them only in order to enliven and nourish, through their influence, the grace-filled powers hidden in you, and then take up your work as a strong man, ready for every good deed. If you keep what you have received to yourself and do not give it a way out through good works, you will not be right, just as one who is estranged from everything belonging to the Church is not right. Because of incorrect zealots of piety, the very structure of a pious life is subjected to criticism; but this does not take away the significance of this structure, nor does it justify the philosophizers who shun it because of these criticisms.

Saturday
Col. 1:3–6; Luke 16:10–15

Ye cannot serve God and mammon (Luke 16:13). A divided thought and divided heart make a person unfit for anything, for *a double-minded man is unstable in all his ways* (James 1:8). He either does nothing, or does and redoes—that is, he builds with one hand and destroys with the other. The source of a truly God-pleasing life is a firm resolution to please God in all things. This resolution directs all of a person's thoughts, desires, and feelings toward one thing, and thus uniting his inward [powers], it makes him strong to perform deeds, bringing unity into all of his activities and imparting to them a single character. Such deeds are successful and fruitful, because they are full of true life. Where do inertia, immobility, and fruitlessness of deeds come from? From inner lifelessness; and inner lifelessness comes from inner division. One single goal is not acknowledged or established as a law of life—deeds are performed haphazardly. Therefore one deed goes in one direction, another goes in another direction, and the building of one's life is never erected. Choose a goal and devote your life to it. The true, main goal is indicated by the God-like nature of man: it is living communion with God. Direct also toward this main goal all personal, scholarly, worldly, civic, commercial, official, and governmental goals. If everyone in society held to this principle, there would be one general tenor to society, and one spirit would fill everyone.

THE NATIVITY OF CHRIST
Gal. 4:4–7; Matt. 2:1–12

Glory to Thee, O Lord! Once again we greet the awaited bright days of Christ's Nativity. Let us be glad and rejoice. In order to raise our festivities to a higher level in these days, the Holy Church has intentionally instituted a fast before them—a certain amount of constraint, so that as we enter the festive period we might feel as though we were coming out into freedom. Nevertheless, the Church in no way desires that we give ourselves over to mere sensual delights and fleshly pleasures. Since the Church has from olden times called these days *sviatki* ("holy days"), they require that our very rejoicing on these days be holy, as they are holy. So that those who rejoice might not forget themselves, the Church has placed a short hymn upon our lips to glorify the newborn Christ, by which the flesh is settled down and the soul is uplifted, showing the proper occupations for these days: "Christ is born, give ye glory," and the rest.[41] Glorify Christ; glorify Him, so that by this doxology your heart and soul might delight, and thereby silence any urge for various other deeds and occupations that might promise some kind of pleasure. Glorify Christ: this does not mean that you have to compose lengthy songs of praise to Christ—no. But if when contemplating or hearing about the birth

---

[41] First irmos of the Canon for the Nativity of Christ.—ED.

of Christ the Savior, you involuntarily cry out from the depths of your soul, "Glory to Thee, O Lord, that Christ is born!"—this is sufficient. This will be a quiet hymn of the heart, which will nevertheless pass through to heaven and enter in to God Himself. Repeat a little more clearly to yourself what the Lord has wrought for us, and you will see how natural this exclamation now is. So that this might be easier for us, we shall compare it to the following incident:

A king promises freedom to a man who is imprisoned in a dungeon and bound with fetters. The prisoner waits a day, then another, then months, and years. He sees no fulfillment of the promise, but does not lose hope, and believes in the king's words. Finally, he sees signs that it is coming soon. His attention increases—he hears a noise; someone is approaching with cheerful words. Now the locks fall and the liberator enters. "Glory to Thee, O Lord!" the prisoner involuntarily cries. "The end of my imprisonment has arrived, and soon I will see God's light!"

Or another incident: A sick man is covered with wounds and paralyzed in all his members. He has tried all medicines and has changed doctors many times. His endurance is exhausted, and he is ready to give himself over to despair. He is told, "There is one more very skilled doctor, who heals everyone from those very illnesses that you have. We have asked him to come, and he has promised to do so." The patient believes them, hope springs up in him, and he waits for the promised one.... One hour passes, then another, and anxiety again begins to torment his soul. Finally, at evening, someone arrives.... The door opens, and the desired visitor enters.... "Glory to Thee, O Lord!" the sick man shouts.

Here is another example: A thundercloud hangs over the face of the earth, and it is covered with darkness. Thunder shakes the foundations of the mountains and lightening tears the sky from one end to the other. All are in fear, as if the end of the world had come. When the thunder passes and the sky clears, everyone breathes freely, saying, "Glory to Thee, O Lord!"

Bring these examples closer to yourself and you will see our whole history in them. The threatening clouds of God's wrath were over us. The Lord—the Peacemaker—has come, and has dispersed the cloud. We were covered with the wounds of sins and passions; the Healer of souls has come and healed us. We were bound by the fetters of slavery; the Liberator has come and released our fetters. Bring all of these examples closer to your heart and take them in with your senses, and you will not be able to refrain from exclaiming, "Glory to Thee, O Lord, that Christ is born!"

I will not try to convey this joy to you with my words; it is inexpressible by any words. The work that was accomplished by the Lord Who is born touches each one of us. Those who enter into communion with Him receive from Him freedom, healing, and peace; they possess all of this and taste of its sweetness. There is no reason to say, "Rejoice!" to those who experience this within themselves, for they cannot help but rejoice. But to those who do not experience it, why say, "Rejoice"? They cannot rejoice. No matter how much you say, "Rejoice at your deliverance," to one bound hand and foot, he will not rejoice. Whence can the joy of healing come to one who is covered with the wounds of sin? How can one who is threatened by the thunder of God's wrath breathe freely? You can only say to him, "Go to the Infant wrapped in swaddling clothes in the manger, and seek deliverance by Him from all the evils that encompass you, for this Infant is Christ, the Savior of the world."

I would like to see everyone rejoicing with this very joy, and not wanting to know any other joys; but not everything that comes from Israel is Israel. Now there will begin empty, wild merriment that inflames the passions.... No matter how much you tell these people to calm down, they only shut their ears and pay no heed. And they always bring these bright days of the Feast to such a point that the merciful Lord is compelled to turn His eyes from us and say: "All of your solemnities are an abomination unto Me" (cf. Is. 1:13–14)! Truly, many of our social festivities are really pagan abominations; that is, some of them are brought to us straight from the pagan world, while others, though they appeared later in time, are penetrated with the spirit of paganism. And it is purposely contrived for such festivities to appear in great quantities during the Feasts of Nativity and Pascha. By getting caught up in them we give the prince of this world—our tormentor, the enemy of God—an excuse to say to God, "Look what You've done for me with Your Nativity and Resurrection! They're all coming to me!" But let the words of the Fiftieth Psalm be repeated more often in the depth of our hearts: *That Thou mightest be justified in Thy words, and prevail when Thou art judged* (Ps. 50:4).

Enlightened Europe is attracting us. Yes, the abominations of paganism that were almost completely cast out of the world were first restored there; they have now come from there to us. Having breathed in that hellish poison, we run around like madmen, forgetting our own selves. But let us remember the year of 1812—why did the French come to us then? God sent them to wipe out all the evil that we had imitated from them. Russia repented then, and God had mercy on her. But now it seems that we have forgotten that lesson. If we come to our senses, of course, nothing will happen. But if we do not come to our senses, who knows? Perhaps the Lord will again send similar teachers, so that they would bring us to our senses and place us on the path of correction. Such is the law of God's righteousness: to cure someone from sin with the thing that enticed him into it. These are not empty words, but a matter that has been confirmed by the voice of the Church. Know, ye Orthodox, that God is not mocked. And knowing this, make merry and rejoice during these days with fear. Illumine the bright Feast with bright deeds, occupations, and festivities, so that all who look upon us would say, "They have holy days—not the kind of amusements practiced by impious and profligates who don't know God."

SCRIPTURAL INDEX

New Testament references follow the King James Version;
Old Testament references follow the Septuagint.

INDEX

Page numbers for illustrations are in boldface italics.

SAINT HERMAN
OF ALASKA
BROTHERHOOD

Since 1965, the St. Herman of Alaska Brotherhood has been
publishing Orthodox Christian books and magazines.

View our catalog, featuring over fifty titles,
and order online, at
www.sainthermanmonastery.com

You can also write us for a free printout of our catalog:

St. Herman of Alaska Brotherhood
P. O. Box 70
Platina, CA 96076
U.S.A.